SAINT·MARY'S COLLEGE OF CALIFORNIA
COLLEGIATE SEMINAR 002

WESTERN TRADITION I

SECOND EDITION

Change the course.

Acknowledgments:

pp. 1–21: From *The History of the Peloponnesian War* by Thucydides, translated by
Rex Warner, with an introduction and notes by M. I. Finley (Penguin Classics 1954,
revised edition 1972). Translation copyright © 1954 by Rex Warner. Introduction and
Appendices copyright © 1972 by M. I. Finley. Reprinted by permission of Penguin
Books Ltd.

pp. 29–63: From *The Comedies* by Terence, translated with an introduction by Betty
Radice (Penguin Classics, 1976). Translation copyright © Betty Radice, 1965, 1967,
1976. Reprinted by permission of Penguin Books Ltd.

pp. 64–94: From *On the Nature of the Universe* by Lucretius, translated by R. E.
Latham, revised with an introduction by John Goodwin (Penguin 1951, 1994).
Translation copyright © R. E. Latham, 1951. Revisions, introduction and notes copy-
right © John Goodwin, 1994.

pp. 95–110: From *Georgics* by Virgil, translated by A. S. Kline. Translation copyright
© by A. S. Kline. Reprinted by permission of the translator.

pp. 111–115: Scripture texts in this work are taken from the *New American Bible*,
revised edition © 2010, 1991, 1986, 1970 Confraternity of Christian Doctrine,
Washington, D.C. and are used by permission of the copyright owner. All Rights
Reserved. No part of the New American Bible may be reproduced in any form without permission in writing from the copyright owner.

Change the course.

530 Great Road
Acton, MA 01720
800-562-2147

Contents

Collegiate Seminar Goals and Outcomes

Collegiate Seminar Vision Statement

The Collegiate Seminar Program seeks to engage Saint Mary's students in a critical and collaborative encounter with the world of ideas as expressed in great texts of the Western tradition in dialogue with and exposure to its encounter with other traditions. Thereby students become part of the Great Conversation. The Program seeks to help them develop as curious, thoughtful members of an intellectual community. Designed to serve the College's goals of a liberal education, the Program strives to put students in possession of their powers to think clearly, critically, and collaboratively, and articulate their ideas effectively—powers that will serve them for the rest of their lives.

Goals of the Collegiate Seminar Program

The Collegiate Seminar Program fosters a genuine sense of collegiality and intellectual community by providing an authentic forum for students to meet and partake of a common experience—the reading and discussion of shared texts under the guidance of faculty from all disciplines. Its participants engage in collaborative dialogue with texts whose ideas shape our world. Through careful reading, shared inquiry, and writing, students improve their skills of analysis and communication. During this process students will develop increased appreciation for these great ideas, and grow in their intellectual curiosity, becoming life-long learners and thinkers. Students will be exposed to a variety of ways of knowing, encouraged in their search for meaning, and learn to accept ambiguity while aiming for clarity.

Seminar Specific Learning Outcomes

As a result of their participation in the Collegiate Seminar Program, students will grow in their ability to:

1. Understand, analyze, and evaluate challenging texts from different genres and periods.
2. Comprehend the intellectual threads that connect works both backward and forward through history.

3. Relate the works studied to their own experience and to notions of authentic humanity.
4. Reflect on prior knowledge and assess one's own process of learning.

Critical Thinking

Critical thinking within Seminar is grounded on the processes of analysis, synthesis and evaluation necessary to read with understanding. Through careful reading, listening, and reflection, which lead to a solid understanding of the texts, critical thinking allows students to make perceptive insights and connections between texts, Seminars and ultimately their life experiences. Critical thinking within Seminar also includes skills that allow for sound judgments to be made when multiple, competing viewpoints are possible. Seminar is a place where reading critically is transformed and integrated into a habit of mind, providing students with the tools to question the authority of the text and the foundations of their own assumptions. In short, critical thinking allows students to recognize, formulate and pursue meaningful questions, which are not only factual but also interpretive and evaluative, about the ideas of others as well as their own.

Critical Thinking Learning Outcomes

As a result of their participation in the Collegiate Seminar Program, students will grow in their ability to:

1. Distinguish the multiple senses of a text (literal and beyond the literal).
2. Identify and understand assumptions, theses, and arguments that exist in the work of authors.
3. Evaluate and synthesize evidence in order to draw conclusions consistent with the text. Seek and identify confirming and opposing evidence relevant to original and existing theses.
4. Ask meaningful questions and originate plausible theses.
5. Critique and question the authority of texts, and explore the implications of those texts.

Written and Oral Communication

A mind is not truly liberated until it can effectively communicate what it knows. Thus the Collegiate Seminar Program seeks to develop strong written and oral communication skills in its students. Students will develop skills that demonstrate an understanding of the power of language to shape thought and experience. They will learn to write and speak logically, with clarity, and with originality, and grow in their intellectual curiosity through the process of writing.

Written and Oral Communication Learning Outcomes

As a result of their participation in the Collegiate Seminar Program, students will grow in their ability to:

1. Recognize and compose readable prose, as characterized by clear and careful organization, coherent paragraphs and well-constructed sentences that employ the conventions of Standard Written English and appropriate diction.
2. Recognize and formulate effective written and oral communication, giving appropriate consideration to audience, context, format, and textual evidence.
3. Analyze arguments so as to construct ones that are well supported (with appropriate use of textual evidence), are well reasoned, and are controlled by a thesis or exploratory question.
4. Use discussion and the process of writing to enhance intellectual discovery and unravel complexities of thought.

Shared Inquiry

Shared inquiry is the act of reasoning together about common texts, questions, and problems. It is a goal of Collegiate Seminar to advance students' abilities to develop and pursue meaningful questions in collaboration with others, even in the context of confusion, paradox, and/or disagreement. Through the habits of shared inquiry students will carefully consider and understand the perspectives and reasoned opinions of others, reconsider their own opinions, and develop rhetorical skills.

Shared Inquiry Learning Outcomes

As a result of their participation in the Collegiate Seminar Program, students will grow in their ability to:

1. Advance probing questions about a common text or other objects of study.

2. Pursue new and enriched understandings of the texts through sustained collaborative inquiry.
3. Reevaluate initial hypotheses in light of evidence and collaborative discussion with the goal of making considered judgments.
4. Engage in reflective listening and inclusive, respectful conversation.

Honor Code and Seminar

The Student Honor Council (of academic 2004–2005) has requested that all Seminar sections discuss the proper use of other persons' opinions in Seminar classes. The Governing Board of Collegiate Seminar proposes the following list of good practices:

Authentic engagement in seminar classes requires that—

1. Students read only the assigned texts in preparation;

2. Students give their own thoughts about the assigned readings;

3. Students do not introduce opinions of experts into the conversation;

4. Student essays present the student's own thoughts on the agreed-upon topic;

5. Instructors advise whether and how essays should respond to, use, or cite opinions which other students have voiced in class.

(CSGB, 5/19/04)

Collegiate Seminar Guidelines for Grading Oral Participation

The following criteria shall be considered in evaluating the oral participation of seminar students:

- Good listening and close attention to the discussion.
- Frequency of contribution to discussion.
- Quality of contributions in terms of forwarding the conversation.
- Clear evidence of reflection upon the reading.
- Ability, with respect to the reading, to describe, propose insights, analyze, see alternatives, compare, and evaluate.
- Ability to counter questions and/or challenge other discussants (including the seminar leader) respectfully.
- Seriousness of engagement, degree of interest in the ideas under discussion, and spontaneity.
- Sense of responsibility for the group's understanding of the text and for the progress of the conversation.

Seminar leaders and students are encouraged to use these criteria to evaluate perfomance as follows:

The student who earns a grade of "A" for oral participation is one who:

1) Is rarely if ever absent from class and is likely to inform the instructor in advance.
2) Is always excellently prepared and demonstrates her/his preparation by consistently offering text-related contributions throughout the discussion.
3) Is self-motivated, entering the discussion with pertinent and useful contributions as appropriate.
4) Is engaged and active in pursuing questions and in testing opinions.

5) Regularly forwards the discussion by drawing comparisons, analyzing problems and questions, offering opinions on interpretations, and responding critically and respectfully to the contributions of others.

6) Listens with active interest to the comments of others; questions others in an effort to understand not only what they are saying but also the reasons and implications of what they are saying.

7) Takes responsibility for the "health and well-being" of the seminar.

The student who earns a grade of "B" for oral participation is one who:

1) Is rarely, if ever, absent from class and is likely to inform the instructor in advance.

2) Is nearly always well prepared and demonstrates her/his preparation by often offering text-related contributions to the discussion.

3) Is often self-motivated, entering the discussion with pertinent and useful contributions as appropriate.

4) Is sometimes engaged and active, sometimes more passive, in pursuing questions and in testing opinions.

5) Sometimes forwards the conversation, sometimes takes a less active role, supporting or questioning the more positive contributions of others.

6) Listens with active interest to the comments of others.

7) Does not obstruct or retard the "health and well being" of the seminar.

The student who earns a grade of "C" for oral participation is one who:

1) Is seldom absent from class.

2) Is generally prepared and demonstrates her/his preparation by offering text-related contributions at some point in the discussion.

3) Regularly contributes to discussion but takes a follower's rather than a leader's role in forwarding the conversation.

4) Listens respectfully to the comments of others.

5) Does not obstruct or retard the "health and well-being" of the seminar.

The student who earns a grade of "D" for oral participation is one who:

1) May be absent from class more than three or four times per semester.

2) May be unprepared for discussion or fail to demonstrate preparation by pertinent text-related contributions to the discussion.

3) Often does not contribute, even as a follower, in the seminar discussion.

4) May fail to listen to others; may engage in disruptive "side conversations."

5) May obstruct or retard the "health and well-being" of the seminar.

The student who earns a grade of "F" for oral participation is one who:

1) May be often absent from seminar.

2) Is unprepared for the majority of classes.

3) Rarely, if ever, contributes to the discussion.

4) Does not listen to others or follow the course of the discussion; may engage in disruptive behavior.

5) May obstruct or retard the seminar.

Saint Mary's College Grading Standards
Collegiate Seminar Program
Seminar 02/14

	The C essay is competent, exhibiting no serious or frequent deficiencies.	*The B essay is strong in most areas.*
Thesis/ Purpose/ Controlling Idea	The C essay addresses the topic and offers a thesis. The thesis, however, may not explore the topic with sufficient complexity or take on a significant intellectual challenge.	The B essay exhibits intellectual engagement. It has a narrowly focused thesis, with a clear sense of purpose and audience. It explores the topic in some depth and with some complexity.
Structure, Organization, and Development	The C essay offers support for its thesis; however, this support may not be evaluated or analyzed thoughtfully, or may tend toward plot summary. The C essay has an introduction, body, and conclusion, generally unified paragraphs, and transitions between paragraphs. However, it may proceed formulaically or mechanically. (e.g. listing examples). The conclusion may not move much beyond the initial thesis.	The B essay proceeds logically and offers appropriate support for its thesis. It is a generally unified essay, with a clear introduction, coherent paragraphs, and effective transitions. Its conclusion does not merely restate the argument, but attempts to draw together preceding insights in a new way.
Language, Style, and Syntax	The C essay employs readable prose, but the sentences may be simple and lack variety. Language may be overly general and wordy.	In the B essay, sentences are sufficiently varied. Language is generally concise and appropriate.
Grammar, Spelling, Punctuation, Formatting, and Documentation of Sources	The C essay employs generally correct grammar, punctuation, formatting, spelling, and documentation. Errors, however, may be serious enough to detract from the effectiveness of the essay.	The B essay employs generally correct grammar, punctuation, formatting, spelling, and documentation. Errors, when they appear, do not detract from the overall effectiveness of the essay.

The F essay is seriously deficient. It may exhibit a poor grasp of the assignment or a lack of familiarity with assigned texts. It may be deficient in one or more of the following areas: purpose, organization and development, language, and mechanics. It may lack a clear thesis or fail to support its thesis.

The A essay excels in all areas.	*The D essay* is deficient in one or more areas.
The A essay has a clearly defined, intellectually challenging focus and a strong sense of purpose and audience. It exhibits depth and complexity in its analysis and originality in its thought.	The D essay may lack a clear thesis, or the thesis may be weak or overly general.
The A essay is distinguished by sound logic. It offers sufficient and appropriate support for the thesis in the form of concrete, specific, and relevant evidence. It is a unified essay that proceeds coherently with an effective introduction, well-developed and unified paragraphs, graceful transitions, and a conclusion that, rather than summarizing previous points, explores the implications of the preceding analysis.	The D essay may fail to provide adequate support for its thesis in the form of textual analysis or other evidence; it may substitute repetition for development or make inaccurate claims. It may lack a clear structure and paragraphs may lack coherence. Transitions may be awkward or nonexistent.
In the A essay, sentences are skillfully crafted and effectively varied; langauge is fresh, precise, and economical. It maintains a consistent and appropriate tone.	The D essay often lacks variety in sentence structure and suffers from inappropriate diction and akward syntax. Language tends to be vague, imprecise, or rambling.
The A essay is almost entirely free of errors in grammar, punctuation, formatting, spelling, and documentation.	A D essay is often characterized by grammatical errors such as fragments, comma splices, agreement errors, or inappropriate shifts in tense, voice, mood, or person. It may also be rife with spelling, punctuation, or formatting errors. It may lack documentation or be improperly documented.

Other common features of failing essays are: faulty logic, ineffective organization, incoherent paragraphs, misreadings, incorrect diction, and so many syntactic and grammatical errors that the essay becomes unreadable.

Kinds of Questions

Questions of Fact

To a question of fact there will be only one answer which can be supported using evidence from the text; this answer may, however, take some effort to discover.

Example: In "The Analogy of the Cave", why do philosophers (those with "beatific vision") appear foolish in the everyday world (such as in the law courts)?

Questions of Interpretation

Your purpose is to make sense of the text. You might ask what conclusions we can draw about the author's meaning, purpose, or basic assumptions. Or you might question the relationship of two statements which seem to be in contradiction. To questions of interpretation, attentive readers can give differing answers, each of which can be supported using evidence from the text.

Example: According to Socrates, the prisoners of "The Analogy of the Cave" are "like us." How does the reading support this view?

Questions of Evaluation

Judge what is presented in the reading. Is what is written true? False? Neither true nor false? Likely? Unlikely? Wrong? Right? Fair? Unfair? Insightful? Obvious? Of course, these categories of judgment (and others like them) are often themselves the very subject of the readings.

Example: Is "The Analogy of the Cave" a good and useful image of human existence? (And what do I mean by "good" or by "useful" or by "image"?)

Chronological Outline of Greek, Roman, and Latin Christian Authors and Historical References

Before Current (Christian) Era (BCE)

1280–1180	Trojan War
753	Founding of Rome
750–620	*Odyssey*
600	Sappho
510	Athenian democratic constitution of Cleisthenes
509	Beginning of the Roman Republic
477	Commencement of Athenian Supremacy
461	Ascendency of Pericles. The *Oresteian Trilogy* of Aeschylus
440	Sophocles exhibits the *Antigone*, and is made one of the ten Athenian generals in the war with Samos
431	Commencement of the Peloponnesian War
430	Plague at Athens. Sophocles, *Oedipus the King*
before 410	Thucydides writes *The History of the Peloponnesian War*
4th century	Plato writes *Meno* in the first half of the century
335–322	Aristotle writes *The Nicomachean Ethics*
322	Suppression of Athenian democracy
300	Euclid teaches geometry in Alexandria
160	Terence writes *The Brothers*
1st century	Lucretius writes *On the Nature of Things* before mid-century
44	Collapse of the Roman Republic and beginning of the Principate
29	Virgil writes *The Georgics*

Current (Christian) Era (CE)

1	Beginning of the Christian Era with the birth of Christ (actually 4 BCE ca.)
1st century	Writing of the New Testament in the last quarter of the century. Plutarch writes *Lives of the Noble Greeks and Romans*, which includes *Coriolanus*

4th century	Constantinian Revolution (transformation of Roman Empire to a Christian Roman Empire)
398	Augustine writes *The Confessions*
525	Boethius writes *On the Consolation of Philosophy*
570	Birth of Mohammed
622	Beginning of the Muslim Era
800	Inauguration of the Frankish Carolingian Empire of the Romans
962	The German Empire of the Romans replaces the Carolingian Empire
1048–1122	Reform of the papacy
1151	Hildegard von Bingen writes *Scivias*
12th/13th c.	Marie de France writes *The Lais*
1198–1303	Ascendancy of the papacy in Europe
1307–1321	Dante Alighieri writes "The Purgatorio" as part of his *Divine Comedy*
1309-1376	Avignon papacy, or Babylonian Captivity of the papacy
1378–1417	Great Schism of the Western Church
1453	Conquest of Constantinople by the Turks and the fall of the Byzantine Eastern Roman Empire

WESTERN
TRADITION I

from the *History of the Peloponnesian War*

Thucydides
Translated by Rex Warner

Pericles' Funeral Oration

In the same winter the Athenians, following their annual custom, gave a public funeral for those who had been the first to die in the war. These funerals are held in the following way: two days before the ceremony the bones of the fallen are brought and put in a tent which has been erected, and people make whatever offerings they wish to their own dead. Then there is a funeral procession in which coffins of cypress wood are carried on wagons. There is one coffin for each tribe, which contains the bones of members of that tribe. One empty bier is decorated and carried in the procession: this is for the missing, whose bodies could not be recovered. Everyone who wishes to, both citizens and foreigners, can join in the procession, and the women who are related to the dead are there to make their laments at the tomb. The bones are laid in the public burial-place, which is in the most beautiful quarter outside the city walls. Here the Athenians always bury those who have fallen in war. The only exception is those who died at Marathon, who, because their achievement was considered absolutely outstanding, were buried on the battlefield itself.

When the bones have been laid in the earth, a man chosen by the city for his intellectual gifts and for his general reputation makes an appropriate speech in praise of the dead, and after the speech all depart. This is the procedure at these burials, and all through the war, when the time came to do so, the Athenians followed this ancient custom. Now, at the burial of those who were the first to fall in the war Pericles, the son of Xanthippus, was chosen to make the speech. When the moment arrived, he came forward from the tomb and, standing on a high platform, so that he might be heard by as many people as possible in the crowd, he spoke as follows:

"Many of those who have spoken here in the past have praised the institution of this speech at the close of our ceremony. It seemed to them a mark of honour to our soldiers who have fallen in war that a speech should be made

1

over them. I do not agree. These men have shown themselves valiant in action, and it would be enough, I think, for their glories to be proclaimed in action, as you have just seen it done at this funeral organized by the state. Our belief in the courage and manliness of so many should not be hazarded on the goodness or badness of one man's speech. Then it is not easy to speak with a proper sense of balance, when a man's listeners find it difficult to believe in the truth of what one is saying. The man who knows the facts and loves the dead may well think that an oration tells less than what he knows and what he would like to hear: others who do not know so much may feel envy for the dead, and think the orator over-praises them, when he speaks of exploits that are beyond their own capacities. Praise of other people is tolerable only up to a certain point, the point where one still believes that one could do oneself some of the things one is hearing about. Once you get beyond this point, you will find people becoming jealous and incredulous. However, the fact is that this institution was set up and approved by our forefathers, and it is my duty to follow the tradition and do my best to meet the wishes and the expectations of every one of you.

'I shall begin by speaking about our ancestors, since it is only right and proper on such an occasion to pay them the honour of recalling what they did. In this land of ours there have always been the same people living from generation to generation up till now, and they, by their courage and their virtues, have handed it on to us, a free country. They certainly deserve our praise. Even more so do our fathers deserve it. For to the inheritance they had received they added all the empire we have now, and it was not without blood and toil that they handed it down to us of the present generation. And then we ourselves, assembled here today, who are mostly in the prime of life, have, in most directions, added to the power of our empire and have organized our State in such a way that it is perfectly well able to look after itself both in peace and in war.

'I have no wish to make a long speech on subjects familiar to you all: so I shall say nothing about the warlike deeds by which we acquired our power or the battles in which we or our fathers gallantly resisted our enemies, Greek or foreign. What I want to do is, in the first place, to discuss the spirit in which we faced our trials and also our constitution and the way of life which has made us great. After that I shall speak in praise of the dead, believing that this kind of speech is not inappropriate to the present occasion, and that this whole assembly, of citizens and foreigners, may listen to it with advantage.

'Let me say that our system of government does not copy the institutions of our neighbours. It is more the case of our being a model to others, than of our imitating anyone else. Our constitution is called a democracy because

[handwritten in margin: how to be a good person.]

power is in the hands not of a minority but of the whole people. When it is a question of settling private disputes, everyone is equal before the law; when it is a question of putting one person before another in positions of public responsibility, what counts is not membership of a particular class, but the actual ability which the man possesses. No one, so long as he has it in him to be of service to the state, is kept in political obscurity because of poverty. And, just as our political life is free and open, so is our day-to-day life in our relations with each other. We do not get into a state with our next-door neighbour if he enjoys himself in his own way, nor do we give him the kind of black looks which, though they do no real harm, still do hurt people's feelings. We are free and tolerant in our private lives; but in public affairs we keep to the law. This is because it commands our deep respect.

'We give our obedience to those whom we put in positions of authority, and we obey the laws themselves, especially those which are for the protection of the oppressed, and those unwritten laws which it is an acknowledged shame to break.

'And here is another point. When our work is over, we are in a position to enjoy all kinds of recreation for our spirits. There are various kinds of contests and sacrifices regularly throughout the year; in our own homes we find a beauty and a good taste which delight us every day and which drive away our cares. Then the greatness of our city brings it about that all the good things from all over the world flow in to us, so that to us it seems just as natural to enjoy foreign goods as our own local products.

'Then there is a great difference between us and our opponents, in our attitude towards military security. Here are some examples: Our city is open to the world, and we have no periodical deportations in order to prevent people observing or finding out secrets which might be of military advantage to the enemy. This is because we rely, not on secret weapons, but on our own real courage and loyalty. There is a difference, too, in our educational systems. The Spartans, from their earliest boyhood, are submitted to the most laborious training in courage; we pass our lives without all these restrictions, and yet are just as ready to face the same dangers as they are. Here is a proof of this: When the Spartans invade our land, they do not come by themselves, but bring all their allies with them; whereas we, when we launch an attack abroad, do the job by ourselves, and, though fighting on foreign soil, do not often fail to defeat opponents who are fighting for their own hearths and homes. As a matter of fact none of our enemies has ever yet been confronted with our total strength, because we have to divide our attention between our navy and the many missions on which our troops are sent on land. Yet, if our enemies engage a detachment of our forces and defeat it, they give themselves credit for having thrown back our entire army; or, if they lose, they claim that they were beaten by us in full strength. There are certain advantages, I think, in our way of meeting danger voluntarily, with an easy mind, instead of with a laborious training, with natural rather than with state-induced courage. We do not have to spend our time practising to meet sufferings which are still in the future; and when they are actually upon us we show ourselves just as brave as these others who are always in strict training. This is one point in which, I think, our city deserves to be admired. There are also others:

'Our love of what is beautiful does not lead to extravagance; our love of the things of the mind does not make us soft. We regard wealth as something to be properly used, rather than as something to boast about. As for poverty, no one need be ashamed to admit it: the real shame is in not taking practical measures to escape from it. Here each individual is interested not only in his own affairs but in the affairs of the state as well: even those who are mostly occupied with their own business are extremely well-informed on general politics—this is a peculiarity of ours: we do not say that a man who takes no interest in politics is a man who minds his own business; we say that he has no business here at all. We Athenians, in our own persons, take our decisions on policy or submit them to proper discussions: for we do not think that there is an incompatibility between words and deeds; the worst thing is to rush into action before the consequences have been properly debated. And this is another point where we differ from other people. We are capable at the same time of taking risks and of estimating them beforehand. Others are brave out of ignorance; and, when they stop to think, they begin to fear. But the man who can most truly be accounted brave is he who best knows the meaning of what is sweet in life and of what is terrible, and then goes out undeterred to meet what is to come.

'Again, in questions of general good feeling there is a great contrast between us and most other people. We make friends by doing good to others, not by receiving good from them. This makes our friendship all the more reliable, since we want to keep alive the gratitude of those who are in our debt by showing continued goodwill to them: whereas the feelings of one who owes us something lack the same enthusiasm, since he knows that, when he repays our kindness, it will be more like paying back a debt than giving something spontaneously. We are unique in this. When we do kindnesses to others, we do not do them out of any calculations of profit or loss: we do them without afterthought, relying on our free liberality. Taking everything together then, I declare that our city is an education to Greece, and I declare that in my opinion each single one of our citizens, in all the manifold aspects of life, is able to show himself the rightful lord and owner of his own person, and do this, more-over, with exceptional grace and exceptional versatility. And to show that this is no empty boasting for the present occasion, but real tangible fact, you have only to consider the power which our city possesses and which has been won by those very qualities which I have mentioned. Athens, alone of the states we know, comes to her testing time in a greatness that surpasses what was imag-ined of her. In her case, and in her case alone, no invading enemy is ashamed at being defeated, and no subject can complain of being governed by people unfit for their responsibilities. Mighty indeed are the marks and monuments of our empire which we have left. Future ages will wonder at us, as the present age wonders at us now. We do not need the praises of a Homer, or of anyone else whose words may delight us for the moment, but whose estimation of facts will fall short of what is really true. For our adventurous spirit has forced an entry into every sea and into every land; and everywhere we have left behind us everlasting memorials of good done to our friends or suffering inflicted on our enemies.

'This, then, is the kind of city for which these men, who could not bear the thought of losing her, nobly fought and nobly died. It is only natural that every one of us who survive them should be willing to undergo hardships in her service. And it was for this reason that I have spoken at such length about our city, because I wanted to make it clear that for us there is more at stake than there is for others who lack our advantages; also I wanted my words of praise for the dead to be set in the bright light of evidence. And now the most important of these words has been spoken. I have sung the praises of our city; but it was the courage and gallantry of these men, and of people like them, which made her splendid. Nor would you find it true in the case of many of the Greeks, as it is true of them, that no words can do more than justice to their deeds.

'To me it seems that the consummation which has overtaken these men shows us the meaning of manliness in its first revelation and in its final proof. Some of them, no doubt, had their faults; but what we ought to remember first is their gallant conduct against the enemy in defence of their native land. They have blotted out evil with good, and done more service to the commonwealth than they ever did harm in their private lives. No one of these men weakened because he wanted to go on enjoying his wealth: no one put off the awful day in the hope that he might live to escape his poverty and grow rich. More to be desired than such things, they chose to check the enemy's pride. This, to them, was a risk most glorious, and they accepted it, willing to strike down the enemy and relinquish everything else. As for success or failure, they left that in the doubtful hands of Hope, and when the reality of battle was before their faces, they put their trust in their own selves. In the fighting, they thought it more honourable to stand their ground and suffer death than to give in and save their lives. So they fled from the reproaches of men, abiding with life and limb the brunt of battle; and, in a small moment of time, the climax of their lives, a culmination of glory, not of fear, were swept away from us.

'So and such they were, these men—worthy of their city. We who remain behind may hope to be spared their fate, but must resolve to keep the same daring spirit against the foe. It is not simply a question of estimating the advantages in theory. I could tell you a long story (and you know it as well as I do) about what is to be gained by beating the enemy back. What I would prefer is that you should fix your eyes every day on the greatness of Athens as she really is, and should fall in love with her. When you realize her greatness, then reflect that what made her great was men with a spirit of adventure, men who knew their duty, men who were ashamed to fall below a certain standard. If they ever failed in an enterprise, they made up their minds that at any rate the city should not find their courage lacking to her, and they gave to her the best contribution that they could. They gave her their lives, to her and to all of us, and for their own selves they won praises that never grow old, the most splendid of sepulchres—not the sepulchre in which their bodies are laid, but where their glory remains eternal in men's minds, always there on the right occasion to stir others to speech or to action. For famous men have the whole earth as their memorial: it is not only the inscriptions on their graves in their own country that mark them out; no, in foreign lands also, not in any visible form but in people's hearts, their memory abides and grows. It is for you to try to be like them. Make up your minds that happiness depends on being free, and freedom depends on being courageous. Let there be no relaxation in face of the perils of the war. The people who have most excuse for despising death are not the wretched and unfortunate, who have no hope of doing well for themselves, but those who run the risk of a complete reversal in their lives, and who would feel the difference most intensely, if things went wrong for them. Any intelligent man would find a humiliation caused by his own slackness more painful to bear than death, when death comes to him unperceived, in battle, and in the confidence of his patriotism.

'For these reasons I shall not commiserate with those parents of the dead, who are present here. Instead I shall try to comfort them. They are well aware that they have grown up in a world where there are many changes and chances. But this is good fortune—for men to end their lives with honour, as these have done, and for you honourably to lament them: their life was set to a measure where death and happiness went hand in hand. I know that it is difficult to convince you of this. When you see other people happy you will often be reminded of what used to make you happy too. One does not feel sad at not having some good thing which is outside one's experience: real grief is felt at the loss of something which one is used to. All the same, those of you who are of the right age must bear up and take comfort in the thought of having more children. In your own homes these new children will prevent you from brooding over those who are no more, and they will be a help to the city, too, both in filling the empty places, and in assuring her security. For it is impossible for a man to put forward fair and honest views about our affairs if he has not, like everyone else, children whose lives may be at stake. As for those of you who are now too old to have children, I would ask you to count as gain the greater part of your life, in which you have been happy, and remember that what remains is not long, and let your hearts be lifted up at the thought of the fair fame of the dead. One's sense of honour is the only thing that does not grow old, and the last pleasure, when one is worn out with age, is not, as the poet said, making money, but having the respect of one's fellow men.

'As for those of you here who are sons or brothers of the dead, I can see a hard struggle in front of you. Everyone always speaks well of the dead, and, even if you rise to the greatest heights of heroism, it will be a hard thing for you to get the reputation of having come near, let alone equalled, their standard. When one is alive, one is always liable to the jealousy of one's competitors, but when one is out of the way, the honour one receives is sincere and unchallenged.

'Perhaps I should say a word or two on the duties of women to those among you who are now widowed. I can say all I have to say in a short word of advice. Your great glory is not to be inferior to what God has made you, and the greatest glory of a woman is to be least talked about by men, whether they are praising you or criticizing you. I have now, as the law demanded, said what I had to say. For the time being our offerings to the dead have been made, and for the future their children will be supported at the public expense by the city, until they come of age. This is the crown and prize which she offers, both to the dead and to their children, for the ordeals which they have faced. Where the rewards of valour are the greatest, there you will find also the best and bravest spirits among the people. And now, when you have mourned for your dear ones, you must depart.'

• • •

Launching of the Sicilian Expedition

At the beginning of spring next year the Athenian delegation came back from Sicily. They were accompanied by the Egestaeans, who brought sixty talents of uncoined silver—a month's pay for sixty ships, which was the number they were going to ask the Athenians to send them.

The Athenians held an assembly and listened to what the Egestaeans and their own delegation had to say. The report was encouraging, but untrue, particularly on the question of the money which was said to be available in large quantities in the treasury and in the temples. So they voted in favour of sending sixty ships to Sicily and appointed as commanders with full powers Alcibiades, the son of Clinias, Nicias, the son of Niceratus, and Lamachus, the son of Xenophanes, who were instructed to help the Egestaeans against the Selinuntines, to reestablish Leontini also, if things went well with them in the war, and in general to make the kind of provisions for Sicily which might seem to them most in accordance with Athenian interests.

Five days later another assembly was held to discuss the quickest means of getting the ships ready to sail and to vote any additional supplies that the generals might need for the expedition. Nicias had not wanted to be chosen for the command; his view was that the city was making a mistake and, on a slight pretext which looked reasonable, was in fact aiming at conquering the whole of Sicily—a very considerable undertaking indeed. He therefore came forward to speak in the hope of making the Athenians change their minds. The advice he gave was as follows:

'It is true that this assembly was called to deal with the preparations to be made for sailing to Sicily. Yet I still think that this is a question that requires further thought—is it really a good thing for us to send the ships at all? I think that we ought not to give such hasty consideration to so important a matter and on the credit of foreigners get drawn into a war which does not concern us. So far as I am concerned personally, I gain honour by it and I am less frightened than most people about my own safety—not that I think that a man is any the worse citizen for taking reasonable care of his own safety and his own property; such men are, in fact, particularly anxious, for their own sakes, that the city should prosper. However, just as in the past I have never spoken against my convictions in order to gain honour, so I shall not do it now, but shall tell you what I think is for the best. I know that no speech of mine could be powerful enough to alter your characters, and it would be useless to advise you to safeguard what you have and not to risk what is yours already for doubtful prospects in the future. I shall therefore confine myself to showing you that this is the wrong time for such adventures and that the objects of your ambition are not to be gained easily.

'What I say is this: in going to Sicily you are leaving many enemies behind you, and you apparently want to make new ones there and have them also on your hands. Possibly you think that the peace treaty which you have made gives you security; and, so long as you make no move, no doubt this treaty will continue to exist in name (for it has become a nominal thing, thanks to the intrigues of certain people here and in Sparta); it will certainly not stop our enemies from attacking us immediately, if in any part of the world any considerable forces of our own should surfer a defeat. In the first place, they only made the peace because of their misfortunes; it was forced on them, and in the matter of prestige we had the advantage. Then also in the treaty itself there are a number of points still not settled. There are some states, too, and important ones as well, who have not yet accepted the peace terms even as they stand. Some of these are openly at war with us, others, because Sparta has not yet made a move, are still holding back, but our truces with them are renewable every ten days, and it is extremely likely that, once they find us with our forces divided (which is just what we are in such a hurry to do), they will be only too eager to make war on us together with the Sicilians, whom they would rather have had as allies in the past than almost any other people. All these are points to be considered; we have not yet come safely into harbour, and this is no time for running risks or for grasping at a new empire before we have secured the one we have already. For the fact is that the Chalcidians in Thrace have been in revolt from us for many years and are still unsubdued; and in other areas, too, we get only a grudging obedience from our subjects. And now we rush to the help of Egesta, of all places—an ally of ours, we say, which has been wronged; meanwhile doing nothing about putting right our own, wrongs which we have suffered all this time from the rebels.

'Yet these rebels, once crushed, could be kept down; whereas even if we did conquer the Sicilians, there are so many of them and they live so far off that it would be very difficult to govern them. It is senseless to go against people who, even if conquered, could not be controlled, while failure would leave us much worse off than we were before we made the attempt. My opinion is, too, that Sicily, as it is at present, is not a danger to us, and that it would be even less of a danger if it came under the control of Syracuse (the possibility with which the Egestaeans are always trying to frighten you). As things are now it is possible that some Sicilians might come against us independently because of their affection for Sparta; but, supposing them to be all under the control of Syracuse, it is hardly likely that one empire would attack another, because if they were to join the Peloponnesians in destroying our empire, they would probably find that their own empire would be destroyed by the same people and for the same reasons. The best way for us to make ourselves feared by the Hellenes in Sicily is not to go there at all; and the next best thing is to make a demonstration of our power and then, after a short time, go away again. We all know that what is most admired is what is farthest off and least liable to have its reputation put to the test; and if anything went wrong with us, they would immediately look down on us and join our enemies here in attacking us. This is, in fact, Athenians, your own experience with regard to Sparta and her allies. Your successes against them, coming so unexpectedly compared with what you feared at first, have now made you despise them and set your hearts on the conquest of Sicily. But one's enemy's misfortunes are insufficient grounds for self-satisfaction; one can only feel real confidence when one has mastered his designs. And we ought to realize that, as a result of the disgrace they have suffered, the Spartans have only one thought, and that is how they can even now regain their own reputation by overthrowing us—as is natural when one considers that military honour is the be-all and the end-all of their existence. So, if we keep our senses, we shall see that what we are fighting for has nothing to do with these Egestaeans in Sicily, who do not even speak our own language: our real problem is to defend ourselves vigorously against the oligarchical machinations of Sparta.

'We should also remember that it is only recently that we have had a little respite from a great plague and from the war, and so are beginning to make good our losses in men and money. The right thing is that we should spend our new gains at home and on ourselves instead of on these exiles who are begging for assistance and whose interest it is to tell lies and make us believe them, who have nothing to contribute themselves except speeches, who leave all the danger to others and, if they are successful will not be properly grateful, while if they fail in any way they will involve their friends in their own ruin.

'No doubt there is someone sitting here who is delighted at having been chosen for the command and who, entirely for his own selfish reasons, will urge you to make the expedition—and all the more so because he is still too young for his post. He wants to be admired for the horses he keeps, and because these things are expensive, he hopes to make some profit out of his appointment. Beware of him, too, and do not give him the chance of endangering the state in order to live a brilliant life of his own. Remember that with such people maladministration of public affairs goes with personal extravagance; remember, too, that this is an important matter, and not the sort of thing that can be decided upon and acted upon by a young man in a hurry.

'It is with real alarm that I see this same young man's party sitting at his side in this assembly all called in to support him, and I, on my side, call for the support of the older men among you. If any one of you is sitting next to one of his supporters, do not allow yourself to be brow-beaten or be frightened of being called a coward if you do not vote for war. Do not, like them, indulge in hopeless passions for what is not there. Remember that success comes from foresight and not much is ever gained simply by wishing for it. Our country is now on the verge of the greatest danger she has ever known. Think of her, hold up your hands against this proposal, and vote in favour of leaving the Sicilians alone to enjoy their own country and manage their own affairs within the boundaries (perfectly satisfactory to us) which now divide us from them—the Ionian sea, for the voyage along the coast, and the Sicilian sea, for the direct voyage. And let the Egestaeans, in particular, be told that, just as they started their war with the Selinun-tines without consulting Athens, so they must themselves be responsible for making peace; and in the future we are not making allies, as we have done in the past, of the kind of people who have to be helped by us in their misfortunes, but who can do nothing for us when we need help from them.

'And I call upon you, the president of the assembly, as you know it is your business to care for the city's interests and as you wish to show yourself a good citizen, to put this question to the vote and allow the Athenians to debate the matter once again. And if you shrink from putting the matter to the vote again, you must remember that you cannot be blamed for a violation of the law when there are so many witnesses here on your side. Consider, too, that in this way you will be acting as the physician for your misguided city, and that the duty of those who hold office is simply this, to do all the good they can to their country, or in any case never to do any harm that can be avoided.'

After this speech of Nicias most of the Athenians who came forward to speak were in favour of making the expedition and not going back on the decision which had already been passed, though a few spoke on the other side. The most ardent supporter of the expedition was Alcibiades, the son of Clinias. He "wanted to oppose Nicias, with whom he had never seen eye to eye in politics and who had just now made a personal attack on him in his speech. Stronger motives still were his desire to hold the command and his hopes that it would be through him that Sicily and Carthage would be conquered—successes which would at the same time bring him personally both wealth and honour. For he was very much in the public eye, and his enthusiasm for horse-racing and other extravagances went beyond what his fortune could supply. This, in fact, later on had much to do with the downfall of the city of Athens. For most people became frightened at a quality in him which was beyond the normal and showed itself both in the lawlessness of his private life and habits and in the spirit in which he acted on all occasions. They thought that he was aiming at becoming a dictator, and so they turned against him. Although in a public capacity his conduct of the war was excellent, his way of life made him objectionable to everyone as a person; thus they entrusted their affairs to other hands, and before long ruined the city.

On this occasion Alcibiades came forward and gave the following advice to the Athenians:

'Athenians, since Nicias has made this attack on me, I must begin by saying that I have a better right than others to hold the command and that I think I am quite worthy of the position. As for all the talk there is against me, it is about things which bring honour to my ancestors and myself, and to our country profit as well. There was a time when the Hellenes imagined that our city had been ruined by the war, but they came to consider it even greater than it really is, because of the splendid show I made as its representative at the Olympic games, when I entered seven chariots for the chariot race (more than any private individual has entered before) and took the first, second, and fourth places, and saw that everything else was arranged in a style worthy of my victory. It is customary for such things to bring honour, and the fact that they are done at all must also give an impression of power. Again, though it is quite natural for my fellow citizens to envy me for the magnificence with which I have done things in Athens, such as providing choruses and so on, yet to the outside world this also is evidence of our strength. Indeed, this is a very useful kind of folly, when a man spends his own money not only to benefit himself but his city as well. And it is perfectly fair for a man who has a high opinion of himself not to be put on a level with everyone else; certainly when one is badly off one does not find people coming to share in one's misfortunes. And just as no one takes much notice of us if we are failures, so on the same principle one has to put up with it if one is looked down upon by the successful: one cannot demand equal treatment oneself unless one is prepared to treat everyone else as an equal. What I know is that people like this—all, in fact, whose brilliance in any direction has made them prominent—are unpopular in their life-times, especially with their equals and also with others with whom they come into contact; but with posterity you will find people claiming relationship with them, even where none exists, and you will find their countries boasting of them, not as though they were strangers or disreputable characters, but as fellow-countrymen and doers of great deeds. This is what I aim at myself, and because of this my private life comes in for criticism; but the point is whether you have anyone who deals with public affairs better than I do. Remember that I brought about a coalition of the greatest powers of the Peloponnese, without putting you to any considerable danger or expense, and made the Spartans risk their all on the issue of one day's fighting at Mantinea, and though they were victorious in the battle, they have not even yet quite recovered their confidence.

'So, in my youth and with this folly of mine which is supposed to be so prodigious, I found the right arguments for dealing with the power of the Peloponnesians, and the energy which I displayed made them trust me and follow my advice. Do not therefore be afraid of me now because I am young, but while I still have the vigour of my youth and Nicias the reputation for being lucky, make the best use you can of what each of us has to offer. Do not change your minds about the expedition to Sicily on the grounds that we shall have a great power to deal with there. The Sicilian cities have swollen populations made out of all sorts of mixtures, and there are constant changes and rearrangements in the citizen bodies. The result is that they lack the feeling that they are fighting for their own fatherland; no one has adequate armour for his own person, or a proper establishment on the land. What each man spends his time on is in trying to get from the public whatever he thinks he can get either by clever speeches or by open sedition—always with the intention of going off to live in another country, if things go badly with him. Such a crowd as this is scarcely likely either to pay attention to one consistent policy or to join together in concerted action. The chances are that they will make separate agreements with us as soon as we come forward with attractive suggestions, especially if they are, as we understand is the case, in a state of violent party strife. As for their hoplites, they have not got so many as they boast of; it is the same with them as with the rest of the Hellenes; the numbers never came up to the estimate made by each state of its own power; in fact the falsification was a very big one, and even in this present war Hellas has barely succeeded in arming herself adequately.

'The position in Sicily, then, is, so far as my information goes, as I have said; indeed, it is even easier than that, since we shall also have a number of non-Hellenic peoples who, through hatred of the Syracusans, will join us in our attack on them. And as for the position at home, if you look at it in the right way you will see that there is nothing here to hinder us. They talk about the enemies we shall leave behind us if we sail, but our fathers left behind them these same enemies when they had the Persians on their hands as well, and so founded the empire, relying solely on their superiority in sea-power. The Peloponnesians have never had so little hope of success against us as they have now. True enough that, if they really had the confidence, they have the strength to invade us by land, but they could do this whether we sailed to Sicily or not. They can do us no harm at all with their fleet, since we shall be leaving behind us a fleet of our own quite capable of dealing with theirs.

'There seems to be, therefore, no reasonable argument to induce us to hold back ourselves or to justify any excuse to our allies in Sicily for not helping them. We have sworn to help them, and it is our duty to help them, without raising the objection that we have had no help from them ourselves. The reason why we made them our allies was not that we wanted them to send us reinforcements here, but in order that they should be a thorn in the flesh for our enemies in Sicily, and so prevent them from coming here to attack us. This is the way we won our empire, and this is the way all empires have been won— by coming vigorously to the help of all who ask for it, irrespective of whether they are Hellenes or not. Certainly if everyone were to remain inactive or go in for racial distinctions when it is a question of giving assistance, we should add very little to our empire and should be more likely to risk losing it altogether. One does not only defend oneself against a superior power when one is attacked; one takes measures in advance to prevent the attack materializing. And it is not possible for us to calculate, like housekeepers, exactly how much empire we want to have. The fact is that we have reached a stage where we are forced to plan new conquests and forced to hold on to what we have got, because there is a danger that we ourselves may fall under the power of others unless others are in our power. And you cannot look upon this idea of a quiet life in quite the same way as others do—not, that is, unless you are going to change your whole way of living and make it like theirs is.

'In the assurance therefore that, in going abroad, we shall increase our power at home, let us set out on this voyage. It will have a depressing effect on the arrogance of the Peloponnesians when they see that we despise the quiet life we are living now and have taken on the expedition to Sicily. At the same time we shall either, as is quite likely, become the rulers of all Hellas by using what we gain in Sicily, or, in any case, we shall do harm to the Syracusans, and so do good to ourselves and our allies. Our security is guaranteed by our navy, so that we can either stay there, if things go well, or come back again; for we shall have naval superiority over all the Sicilians put together.

'Do not be put off by Nicias's arguments for non-intervention and his distinctions between the young and the old. Let us instead keep to the old system of our fathers who joined together in counsel, young and old alike, and raised our state to the position it now holds. So now in the same way make it your endeavour to raise this city to even greater heights, realizing that neither youth nor age can do anything one without the other, but that the greatest strength is developed when one has a combination where all sorts are represented—the inferior types, the ordinary types, and the profoundly calculating types, all together. Remember, too, that the city, like everything else, will wear out of its own accord if it remains at rest, and its skill in everything will grow out of date; but in conflict it will constantly be gaining new experience and growing more used to defend itself not by speeches, but in action. In general, my view is that a city which is active by nature will soon ruin itself if it changes its nature and becomes idle, and that the way that men find their greatest security is in accepting the character and the institutions which they actually have, even if they are not perfect, and in living as nearly as possible in accordance with them.'

This was the speech of Alcibiades. After listening to him, and to the Egestaeans and to some exiles from Leontini who came forward as suppliants, reminding them of their oaths and begging for help, the Athenians became much more eager than before to make the expedition. Nicias realized that there was no longer any hope of diverting them from their course by using the arguments that he had used already, but thought that there was a possibility of making them change their minds if he were to make an exaggerated estimate of the forces required. He therefore came forward again and spoke as follows:

'I see, Athenians, that you are quite determined on the expedition, and I hope it may turn out as we all wish. I shall now tell you what my opinion is as things stand at present. We are going to set out against cities which are, according to my information, of considerable strength, not subjects of one another and not wanting the kind of change by which they would be glad to escape from some oppressive government and accept a new government on easier terms; very unlikely, in fact, to give up their freedom in order to be ruled by us. The numbers also of the Hellenic cities are very large for one island. Apart from Naxos and Catana, which I expect will join us because of their racial connexion with Leontini, there are seven other cities equipped with military and naval forces very much along the same lines as our own, particularly Selinus and Syracuse, our main objectives. They have great numbers of hoplites and archers and javelin-throwers, great numbers of triremes, and plenty of men to form the crews. They have money, not only in the hands of private people, but also in the temples of Selinus, and Syracuse also receives the payment of first-fruits from some of the native peoples. But the greatest advantage they have over us is in the number of their horses and in the fact that they grow their own corn and do not have to import any.

'To deal with a power of this kind we shall need something more than a fleet with an inconsiderable army. We must have in addition a large army of infantry to sail with us, if we want our actions to come up to what we have in mind, and are not to be restricted in our movements by the numbers of their cavalry; especially if the cities are frightened of us and combine among themselves, leaving us with no friends except the Egestaeans to provide us with cavalry with which to meet them. It would be disgraceful if we were forced to retire or to send back later for reinforcements owing to insufficient foresight to begin with. We must start, then, with a force that is large enough for its task, and we must realize that we are going to sail a long way from our own country on an expedition very different from any of those which you may have undertaken against any of your subjects in this part of the world, when you have had your alliance to fall back on and when supplies have been easy to obtain from friendly territory. Instead of this, we are cutting ourselves off from home and going to an entirely different country, from which during the four winter months it is difficult even for a messenger to get to Athens.

'I think, therefore, that we ought to take a large army of hoplites from Athens and from our allies—from the subject states, and also any whom we can persuade or hire to come with us from the Peloponnese. We must have large forces of archers and of slingers, so as to hold our own against the enemy cavalry. And we must have a very decided superiority at sea, so as to make it easier for us to bring in our supplies. We must take our own corn from here (wheat, that is to say, and parched barley), and a proportion of bakers from the mills must be requisitioned and paid for their services, so that, in case we are ever weather-bound, the expedition may have its supplies; for not every city will be able to receive a force as large as ours will he. In other respects, too, we must equip ourselves to the best of our ability in order to avoid having to depend on other people, and in particular we must take with us as much money as possible from here, since you may be sure that so far as the money at Egesta is concerned, and which is supposed to be all ready for us, it is more likely to be there in theory than in fact.

'So we must leave Athens with a force that is not only a match for their forces, except in the numbers of hoplites available for a pitched battle, but actually much superior to them in every direction; and even so we shall find it hard enough to conquer the enemy and come off safely ourselves. We must act on the assumption that we are going off to found a city among foreigners and among enemies, and that those who do this have either to become masters of the country on the very first day they land in it, or be prepared to recognize that, if they fail to do so, they will find hostility on every side. Fearing this and knowing that we shall have need of much good counsel and more good fortune (a hard thing to be sure of, since we are but men), I wish to leave as little as possible to fortune before I sail, and to set out with an army that, according to all reasonable probability, should be secure. This I believe to be the best way to guarantee the general interests of the city and the safety of those of us who are going to serve in the campaign. If anyone thinks differently, I invite him to take the command instead of me.'

In making this speech Nicias thought that either the Athenians would be put off by the scale of the armament required, or, if he was forced to make the expedition, he would in this way sail as safely as possible.

The Athenians, however, far from losing their appetite for the voyage because of the difficulties in preparing for it, became more enthusiastic about it than ever, and just the opposite of what Nicias had imagined took place. His advice was regarded as excellent, and it was now thought that the expedition was an absolutely safe thing. There was a passion for the enterprise which affected everyone alike. The older men thought that they would either conquer the places against which they were sailing or, in any case, with such a large force, could come to no harm; the young had a longing for the sights and experiences of distant places, and were confident that they would return safely; the general masses and the average soldier himself saw the prospect of getting pay for the time being and of adding to the empire so as to secure permanent paid employment in future. The result of this excessive enthusiasm of the majority was that the few who actually were opposed to the expedition were afraid of being thought unpatriotic if they voted against it, and therefore kept quiet.

Finally one of the Athenians came forward and addressed Nicias personally, telling him that there was no need to make excuses or to delay matters any further; instead let him now say in front of everyone what forces the Athenians were to vote for him. Nicias spoke reluctantly, and said that he would go further into this with his colleagues in a quieter atmosphere, but, so far as he could see at present, they ought to sail with at least 100 triremes; transports would come from the Athenian shipping in whatever number was decided upon, and others should be sent for from the allies; the total force of hoplites, Athenian and allied, should be not less than 5,000 and, if possible, more; the rest of the force should be in proportion—archers from Athens and from Crete, slingers—all this and anything else that seemed necessary should be got ready and taken with them.

When the Athenians heard this, they immediately voted that the generals should have full powers with regard to the numbers of the army and to the expedition in general, to act as they thought best. After this the preparations began; instructions were sent to the allies, lists of those to be called up were made in Athens. It was all the easier to provide for everything as the city had just recovered from the plague and the years of continuous war, and as a number of the young had grown to manhood, and capital had accumulated as a result of the truce.

While these preparations were going on it was found that in one night nearly all the stone Hermae[1] in the city of Athens had had their faces disfigured by being cut about. No one knew who had done this, but large rewards were offered by the state in order to find out who the criminals were, and there was also a decree passed guaranteeing immunity to anyone, citizen, alien, or slave, who knew of any other sacrilegious act that had taken place and would come forward with information about it. The whole affair, indeed, was taken very seriously, as it was regarded as an omen for the expedition, and at the same time as evidence of a revolutionary conspiracy to overthrow the democracy.

Information was in fact forthcoming from some resident aliens and some personal servants. They had nothing to say about the Hermae, but told of some other cases which had happened previously when statues had been defaced by young men who were enjoying themselves after having had too much to drink, and also of mock celebrations of the mysteries held in private houses. One of those accused was Alcibiades, and this fact was taken up by those who disliked him most because he stood in the way of their keeping a firm hold themselves of the leadership of the people, and who thought that, if they could drive him out, they would step into the first place. They therefore exaggerated the whole thing and made all the noise they could about it, saying that the affair of the mysteries and the defacement of the Hermae were all part of a plot to overthrow the democracy, and that in all this Alcibiades had had a hand; evidence for which they found in the unconventional and undemocratic character of his life in general.

Alcibiades denied the charges made against him on the spot and was prepared to stand his trial before sailing on the expedition, the preparations for which had now been completed, and to be examined as to whether he had done any of the things with which he was accused; he should suffer the penalty, if found guilty, and, if acquitted, should take up his command. He begged them not to listen to attacks made on him in his absence, but, if he was really guilty, to put him to death there and then, and he pointed out how unwise it would be to send him out in command of such a large army with such serious accusations still hanging over his head. His enemies, however, were afraid that, if the case was brought on at once, he would have the goodwill of the army and that the people would be lenient to him because of the popularity he had won by getting the Argives and some of the Mantineans to join in the expedition. They therefore did all they could to put things off and prevent the trial taking place, and produced some more speakers who said that Alcibiades ought to sail now, and not hold up the departure of the army, but that he should be tried on his return within a fixed number of days. Their plan was to bring some more serious accusation against him (which they could do all the more easily when he was away) and then to send for him and bring him back to stand his trial. It was decided, therefore, that Alcibiades should sail.

After this, when it was already midsummer, they put to sea for Sicily. Most of the allies, with the ships carrying corn and the smaller craft and the rest of the equipment, had previously received instructions to assemble at Corcyra, so as to cross the Ionian sea from there in one body to the promontory of Iapygia. But the Athenians themselves and any of their allies who were in Athens at the time went down to Piraeus at dawn on the day appointed and manned the ships for putting out to sea. The rest of the people, in fact almost the entire population of Athens, citizens and foreigners, went down to Piraeus with them. Those who were natives of the country all had people to see off on their way, whether friends or relatives or sons, and they came full of hope and full of lamentation at the same time, thinking of the conquests that might be made and thinking, too, of those whom they might never see again, considering the long voyage on which they were going from their own country. At this moment when they were really on the point of parting from each other with all the risks ahead, the danger of the situation came more home to them than it had at the time when they voted for the expedition. Nevertheless they were heartened with the strength they had and with the sight of the quantities of every kind of armament displayed before their eyes. As for the foreigners and the rest of the crowd, they came merely to see the show and to admire the incredible ambition of the thing.

Certainly this expedition that first set sail was by a long way the most costly and the finest-looking force of Hellenic troops that up to that time had ever come from a single city. In numbers of ships and hoplites it was no greater than the force which Pericles took to Epidaurus and the same force which went against Potidaea with Hagnon, which consisted of 4,000 Athenian hoplites, 300 cavalry, and 100 triremes, with the addition of fifty more ships from Lesbos and Chios and many allied troops as well. That force, however, went only on a short voyage and was only equipped in the ordinary way, whereas this expedition was planned with a view to its being away for a long time and was equipped for both kinds of fighting, whichever should be required, both with warships and with ground troops. The fleet, was in a high state of efficiency and had cost a lot of money both to the captains and the State. Every sailor received a drachma a day from the Treasury, which also provided empty ships (sixty fighting ships and forty for the transport of hoplites) all manned with the best crews available. The captains, too, offered extra pay, in addition to that provided by the State to the *thranitae* and the rest of the crews, and they went to great expense on figure-heads and general fittings, every one of them being as anxious as possible that his own ship should stand out from the rest for its fine looks and for its speed. As for the land forces, they had been chosen from the best men who were liable for calling-up, and there had been much rivalry and much pains spent by everyone on his armour and personal equipment. It therefore happened that there was not only all this competition among the Athenians themselves, each with regard to his own particular piece of responsibility, but to the rest of Hellas it looked more like a demonstration of the power and greatness of Athens than an expeditionary force setting out against the enemy. It would have been found that a grand total of many talents of money were being taken out of the city, if one reckoned up the sums spent by the State and the private expenses of those who were serving—a total which would include what the State had already spent and what was being sent out in the hands of the generals, what individuals had spent on personal equipment, what the captains had spent and were still to spend on their ships; and, in addition to all this, there would have to be included the money for private expenses which everyone was likely to have taken with him over and above his pay from the State on an expedition which was to last for a long time, and also what the soldiers or traders took with them for purposes of exchange. And what made this expedition so famous was not only its astonishing daring and the brilliant show that it made, but also its great preponderance of strength over those against whom it set out, and the fact that this voyage, the longest ever made by an expedition from Athens, was being undertaken with hopes for the future which, when compared with the present position, were of the most far-reaching kind.

When the ships were manned and everything had been taken aboard which they meant to take with them on the voyage, silence was commanded by the sound of the trumpet, and the customary prayers made before putting to sea were offered up, not by each ship separately, but by them all together following the words of a herald. The whole army had wine poured out into bowls, and officers and men made their libations from cups of gold and of silver. The crowds on the shore also, the citizens and others who wished well to the expedition, joined together in the prayers. Then, when the hymn had been sung and the libations finished, they put out to sea, first sailing out in column, and then racing each other as far as Aegina. So they made good speed on their way to Corcyra, where the other force of their allies was assembling.

Note

[1] These are a national institution, the well-known square-cut figures, of which there are great numbers both in the porches of private houses and in the temples.

from *Elements* (Books I–XIII)
Definitions, Postulates, Common Notions, and Propositions 1–3 from Book I

Euclid
Based on the Translation by Sir Thomas L. Heath

Book I

Definitions

1. A point is that which has no part.
2. A line is breadthless length.
3. The extremities of a line are points.
4. A straight line is a line which lies evenly with the points on itself.
5. A surface is that which has length and breadth only.
6. The extremities of a surface are lines.
7. A plane surface is a surface which lies evenly with the straight lines on itself.
8. A plane angle is the inclination to one another of two lines in a plane which meet one another and do not lie in a straight line.
9. And when the lines containing the angle are straight, the angle is called rectilineal.
10. When a straight line set up on a straight line makes the adjacent angles equal to one another, each of the equal angles is right, and the straight line standing on the other is called a perpendicular to that on which it stands.
11. An obtuse angle is an angle greater than a right angle.
12. An acute angle is an angle less than a right angle.
13. A boundary is that which is an extremity of anything.
14. A figure is that which is contained by any boundary or boundaries.

15. A circle is a plane figure contained by one line such that all the straight lines falling upon it from one point among those lying within the figure are equal to one another;

16. And the point is called the center of the circle.

17. A diameter of the circle is any straight line drawn through the center and terminated in both directions by the circumference of the circle, and such a straight line also bisects the circle.

18. A semicircle is the figure contained by the diameter and the circumference cut off by it. And the center of the semicircle is the same as that of the circle.

19. Rectilineal figures are those which are contained by straight lines, trilateral figures being those contained by three, quadrilateral those contained by four, and multilateral those contained by more than four straight lines.

20. Of trilateral figures, an equilateral triangle is that which has its three sides equal, an isosceles triangle that which has two of its sides alone equal, and a scalene triangle is that which has its sides unequal.

21. Further, of trilateral figures, a right-angled triangle is that which has a right angle, an obtuse-angled triangle that which has an obtuse angle, and an acute-angled triangle that which has its three angles acute.

22. Of quadrilateral figures, a square is that which is both equilateral and right-angled; an oblong that which is right-angled but not equilateral; a rhombus that which is equilateral but not right-angled; and a rhomboid that which has its opposite sides and angles equal to one another but is neither equilateral nor right-angled. And let quadrilaterals other than these be called trapezia.

23. Parallel straight lines are straight lines which, being in the same plane and being produced indefinitely in both directions, do not meet one another in either direction.

Postulates

Let the following be postulated:

1. To draw a straight line from any point to any point.
2. To produce a finite straight line continuously in a straight line.
3. To describe a circle with any center and distance.

4. That all right angles are equal to one another.

5. That, if a straight line falling on two straight lines makes the interior angles on the same side less than two right angles, the two straight lines, if produced indefinitely, meet on that side on which are the angles less than the two right angles.

Common Notions

1. Things which are equal to the same thing are also equal to one another.

2. If equals be added to equals, the wholes are equal.

3. If equals be subtracted from equals, the remainders are equal.

4. Things which coincide with one another are equal to one another.

5. The whole is greater than the part.

Propositions

Proposition 1

On a given finite straight line to construct an equilateral triangle.

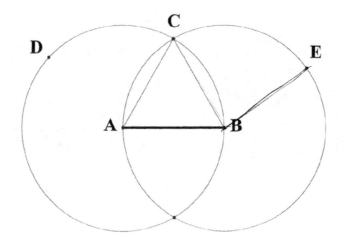

Let AB be the given finite straight line.

Thus it is required to construct an equilateral triangle on the straight line AB.

With center A and distance AB let the circle BCD be described; again, with center B and distance BA let the circle ACE be described; and from the point C, in which the circles cut one another, to the points A, B let the straight lines CA, CB be joined.

Now, since the point A is the center of the circle CDB,

AC is equal to AB.

Again, since the point B is the center of the circle CAE,

BC is equal to BA.

But CA was also proved equal to AB; therefore each of the straight lines CA, CB is equal to AB.

And things which are equal to the same thing are also equal to one another;

therefore CA is also equal to CB.

Therefore the three straight lines CA, AB, BC are equal to one another.

Therefore the triangle ABC is equilateral; and it has been constructed on the given finite straight line AB, (being) what it was required to do.

Proposition 2

To place at a given point (as an extremity) a straight line equal to a given straight line.

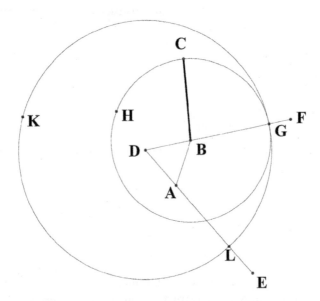

Let A be the given point, and BC the given straight line.

Thus it is required to place at the point A (as an extremity) a straight line equal to the given straight line BC.

From the point A to the point B let the straight line AB be joined; and on it let the equilateral triangle DAB be constructed.

Let the straight lines AE, BF be produced in a straight line with DA, DB; with center B and distance BC let the circle CGH be described; and again, with center D and distance DG let the circle GKL be described.

Then, since the point B is the center of the circle CGH,

BC is equal to BG.

Again, since the point D is the center of the circle GKL,

DL is equal to DG.

And in these DA is equal to DB;

therefore the remainder AL is equal to the remainder BG.

But BC was also proved equal to BG;

therefore each of the straight lines AL, BC is equal to BG.

And things which are equal to the same thing are also equal to one another;

therefore AL is also equal to BC.

Therefore at the given point A the straight line AL is placed equal to the given straight line BC, (being) what it was required to do.

Proposition 3

Given two unequal straight lines, to cut off from the greater a straight line equal to the less.

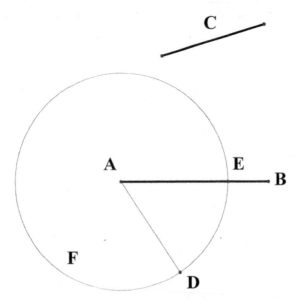

Let AB, C be the two given unequal straight lines and let AB be the greater of them.

Thus it is required to cut off from AB the greater a straight line equal to C the less.

At the point A let AD be placed equal to the straight line C; and with center A and distance AD let the circle DEF be described.

Now, since the point A is the center of the circle DEF,

AE is equal to AD.

But C is also equal to AD.

Therefore each of the straight lines AE, C is equal to AD;

so that AE is also equal to C.

Therefore, given the two straight lines AB, C, from AB the greater AE has been cut off equal to C the less, (being) what it was required to do.

The Brothers

Terence
Translated by Betty Radice

Production Notice

The Brothers by Terence: performed at the funeral games for Lucius Aemilius Paulus held by Quintus Fabius Maximus and Publius Cornelius Africanus.[1]

Produced by Lucius Ambivius Turpio and Lucius Hatilius (or Atilius) of Praeneste.

Music composed by Flaccus, slave of Claudius, for Sarranian[2] pipes throughout.

Greek original by Menander.

The author's sixth play, written during the consulship of Marcus Cornelius Cethegus and Lucius Anicius Gallus.[3]

Synopsis

Demea has two young sons. He gives Aeschinus to his brother Micio for adoption and keeps Ctesipho. The latter is captivated by the charms of a lute-player while under his stern father's strict authority; his brother Aeschinus keeps the secret, takes on himself the scandal and intrigue of the affair, and ends by abducting the girl from a slave-dealer. Aeschinus has also seduced an Athenian citizen, a girl in humble circumstances, and promised to make her his wife. Demea grumbles and scolds; but soon the truth is revealed, Aeschinus marries the girl he wronged, and Ctesipho is allowed to have his lute-player.

Characters

DEMEA }	*elderly brothers. Micio lives in Athens and*
MICIO }	*Demea farms just outside*
AESCHINUS }	*Demea's sons. Aeschinus has been adopted as his*
CTESIPHO }	*son by Micio*
SYRUS	*a slave, Micio's head servant*

29

DROMO ⎱ *two of Micio's house slaves*
STEPHANIO ⎰
PARMENO   *Aeschinus's personal slave*
SOSTRATA   *a widow, Micio's next-door neighbour*
PAMPHILA   *her daughter*
CANTHARA   *her old nurse*
GETA   *her slave and house servant*
HEGIO   *a neighbour and friend of her late husband*
SANNIO   *a slave-dealer*
BACCHIS   *a music-girl*

*

The scene is laid in Athens in front of the houses of Micio and Sostrata. To the audience's right the street leads to the centre of the town and the harbour, to the left to the country

Author's Prologue to *The Brothers*

The poet is well aware that his writing is scrutinized by unfair critics, and that his enemies are out to depreciate the play we are about to present; he therefore intends to state the charge against himself in person, and you shall judge whether his conduct deserves praise or blame. Joined in Death is a comedy by Diphilus.[4] Plautus made a Latin play out of it with the same name. In the beginning of the Greek play there is a young man who abducts a girl from a slave-dealer. Plautus left out this incident altogether, so the present author took it for his Brothers and translated it word for word. This is the new play we are going to act; watch carefully and see if you think the scene is a plagiarism or the restoration of a passage which had been carelessly omitted.

As to the spiteful accusation that eminent persons[5] assist the author and collaborate closely with him: his accusers may think it a grave imputation, but he takes it as a high compliment if he can win the approval of men who themselves find favour with you all and with the general public, men whose services in war, in peace, and in your private affairs, are given at the right moment, without ostentation, to be available for each one of you.

After this, you must not expect an outline of the plot—the old men who come on first will explain part of it, and the rest will be clear during the action of the play. Make sure that your goodwill gives the author fresh enthusiasm for his work.

[MICIO *comes out of his house calling to the servants within; as there is no answer he comes forward, and is revealed as a dapper middle-aged bachelor.*]

MICIO: Boy! . . . Then Aeschinus didn't come home last night from that dinner-party, nor any of the servants he took with him. It's true what they say: you may have stayed away from home or be late coming back, but you'll have a better reception from your angry wife for all her hard words and suspicions than you'll get from your loving parents. Suppose you're late; your wife merely imagines you're in love or someone loves you, or you are drinking and enjoying yourself and like to go off alone while she mopes by herself. Now look at me when my son hasn't returned, full of fancies and forebodings. The boy may have caught a chill or fallen down and broken a leg . . . . Why on earth should a man take it into his head to get himself something to be dearer to him than his own self? It's not as if he's my own son—he's my brother's, and my brother and I have had quite different tastes since boyhood. I've always chosen an easy life, stayed in town and enjoyed my leisure; and my married friends count me lucky never to have taken a wife. My brother's the opposite in every way—lived in the country, always saved, and chose the hard way; he married and had two sons, then I adopted the elder and brought him up from boyhood, and regarded him as my own. I've loved him like my own son: he has been my joy and sole delight. And I do all I can to ensure that he returns my affection. I give him money, turn a blind eye, don't feel called on to exercise my authority in everything; in fact, I've brought him up not to hide from me those youthful misdeeds which other sons conceal from their fathers. For a young man who has acquired the habit of telling lies and deceiving his father, and has the effrontery to do so, will do this all the more to everyone else. A gentleman's children should be treated honourably and like gentlemen. They can be restrained better that way, I believe, than through fear. But none of this suits my brother—he has different ideas. He keeps coming to me crying 'What are you doing, Micio? Why are you ruining our boy? Why do you let him drink and go after women, pay his bills for all this, and give him so much to spend on clothes? You've no sense.' Well, he has no feeling. It's beyond all right and reason, and it's quite wrong (in my view, at any rate) to hold that there's more weight and stability in authority imposed by force than in one which rests on affection. This is my system and the theory I have evolved; if the threat of punishment alone drives a man to do his duty, he'll be careful only so long as he thinks he may be detected: once he hopes not to be found out, he falls back into his old ways. But a man won by kindness is sincere in his behaviour, eager to make you a return, and stays the same whether he's with you or not. A father's duty then is to train his son to choose the right course of his own free will, not from fear of another; this marks the difference between a father and a tyrant in the home. If he fails to do this, he should admit he doesn't know how to manage his children. . . . But I do believe that's the man himself. . . . Yes it is, and I can see something has made him cross; I suppose I'm in for a scolding as usual, [DEMEA *comes on right from the town: shabby and workworn, he looks older than his years.*] Glad to see you well, Demea.

DEMEA: Good, I was looking for you.

MICIO: You look put out. Why?

DEMEA: Put out indeed! Can you ask me why, with a son like Aeschinus on our hands?

MICIO [*aside*]: I told you so. [*Aloud*] What has he done?

DEMEA: Done? He has neither shame nor scruple nor fear of the law! Never mind his past deeds; look at his latest exploit!

MICIO: Well, what *is* it?

DEMEA: Breaking open a door, bursting into someone else's house, beating the master and the entire household pretty well to death, and making off with the girl he's carrying on with. The scandal's all over the town. I can't tell you, Micio, how many people came up to tell me; everyone's talking about it. Good heavens, if he needs an example, why on earth can't he look at his brother, thrifty, sober, living in the country, and managing his affairs in very different style? I'm talking of Aeschinus, but it's you I mean, Micio; you have let him go astray.

MICIO: Is anything as unjust as a narrow-minded man! He can only see right in what he has done himself.

DEMEA: What do you mean?

MICIO: Simply that you are all wrong, Demea. It's no crime, believe me, for a young man to enjoy wine and women; no, and neither is it to break open a door. If you and I didn't do these things it was only because we hadn't the money. Are you claiming credit now for your conduct when it was only restricted by poverty? How unfair! If we had had the means, we should have done the same. As for that boy of yours, if you had any humanity you would let him behave as a young man should, here and now; if not, he will only wait to bundle your corpse out of the house before carrying on just the same when he's past the right age.

DEMEA: Good heavens, man, you drive me mad! No crime for a young man—

MICIO: Now listen to me, instead of going on and on about this. You gave me your son to adopt; he's my son now. If he does wrong, it's my affair, Demea; I meet most of the bills. He dines and wines and reeks of scent: I pay for it all. He keeps a mistress: I shall pay up as long as it suits me, and when it doesn't, maybe she will shut her door on him. He has broken a door-lock; I'll have it mended. He has torn someone's clothes; they can be repaired. Thank God I have the means to do so, and so far it hasn't worried me. Once and for all, either shut up or name anyone you like to judge between us; I'll prove it's you who are more in the wrong.

DEMEA: Damn it all, why not learn how to be a father from others who really know!

MICIO: You may be his natural father, but morally he is my son.

DEMEA: You? A moral father?

MICIO: Oh, if you are going on, I'm off.

DEMEA: Leaving me like this?

MICIO: Why should I listen to the same tale again and again?

DEMEA [*after a pause*]: I'm worried, Micio.

MICIO: So am I worried, Demea, but we must stick to our own worries. You look after one boy and I the other. If you worry about both, it's as good as demanding back the son you gave me.

DEMEA: No, no, Micio.

MICIO: Well, that's how it seems to me.

DEMEA: All right, have it your own way. . . . Let him squander his money, ruin others and himself; it's no concern of mine. And if ever again a single word—

MICIO: Temper again, Demea?

DEMEA: Don't you believe me? But am I asking for him back? All the same, it's hard: he's my flesh and blood. . . . If I oppose—All right, I've done. You want me to look after one son, and so I do. Thank heaven he's a boy after my own heart. The one you've got will learn some day—but I won't be too hard on him. [*He goes off right towards the town.*]

MICIO: There's something in what he says, but it's not the whole story. I don't really like it, but I wasn't going to show him I was upset. However much I try to placate him, I only start arguing and put him off; he's that sort of man. He's being unreasonable, and if I were to add to his fury or even try to share it, I should soon be as crazy as he is. All the same, Aeschinus has treated me pretty badly over this. He has been the round of the whores, and they've all cost money; then only the other day he got sick of them, I suppose, and announced his intention of marrying. I hoped he was growing up and settling down, and I was delighted. Now it's all starting again!

But in any case I must know the facts and find the boy if he's still in town. [*He goes off towards the town.*]

[The young man, AESCHINUS, comes on from the other direction with the music-girl, BACCHIS, and his slave, PARMENO, followed by the slave-dealer, SANNIO.]

SANNIO: Help, help, everyone, help a poor innocent man! I need your help!

AESCHINUS [*to the girl*]: Don't worry, now just stand here. Don't look round, there's no danger, he shan't touch you while I'm here.

SANNIO: I'll have her in spite of all—

AESCHINUS: He's a scoundrel but he won't want to risk a second thrashing today.

SANNIO: Aeschinus, listen; you can't say you don't know my character. I'm a slave-dealer—

AESCHINUS: I know.

SANNIO:—but as honest a man as ever was. You may apologize afterwards and say you meant me no harm, but I shan't give that [*snapping fingers*] for it. Take it from me, I'll have my rights, and you'll pay with more than words for what you've done to me. I know what you'll say: 'I'm sorry, I'm willing to swear you were attacked without provocation.' Meanwhile the way I've been treated is a disgrace.

AESCHINUS [*to* PARMENO]: Go on, get a move on and open the door.

SANNIO: You aren't listening to what I say?

AESCHINUS [*to the girl*]: Quick, go inside.

SANNIO: No you don't!

AESCHINUS: Stand over him, Parmeno, you're too far off; here, close up to him; that's right. Now watch, don't take your eyes off mine, and when I give the wink, be quick and plant your fist straight in his jaw.

SANNIO: Just let him try!

AESCHINUS: Now look out! [*With a look at* PARMENO, *who gives* SANNIO *a violent blow.*] Let go that girl!

SANNIO: It's monstrous!

AESCHINUS: He'll give you another if you don't watch out! [*He does.*]

SANNIO: Oh, oh!

AESCHINUS: I didn't wink, but it's a fault on the right side. [*To the girl*] Now go in.

[PARMENO takes the girl into MICIO's house]

SANNIO: What's all this? Are you king here, Aeschinus?

AESCHINUS: If I were I'd see you got the reward you merit.

SANNIO: What do you want with me?

AESCHINUS: Nothing.

SANNIO: Do you know the sort of man I am?

AESCHINUS: I don't want to.

SANNIO: Have I ever touched anything of yours?

AESCHINUS: If you had, you'd suffer for it.

SANNIO: The girl's mine; I paid cash for her. What right have you to detain her? Answer me that.

AESCHINUS: You'd do better to stop this row outside my house. And if you go on making a nuisance of yourself, you'll find yourself *inside* being whipped within an inch of your life.

SANNIO: I'm a free man—you can't whip me.

AESCHINUS: Can't I?

SANNIO: You brute! Is this where all free men are supposed to be equal?

AESCHINUS: If you've quite finished making a scene, you pimp, be so good as to listen to me.

SANNIO: Who's making a scene? I or you?

AESCHINUS: Drop it. Talk business.

SANNIO: What business? What talk?

AESCHINUS: Are you ready now to hear something to your advantage?

SANNIO: I'm all ears, as long as it's a fair deal.

AESCHINUS: Bah! Now a pimp wants me to stick to fair dealing!

SANNIO: I know I'm a pimp, the bane of youth, a plague and a liar, but I never did any harm to *you*.

AESCHINUS: No, that's the only thing to come.

SANNIO: Go back to where you began, please, Aeschinus.

AESCHINUS: You paid two thousand drachmas for that girl, and much good may it do you! I'll pay you the same.

SANNIO: What if I refuse to sell? Will you use force?

AESCHINUS: No—

SANNIO: Good; I was afraid you would.

AESCHINUS: The girl is free-born and shouldn't be sold at all. That's my view and I'm laying hands on her to set her free. Now make up your mind, take the money or get up a case. You can be thinking it over till I come back: you pimp. [*He goes into* MICIO's *house.*]

SANNIO: Gods above, I don't wonder folk go mad with the injustice done them! That fellow has dragged me out of my house, beaten me, carried off my girl under my nose, rained blows galore on my wretched back, and on top of all he has done insists I hand her over at cost price. Supposing it's a fair offer, and he's demanding his rights. Well, I'm willing, as long as he pays up. But I can predict just what will happen; once I agree to sell for a price he'll have witnesses on the spot to prove I *have* sold her. As for the money—moonshine. 'Soon,' he'll say: 'come back tomorrow.' I can put up with that too, so long as he pays up in the end, although it's a swindle. But I have to face facts: when you follow my profession you must put up with insults from these young men and keep your mouth shut. Well, nobody's going to pay me here. I'm only wasting time totting up accounts like this.

[SYRUS *comes out of* MICIO's *house talking to* AESCHINUS *within: he is a smart middle-aged manservant.*]

SYRUS: All right, sir, I'll see the man myself. He'll be only too keen to take the money when I've dealt with him, and think himself well treated into the bargain. [*Coming forward*] What's this I hear, Sannio? Have you been having a scrap with my master?

SANNIO: Scrap? I never saw a fight on worse terms than the one we've just had. He dealt all the blows and I took them till we're both worn out.

SYRUS: It was your own fault.

SANNIO: What should I have done?

SYRUS: Humoured him: he's young.

SANNIO: What else did I do? I let him punch me on the jaw.

SYRUS: Come, you know what I mean. Forget money on occasion; that's sometimes the best way to make it. If you were afraid that if you gave up a fraction of your rights and humoured the young man you wouldn't get your cash back—and with interest—you really are a prize fool.

SANNIO [*sulkily*]: I don't pay down cash for expectations.

SYRUS: You'll never make your fortune, Sannio; you've no idea how to set your traps.

SANNIO: Maybe your way's best, but I'm not sharp enough. I've always liked to make what I could on the spot.

SYRUS: Go on, I know you. It's well worth two thousand to you to keep on the right side of my young master; and besides, I'm told you are off to Cyprus and [*ignoring* SANNIO's *interruption*] you've made all your purchases to take there and hired a boat. I know you can't give your mind to this now, but once you're back again you'll fix things up with him all right.

SANNIO: I'm not going anywhere! [*Aside*] Damn it: that's what set them on to this.

SYRUS [*aside*]: That stung him; he's afraid.

SANNIO [*aside*]: Curse him, look what a moment for a holdup! All those women and other things are bought ready to take over to Cyprus. If I miss the market there, it's a hell of a loss. If I drop this matter now and take it up when I'm back again—no go, it'll have gone stale and all I'll get will be 'Why come now? Why did you allow it? Where have you been?' It would be better to cut my losses than go on waiting here now or bring a case later on.

SYRUS: Have you finished working out what you stand to gain?

SANNIO: Is this the right way for him to behave? Should Aeschinus set about getting the girl away from me by force?

SYRUS [*aside*]: He's wavering: one word more. See if you like this better, Sannio. Rather than risk saving or losing the whole sum, halve it. He'll scrape up a thousand from somewhere.

SANNIO: No, no! Now can't a poor man be sure of his capital? Has your master no shame? Thanks to him every tooth in my head is loose and my skull is one great bump with his blows. Now he wants to cheat me, does he? I'm not going.

SYRUS: As you please. Anything more, or can *I* go?

SANNIO: No, damn it, please listen, Syrus. Never mind how I've been treated, sooner than go to law just let me have back the money I paid for her. Up to now I know you've had no proof of my friendship, Syrus, but you'll see I'll be grateful and remember you.

SYRUS [*accepting the proffered bribe*]: I'll do my best. Look, here comes Ctesipho, all smiles about his mistress.

SANNIO: Now what about my request?

SYRUS: Wait a minute.

[*Enter* CTESIPHO *from the town, right, a volatile young man in high spirits.*]

CTESIPHO [*not seeing the others*]: Any man's welcome in time of need, but the real joy comes when your helper is the very man you want! Aeschinus my brother, how can I find words to praise you? At least I'm sure that nothing I can say will be too good for you, and I know, too, that no one alive has what I possess—a brother who stands first among men in every virtue!

SYRUS: Sir—

CTESIPHO: Oh Syrus, where is Aeschinus?

SYRUS: In there, at home, waiting for you.

CTESIPHO [*in raptures*]: Ah!

SYRUS: What do you mean by that?

CTESIPHO: What indeed! It's all his doing, Syrus, that I can live today! The splendid fellow! He put my interests before all his own, took on himself all the hard words and gossip, my own trouble and misdeeds; no one could do more. Who's that at the door?

SYRUS: Wait, it's your brother coming out. [AESCHINUS *comes out of the house.*]

AESCHINUS: Where's that dirty liar?

SANNIO [*aside*]: That's me he wants. Anything in his hand? Damn it, nothing.

AESCHINUS: Ah, good, I was looking for you, Ctesipho. How are you? Everything's settled now, so you can cheer up.

CTESIPHO: I can indeed, with a brother like you, Aeschinus, my own dear
  Aeschinus! I daren't praise you more to your face, or you might take it for
  flattery rather than true gratitude.

AESCHINUS: Come, come, you idiot, surely we know each other well enough
  by now. . . . I'm only sorry we heard of it so late and had almost reached
  the point of finding it impossible for anyone to help you, though we all
  wanted to.

CTESIPHO: I was ashamed—

AESCHINUS: Not ashamed but stupid, to let a little thing like that nearly drive
  you out of the country. It doesn't bear speaking of. God forbid such a
  thing!

CTESIPHO: I'm sorry.

AESCHINUS [*to* SYRUS]: And now what has Sannio to say?

SYRUS: Oh, he's calmed down.

AESCHINUS: I'm going to town to settle up with him. You go in to her, Ctesipho.

SANNIO [*to* SYRUS]: Try now, Syrus. [CTESIPHO *goes in.*)

SYRUS [*to* AESCHINUS]: Let's go, sir. This chap's in a hurry to be off to Cyprus.

SANNIO: Not so much hurry as you'd like! I've got time, and here I'll wait.

SYRUS: You'll be paid, don't worry.

SANNIO: But will he pay in full?

SYRUS: He will. Now shut up and come along.

SANNIO: I'm coming.

  [AESCHINUS *and* SANNIO *go off right;* SYRUS *is following when* CTESIPHO
  reappears.]

CTESIPHO: Hi, Syrus!

SYRUS: Well, what is it?

CTESIPHO: Do please pay that horrible man as soon as you can. If he carries on
  worse than this it may reach my father's ears, and that'll be the death of
  me—for ever.

SYRUS: I'll see it shan't. [*With growing self-importance*] Now, courage, sir; enjoy
  yourself with your lady indoors, and have dinner laid and all ready for us.
  I'll see this business settled and then come home with the fish.

CTESIPHO: Yes, do. Everything's so marvellous we must celebrate today.

  [*He goes back into* MICIO'*s house and* SYRUS *goes off after the others.
  After a short pause* SOSTRATA *comes out of her house, followed by the
  nurse,* CANTHARA.]

SOSTRATA: Please, nurse, how is my daughter? How are things going?

CANTHARA: How are things? All right, I hope, ma'am. My poor dear, your
  pains are only just beginning. . . . You're not worrying already, as if you'd
  never seen a birth nor had a baby yourself?

SOSTRATA: Alas, I'm friendless, we are two women alone—even Geta isn't here and I've no one to send for the midwife or to fetch Aeschinus.

CANTHARA: Bless you, he'll soon be here; he never lets a day pass without coming, whatever happens.

SOSTRATA: He's my sole comfort in my woes.

CANTHARA: And you couldn't have done better, ma'am, as it turns out, once the damage was done, at least as regards him—such a nice young man, well-born and good-hearted, coming from a grand home like his!

SOSTRATA: Yes, you're right; heaven keep him safe for us.

[SOSTRATA's *elderly slave,* GETA, *rushes on right in a state of great agitation, without seeing the women.*]

GETA: Here's a state of affairs! O world, unite, take counsel, seek a remedy, but what good will it do—such trouble as I'm in, and my mistress and her daughter too! O misery! Beset on all sides and no way out! Violence, destitution, injustice, desertion, disgrace! What times! What crimes! O wicked world, O vile wretch!

SOSTRATA: Heavens, why is Geta running about in such a state?

GETA: Honour, his promised word, pity, nothing could hold him back and turn him from his purpose—nor the thought that the poor girl he vilely seduced was just about to bear his child!

SOSTRATA: What *is* he saying? I still can't understand.

CANTHARA: Let's go nearer, ma'am, please.

GETA [*dancing about*]: O woe! I'm nearly out of my mind with fury. I'd like nothing better than to see that household in front of me—I'd vent my rage on the lot while my blood is roused! I'd have vengeance enough if I could wreak it on them! First I'd choke the life out of that old villain who brought up this monster, then that Syrus who put him up to this, how I'd smash him up! I'd grab him by the waist and fling him up, I'd dash his head on the ground and spatter his brains in the street! I'd take that young man and gouge out his eyes and pitch him headlong! As for the rest of them, I'd rush and knock them out, hit and hammer and stamp them underfoot! [*Pausing to get his breath back*] . . . Now I'd best hurry and tell the mistress what's gone wrong. [*He moves towards the house.*]

SOSTRATA: Let's call him. Geta!

GETA: Don't bother me, whoever you are.

SOSTRATA: It's me, Sostrata.

GETA: Where? I was looking for you, madam.

SOSTRATA: And I was waiting for you. You're back in the nick of time.

GETA: Madam—

SOSTRATA: What is it? You're trembling.

GETA: Oh—

CANTHARA: What's the hurry, Geta? Get your breath back.

GETA: We are quite—

SOSTRATA: Quite what?

GETA: Done for. Ruined.

SOSTRATA: For heaven's sake, explain.

GETA: Now—

SOSTRATA: Now what, Geta?

GETA: Aeschinus—

SOSTRATA: What has he done?

GETA: He's broken away from us all.

SOSTRATA: No, it can't be. . . . But *why*?

GETA: He has found a new girl—

SOSTRATA: O heaven help me!

GETA: And he makes no secret of it. He carried her off quite openly from the pimp.

SOSTRATA: Are you quite sure?

GETA: Quite, madam. I saw it with my own eyes.

SOSTRATA: Oh no, no. What can one believe? Who can be trusted? Our Aeschinus, the life of us all, in whom we put all our hopes and everything, who swore he could not live a day without her! And he promised he would put the baby in its grandfather's arms and beg the old man's leave to marry her!

GETA: Madam, try to stop crying and think of the future; what ought we to do? Put up with it and say nothing, or tell someone?

CANTHARA: Heavens, man, are you crazy? Do you think this the sort of news to spread around?

GETA: No, I don't. First; the facts show he cares nothing for us. If we make this public now, he'll deny it, I'm sure, and we'll risk your reputation, madam, and your daughter's life. And then, however much he might admit this is his doing, as he loves someone else it won't help your daughter to be married to him. So whichever way you look at it, best keep it quiet.

SOSTRATA [*after a pause for thought*]: No, not for the world! I won't.

GETA: What will you do then?

SOSTRATA: I'll tell everything.

CANTHARA: Oh my dear lady, think what you are doing.

SOSTRATA: Things couldn't be worse than they are now. In the first place she has no dowry, and then she's lost the next best thing—her reputation is ruined and she can't be married without one. There's just one thing we can do; if he denies it, I've got proof in the ring he sent her. Finally, my conscience is clear; no money, nothing unworthy of her or me has passed between us. I shall take him to court.

GETA [*dubiously*]: Very well, I suppose you're right.

SOSTRATA: Geta, you be off as fast as you can to her relative Hegio and tell him the whole story. He was my husband's dearest friend and has always looked after us.

GETA: Just as well, for no one else will. [*He goes off right.*]

SOSTRATA: You hurry too, Canthara, run and fetch the midwife; she mustn't keep us waiting when she's needed.

[CANTHARA *goes off to the town, right, and* SOSTRATA *into her house. After a short pause* DEMEA *comes back from the town.*]

DEMEA: I'm finished. Ctesipho, my own son, was with Aeschinus, they say, and had a hand in this abduction. This is the last straw, if the one who's still some good can be led astray by the other. Where am I to look for the boy? In some low dive I suppose, taken by that dissolute brother of his, you may be sure. [*Looking down the street, right*] Now here comes Syrus: he'll know where he is, but he's one of the gang and if he guesses I'm trying to find him he'll never say a word, the brute! I won't let him see that's what I want.

[SYRUS *comes back from the town with a basket of fish, pretending not to see* DEMEA.]

SYRUS [*aside*]: Well, we told the whole tale to our old man, just as it happened, and I never saw anyone better pleased.

DEMEA: Ye gods, the stupidity of the man!

SYRUS: He congratulated his son and thanked me for the advice I gave him. . . .

DEMEA: I shall explode!

SYRUS: He counted out the cash on the spot, and then gave me something to spend—which I've done to my liking [*looking in the basket*].

DEMEA: Here's the fellow for your orders if you want the job well done!

SYRUS: Why, sir, I didn't see you. What's the matter?

DEMEA: Matter? I never cease to marvel at the way you people behave.

SYRUS: Silly I know, in fact to be honest it's ridiculous. [*Calls indoors as he hands in the basket*] Gut all these fish, Dromo, except that biggest conger. Let it swim in water for a bit and it can be filleted when I come back, not before.

DEMEA: It's a scandal!

SYRUS [*virtuously*]: I don't like it either, sir, I often protest. [*Calls indoors*] This salt fish, Stephanio, see it's properly soaked.

DEMEA: Heavens above, does the man do it deliberately, or think he'll gain merit if he ruins my son? Damn it, I can see the day when that young man will have to leave home penniless and serve overseas.

SYRUS: Ah, sir, you can look to the future as well as seeing what's under your nose: that's true wisdom.

DEMEA: Tell me, is that girl still in your house?

SYRUS: She's there, indoors.

DEMEA: And she'll be kept there?

SYRUS: I suppose so; your son's crazy about her.

DEMEA: Impossible!

SYRUS: It's his father's foolish weakness, sir. He spoils him dreadfully.

DEMEA: I'm sick and tired of the man!

SYRUS: Ah, there's a world of difference between you and him, sir, and I don't say this just to your race. You're all wisdom, from top to toe; he's nothing but notions. Now *you* wouldn't have let your son carry on like this.

DEMEA: Of course not. I should have got wind of it at least six months before it all began.

SYRUS: No need to tell *me*, sir, how watchful you'd be.

DEMEA: So long as Ctesipho stays as he is, that's all I want.

SYRUS: Like father, like son, that's all we want.

DEMEA: What about him? Have you seen him today?

SYRUS: Ctesipho? [*Aside*] I'll pack this one off to the country. [*Aloud*] He's been up at the farm for some time I believe.

DEMEA: Are you quite sure?

SYRUS: Oh yes, sir, I went along with him myself.

DEMEA: Splendid. I was afraid he was hanging around here.

SYRUS: And what a temper he was in!

DEMEA: What about?

SYRUS: Oh, he'd had a row in town with his brother over that girl.

DEMEA: Really?

SYRUS: Yes, he spoke out all right. Just as the money was being counted out, up he came unexpectedly: 'Oh, Aeschinus!' he cried, 'Fancy you doing this! Think of the disgrace to the family!'

DEMEA: I could weep for joy.

SYRUS: 'It's not just money you are wasting, it's your life.'

DEMEA: Bless him, he's a chip off the old block; I have hopes of him.

[SYRUS *shrugs his shoulders expressively.*]

DEMEA [*ignoring this*]: He's full of maxims like that.

SYRUS: Naturally; he could learn them all at home.

DEMEA: I spare no pains, let slip no chance, and give him a sound training; in fact I'm always telling him to look at other men's lives as in a mirror, and choose from them an example for himself. 'Do this' I say—

SYRUS: And quite right too.

DEMEA: 'Avoid that'—

SYRUS: Splendid.

DEMEA: 'This does you credit'—

SYRUS: That's the way.

DEMEA: 'There you'll be wrong'—

SYRUS: Perfect.

DEMEA: 'And then'—

SYRUS: Excuse me, sir, I haven't time at the moment to listen to you. I've got just the fish I wanted and I must see they're not spoiled. It's as bad a fault in us servants not to see to such things as it is in you and yours, sir, not to do what you've just been saying, and as far as I can I train the other servants on the same lines as you. 'This is too salt,' I say, 'this is burnt to a cinder, this is not cleaned properly; but that's just right, remember to do that next time.' I spare no pains to give all the advice I can, as I understand it, and I end up by telling them to look in the pans like a mirror, sir, while I tell them what they ought to do. All this sounds silly I know, but what would you have us do? You have to take men as they are . . . . Anything else you want, sir?

DEMEA [*angrily*]: Only that you all had more sense.

SYRUS: You're off to the country now?

DEMEA: At once.

SYRUS [*blandly*]: Well, if no one takes your good advice, you're not really doing much good here, are you, sir? [*He goes into Micio's house.*]

DEMEA: Off to the country then, as the boy I wanted here is there already. He belongs to me, and he's the one to worry about. As for the other one, Micio can see to him, as that's what he wants. Now who can I see coming? My comrade Hegio I do believe, if my eyes don't deceive, me, my old boyhood friend, a man of worth and honour of the good old sort, and heaven knows we've all too few citizens like him! It will be a long day before the country suffers anything from *him*. I *am* pleased; as long as I can still set eyes on one of his kind, life's worth living. I'll wait here to greet him and have a word with him.

[GETA *returns right, talking to* HEGIO, *and not seeing* DEMEA]

HEGIO: Good heavens, Geta, what a monstrous story. Can it be true?

GETA: It's a fact, sir.

HEGIO: Such ungentlemanly conduct in a member of that family! Aeschinus, this is not like your father's son!

DEMEA [*aside*]: He must have heard about that girl. *He* can feel it, though it's not his son, while the boy's own father thinks nothing of it. Damn it, I wish Micio were here to listen to him!

HEGIO: They must do the right thing; they shan't get away with this.

GETA: We pin all our hopes on you, sir: you're all we have and we all look to you as our father and protector. Our old master entrusted us to you with his dying words, and if you abandon us we're lost.

HEGIO: Never: don't talk like that. I can't do enough when duty calls me.

DEMEA: I'll meet him. [*Coming forward*] Hegio, I hope with all my heart I see you well.

HEGIO [*coldly*]: Oh, I was looking for you. The same to you, Demea.

DEMEA: You wanted me?

HEGIO: Yes. Your elder son Aeschinus, the one you gave to your brother to adopt, has shown himself neither an honest man nor a gentleman.

DEMEA: What do you mean?

HEGIO: You knew our old friend Simulus—

DEMEA: Of course I did.

HEGIO: Your son has seduced his daughter.

DEMEA: Oh no!

HEGIO: Wait, Demea; you haven't heard the worst.

DEMEA: Can anything be worse?

HEGIO: Yes indeed. This could have been borne somehow—there were excuses: darkness, passion, drink, and youth; it is human nature. When he realized what he had done, he went of his own accord to the mother, weeping, begging, praying, promising, and swearing to marry the girl. He was forgiven and trusted, and the matter was hushed up. The girl was pregnant, and today her time is near. How our fine gentleman has bought himself another girl to live with, a music-girl, heaven help us, and the other is abandoned.

DEMEA: Are you sure this is true?

HEGIO: The girl is here and her mother too, and the facts are obvious; then there's Geta, an honest man as slaves go, and an active one—he's the prop and mainstay of the whole household. Take him, tie him up, get the truth out of him!

GETA: Put me on the rack, sir, if that's not the truth. Besides, the boy won't deny it; bring him face to face with me.

DEMEA [*aside*]: I'm ashamed. I can't think what to do or say to him.

PAMPHILA [*from inside the house*]: Ah, the pain! Juno Lucina, help me, save me, save me!

HEGIO: What, has her labour started?

GETA: It must have, sir.

HEGIO: Now you can hear her calling on the honour of your family, Demea. Do what you must do, and let it be of your own good will. I pray heaven you will take the proper course, but if your intentions are otherwise, I warn you I shall defend this girl and her dead father with all my power. He was my relative, and we were brought up together from our earliest childhood; we stood together in peace and war, and together we faced the hardships of poverty to the end. Hence I shall make every effort, do all I can, go to law if need be, lay down my life in feet, before I fail these women. . . . What is your answer?

DEMEA [*at a loss*]: I'll find my brother, Hegio, and do what he advises.

HEGIO: But bear this in mind, Demea. The more easy your life, the higher you people rise in power, wealth, good fortune and rank, the more you must judge rightly what is right and fair, if you want to be known as honest men. [*He turns away.*]

DEMEA: Just a moment; everything proper shall be done.

HEGIO: That is no more than your duty. Geta, take me in to Sostrata.

[*They go into* SOSTRATA'*s house.*]

DEMEA: I warned him this would happen. I only hope it will end here! But indulgence carried so far is bound to end in disaster of some sort. I'll go and find my brother and pour out the whole story. [*He goes off right.*]

HEGIO [*coming out of the house*]: Bear up, Sostrata, and do what you can to comfort her. I'll find Micio, if he's in town, and tell him exactly what has happened. If he intends to do his duty, let him do it. But if he has other ideas, he must give me an answer so that I know at once what steps to take.

[*He goes off, right, towards the town. Almost immediately* CTESIPHO *and* SYRUS *come out of* MICIO'*s house.*]

CTESIPHO: Do you really mean my father's gone off to the country?

SYRUS: Yes, some time ago.

CTESIPHO: Go on, please, tell me about it.

SYRUS: He's at the farm, busy with something at this very moment, I expect.

CTESIPHO: I hope he is! And so long as he doesn't kill himself, I wish he'd end up so tired that for the next three days he'd be unable to get out of bed!

SYRUS: Hear, hear; or something even better.

CTESIPHO: Agreed. I do so much want to spend this whole day as happily as I began. There's only one thing I don't like about our farm—it's too near. If it were farther off he couldn't be back before dark. As it is, I know what'll happen: he won't find me there, so he'll come running back here to ask me where I've been. 'I haven't seen you all day.' What's the answer to that?

SYRUS: Can't you think of anything?

CTESIPHO: Nothing at all.

SYRUS: The more fool you. Haven't you a dependant, a companion, or a friend?

CTESIPHO: Yes I have. What then?

SYRUS: You could have been doing business with them.

CTESIPHO: But I wasn't. I can't say that.

SYRUS: Yes you can.

CTESIPHO [*dubiously*]: That might account for the day. . . . If I spend the night here, what excuse have I then?

SYRUS: Oh, if only people made a habit of doing business with their friends by night as well! Never mind, don't worry, I know him and his ways. Let him see the with fury, but I'll soon have him as quiet as a lamb.

CTESIPHO: How?

SYRUS: He likes to hear the best of you. I can sing your praises to heaven and go through the list of all your virtues.

CTESIPHO: *My* virtues?

SYRUS: Yours all right. I can have the old man crying like a child for joy. Now look out!

CTESIPHO: What is it?

SYRUS: Talk of the devil. . . .[6]

CTESIPHO: Is it my father?

SYRUS: His very self.

CTESIPHO: Oh, Syrus, what are we to do?

SYRUS: Quick, go in. I'll see to it.

CTESIPHO: If he wants me you haven't seen me, do you hear?

SYRUS: You shut up!

[*He pushes* CTESIPHO *into the house and stands back, by the door.* DEMEA *returns from the town.*]

DEMEA: Just my luck! First I can't find my brother anywhere; then while I'm looking for him I run into one of the farm hands and he tells me Ctesipho is *not* at the farm. Now I don't know what to do.

CTESIPHO [*putting his head out*]: Syrus!

SYRUS: What?

CTESIPHO: Is it me he wants?

SYRUS: Yes.

CTESIPHO: Then I'm done for.

SYRUS: Bear up.

DEMEA [*still talking to himself*]: Nothing but bad luck . . . what the devil does it mean? I can't make it out. Maybe I'm to believe I was born for nothing but misery. I was the first to guess our troubles, the first to find everything out, the first to give the bad news. Whatever happens, I'm the one who suffers.

SYRUS [*aside*]: He makes me laugh. The first to know! He's the only one who hasn't a clue.

DEMEA: Now I'm back to see if Micio's home again.

CTESIPHO [*peeping out*]: Syrus! For heaven's sake don't let him in here.

SYRUS: Be quiet, can't you? I'll do my best.

CTESIPHO: Yes, I dare say, but I just can't trust you. I'll find a room and lock myself in with her, that'll be safest.

SYRUS: All right. I'll move him on, anyway.

DEMEA: There's that scoundrel Syrus.

SYRUS [*aloud, pretending not to see* DEMEA]: How the devil can anyone carry on here at this rate! I should just like to know how many masters I'm supposed to have. It's a dog's life!

DEMEA: What's all this whining about? What can he want? Now then, my man, is my brother at home?

SYRUS: Why the hell do you call me your man? I'm finished.

DEMEA: What's the matter with you?

SYRUS: Matter? Ctesipho's pretty well pummelled me to death, and that girl too.

DEMEA: What's that you say?

SYRUS: Just you take a look at the way he's split my lip.

DEMEA: Why was that?

SYRUS: He says it was all my doing that the girl was bought.

DEMEA: I thought you said just now that you'd gone with him to the farm.

SYRUS: So I did, but he came back in a towering rage. He spared nothing. Fancy not being ashamed to beat an old man like me! Why it seems only yesterday I held him in my arms and he was only *so* high.

DEMEA: Splendid! You're your father's son, Ctesipho! Why, you're a man at last!

SYRUS: Splendid indeed! If he's any sense he'll keep his fists to himself in future.

DEMEA: Well done!

SYRUS: Oh very, beating up a wretched girl and a poor slave who didn't dare hit back. Oh yes, well done!

DEMEA: Couldn't be better. He sees as I do that you're at the bottom of all this. Now, is my brother at home?

SYRUS [*sulkily*]: No he isn't.

DEMEA: I wonder where I can find him.

SYRUS: I know all right, but I'm certainly not telling you.

DEMEA: You say that?

SYRUS: Yes, I do.

DEMEA: Then I'll knock your head off here and now.

SYRUS: Well, there's a man. . . . I don't know his name, but I know where to find him.

DEMEA: Tell me then.

SYRUS: You know this colonnade near the meat market, down that way?

DEMEA: Of course I do.

SYRUS: Go straight up the street past it. Then there's a turning going downhill; go straight down and you'll see a chapel on this side and next to it that alley—

DEMEA: Which one?

SYRUS: Where there's a big fig-tree.

DEMEA: I know.

SYRUS: Go on through it.

DEMEA [*after some thought*]: That alley hasn't *got* a way through.

SYRUS: So it hasn't. What a fool I am! My mistake. Go back to the colonnade. Yes, this is a much shorter way and less chance of going wrong. Do you know Cratinus's house, that rich fellow's?

DEMEA: Yes.

SYRUS [*rapidly*]: Go past it, turn left, straight up the street, come to the Temple of Diana, then turn right and before you come to the town gate just by the pond there's a small flour mill and a workshop opposite. . . . That's where he is.

DEMEA [*suspiciously*]: What's he doing there?

SYRUS [*airily*]: Oh, giving orders for some seats . . . for sitting in the sun . . . to be made with oak legs.

DEMEA: For one of your drinking-parties I suppose. Very nice too! I'll be off. [*He goes off to the town, right.*]

SYRUS: That's right, go; and today I've given you the marching orders you deserve, old drybones. Well, Aeschinus is horribly late, lunch is spoiling, and Ctesipho—all he wants is love. That gives me time for myself. I'll go and have a sip of the wine and a pick at all the best bits . . . a nice easy way to spin out a day like this.

[*He goes into the house.* MICIO *and* HEGIO: *Come on right together from the town.*]

MICIO: I really can't see I deserve your praise for this, Hegio. The offence was on our side, and it is no more than my duty to put things right. I know there are men who see a wanton insult in any criticism of their conduct and deliberately turn the attack on their critics, but did you think I was one of them? Are you thanking me for being different?

HEGIO: No, no, of course not. I never thought you other than you are, Micio. But now please come with me to the girl's mother and tell her in person all you've said to me, that all her suspicions of Aeschinus were on account of his brother and that music-girl.

MICIO: Let us go in then, if we must and you think it's the right thing.

HEGIO: That's good of you. She's wearing herself out with grief and worry, and you can take this weight off her mind. It will be a duty well done. But if you prefer, I can tell her what you've said to me.

MICIO: No, I'll go.

HEGIO: It really is good of you. People who are not so lucky in life somehow always tend to be a bit suspicious and ready to take offence at everything; I suppose their poverty makes them feel inadequate. If you can explain to her yourself she'll take it better.

MICIO: True: how right you are.

HEGIO: Come in with me then.

MICIO: Certainly.

[*They go into* SOSTRATA's *house; there is a short pause, then* AESCHINUS *hurries on right and paces about distractedly.*]

AESCHINUS: This is sheer torture! I never thought to receive such a cruel blow. I just can't think what I'm to do with myself or what to do at all. I'm numb with terror, dazed with fear, robbed of reasoning power! How can I find a way out of this confusion? This awful suspicion—it all seemed so natural! Sostrata is convinced I bought this girl for myself—so I discovered from the old woman when I caught sight of her on her way to fetch the midwife; I ran up and asked her how Pamphila was, whether labour had started and the midwife had been sent for. 'Get out!' was all she said. 'Clear off, Aeschinus, we've had enough of your lying words and your broken promises !' 'What on earth do you mean by that?' I said. 'Good-bye, you can keep the girl you've chosen.' I guessed at once what they suspected, but held my tongue—one word about my brother to that old gossip and all would be out.

Now what can I do? Say the girl is my brother's? But this mustn't get abroad at all costs. I can't let it out if it's still possible to keep the secret. . . . Besides, I doubt if they would believe me: it all hangs together and sounds likely enough. It was I who carried off the girl and I who paid the money, and our house she was brought to. This at least was all my doing, I admit. If only I'd told it all to my father however I'd managed it! I could have persuaded him to let me marry Pamphila. . . . [*After a pause*] Here I am, still putting things off! Now's the time, Aeschinus, to pull yourself together! And first of all I'll go to the women and clear myself. [*He moves towards* SOSTRATA's *house.*] Here's the door. . . . No, I can't face it. . . . I'm a poor thing, I can never raise a hand to this door without a shudder. . . . [*He makes a tremendous effort and knocks loudly*] Anyone there? It's Aeschinus. Open the door, somebody, at once! Someone's coming out; I'll stay over here.

[MICIO *comes out of* SOSTRATA's *house speaking back to her.*]

MICIO: Do as I say, Sostrata, both of you, while I find Aeschinus and tell him our arrangements. [*Coming forward*] Someone knocked—who was it?

AESCHINUS [*aside*]: Heavens, it's my father; I'm done for!

MICIO: Aeschinus!

AESCHINUS [*aside*]: What can he want?

MICIO: Was it you who knocked? [*Aside*] No reply; I think I must tease him a bit—he deserves it for never wanting to trust me over this. [*Aloud*] Can't you answer me?

AESCHINUS [*in confusion*]: *I* didn't knock—at least I don't think I did.

MICIO: No? I was just wondering what you were doing here. [*Aside*] He's blushing: all's well.

AESCHINUS: Excuse me, father, but what took you there? [*pointing to* SOSTRATA's *house*].

MICIO: No business of mine. A friend brought me here just now—to act as a witness.

AESCHINUS: Witness for what?

MICIO [*watching him closely*]: I'll tell you. There are some women living here, in a poor way. I don't think you know them, in fact I am sure you can't, for they have not been here long.

AESCHINUS: Well, what then?

MICIO: There is a girl with her mother—

AESCHINUS: Go on—

MICIO: The girl has lost her father, and this friend of mine is her next-of-kin; so he must marry her. That's the law.[7]

AESCHINUS [*aside*]: No—I can't bear it.

MICIO: What was that?

AESCHINUS: Nothing: it's all right: go on.

MICIO: He has come to take her away to Miletus—where he lives.

AESCHINUS: What, to take the girl away with him?

MICIO: That's right.

AESCHINUS: All the way to Miletus did you say?

MICIO: I did.

AESCHINUS [*aside*]: Oh my head reels! [*Aloud*] But the women—what do they say?

MICIO: What do you expect? Nothing, in fact. The mother has a trumped-up story about the girl having a baby by another man, whom she won't name. He came first, she says, so the girl ought not to be married to my friend.

AESCHINUS: Then don't you think that's right?

MICIO: No, I don't.

AESCHINUS: You don't? And will he really take her away, father?

MICIO: Why on earth shouldn't he?

AESCHINUS [*in a passionate outburst*]: It was cruel of you both, it was heartless, and if I must speak plainly, father, it was—it was—downright dishonourable!

MICIO: But *why*?

AESCHINUS: You ask me why? What about the unhappy man who first loved her and for all I know, poor wretch, still loves her desperately? What do you suppose *he* will feel when he sees her torn from his arms and carried off before his very eyes? I tell you, father, it's a sin and a scandal!

MICIO: How do you make that out? Who promised this girl in marriage and who gave her away? Who was the bridegroom and when was the wedding? Who witnessed it? She was meant for another—why did this man take her?

AESCHINUS: Then was this girl to sit at home, at her age, waiting for a relative to turn up from heaven knows where? You could have said *that*, father, and stuck to it.

MICIO: Nonsense! I had come to help a friend; was I to turn against him? In any case, Aeschinus, the girl is no concern of ours. Why should we bother about them? Let us go. . . . But what's the matter? Why are you crying?

AESCHINUS: Father, please listen. . . .

MICIO [*gently*]: My son, I have heard the whole story; I understand, for I love you, so all you do touches my heart.

AESCHINUS: Then I'll try to deserve your love in future all your life, father—I feel so guilty and ashamed of what I've done that I can't look you in the face.

MICIO: I believe you; I know you are honourable at heart. But I worry about you and your heedless ways. What sort of a country do you think you live in? You seduced a girl you should never have touched. That was your first fault, and quite bad enough, though no more than human: honest men have done the same before you. But afterwards, tell me, did you give it a thought? Or did you look ahead at all and think what you should do and how to do it? If you were ashamed to confess to me yourself, how was I to find out? You delayed and did nothing while nine months went by. This was the greatest wrong you could do, to yourself, to that poor girl, and the child. Well: did you think you could leave everything to the gods and go on dreaming? And that she would be brought to you as a bride without your lifting a finger? I trust you are not so thoughtless in all your personal affairs. [*Changing his tone, after a pause*] Cheer up, you shall marry her.

AESCHINUS: What?

MICIO: I said, Cheer up.

AESCHINUS: Father, for pity's sake, are you making fun of me now?

MICIO: No, I'm not. Why should I?

AESCHINUS: I don't know, except that I'm so desperately anxious for this to be true that I'm afraid it isn't.

MICIO: Go indoors, and pray the gods to help you bring home your wife. Off with you.

AESCHINUS: What? My wife? Will it be soon?

MICIO: Yes.

AESCHINUS: How soon?

MICIO: As soon as possible.

AESCHINUS [*hugging him*]: Damn me, father, if I don't love you more than my own eyes!

MICIO [*gently disengaging himself*]: What, more than—her?

AESCHINUS: Well, just as much.

MICIO [*ironically*]: Very kind of you.

AESCHINUS [*suddenly remembering*]: But where's that man from Miletus?

MICIO [*airily*]: Lost, gone, on board his ship. . . . *Now* what's stopping you?

AESCHINUS: Father, you go, you pray to the gods. They'll be more likely to listen to you, I know; you're so much better than I.

MICIO: I *am* going in: there are preparations to be made. You be sensible and do what I say. [*He goes into* MICIO's *house.*]

AESCHINUS [*coming forward*]: What do you think of that? Is this what it means to be a father or a son? A brother or a friend couldn't do more for me. Oh, he's a man to love and cherish in one's heart! Wonderful! If he can be so kind I'll be sure never to be foolish again or do anything he doesn't like. This lesson will be a warning. But I must hurry indoors or I shall delay my own wedding!

[*He goes into* MICIO's *house, and almost at once* DEMEA *comes on wearily, back from his search.*]

DEMEA: I've walked and walked till I'm worn out. Curse you, Syrus, and your directions! I trailed all over the town, to the gate and the pool and everywhere, and found no sign of a workshop at all nor a soul who said he'd seen my brother. Well, my mind is made up: I'm sitting down here outside his house to wait till he comes back.

[MICIO *comes out of his house talking to* AESCHINUS *inside.*]

MICIO: I'll go across and tell them we are all ready now.

DEMEA: Here he is. I've been looking for you for hours, Micio.

MICIO: What for?

DEMEA: I've more news for you: more wicked deeds of that good young man of yours.

MICIO: What, again!

DEMEA: Unheard-of crimes, appalling ones!

MICIO [*impatiently*]: That'll do.

DEMEA: You've no idea of what he is—

MICIO: Yes I have.

DEMEA [*in a fury*]: You fool, you imagine I'm talking about that music-girl: this time it's an honest girl who is Athenian born.

MICIO [*quietly*]: I know.

DEMEA: You know? And you allow it?

MICIO: Why shouldn't I?

DEMEA: How can you be so calm? Aren't you furious?

MICIO: No. It's true I should prefer—

DEMEA: And now there's a child.

MICIO [*sincerely*]: Heaven bless it!

DEMEA: The girl has nothing—

MICIO: So I heard.

DEMEA: She'll have to be married without a dowry —

MICIO: Evidently.

DEMEA: What's to be done now?

MICIO: What the situation requires. She shall be moved from that house to this [*pointing to* SOSTRATA's *house and his own*].

DEMEA: Good God! Is that the proper thing to do?

MICIO: What more *can* I do?

DEMEA: What indeed! If you really have no feelings about all this, it would surely be only human to *pretend* you have.

MICIO: But I've arranged for him to marry the girl; everything is settled and the wedding is on the way; I've removed all their fears; that is what seems to me only human.

DEMEA [*thoughtfully, after a pause*]: But are you really pleased, Micio, with what you've done?

MICIO: If I could alter the situation—no. But as things are, I can't; so I must accept it quietly. Life is like a game of dice; if you don't get the throw you need most, you must use skill to make the best of what turns up.

DEMEA [*furious again*]: Make the best indeed! And this skill of yours has thrown away two thousand drachmas on that music-girl! Now she'll have to be sold for what she'll fetch, or given away if no one makes an offer.

MICIO: No; I have no intention of selling her.

DEMEA: Then what *do* you propose to do?

MICIO: She shall stay with us.

DEMEA: Heavens above, is he going to keep a mistress in the same house as his wife?

MICIO: Why not?

DEMEA: Are you really in your right mind?

MICIO: I think so.

DEMEA [*with heavy sarcasm*]: God help me, all this tomfoolery makes me wonder if your idea is to have this girl to partner your own singing.

MICIO: Perhaps it is.

DEMEA: And the new bride to join in!

MICIO: Of course.

DEMEA: The three of you dancing hand-in-hand—

MICIO: Certainly.

DEMEA: Certainly?

MICIO [*seizing him by the hand*]: With you to make a fourth if we want one!

DEMEA [*shaking himself free with a cry of disgust*]: Have you no sense of shame?[8]

MICIO [*suddenly serious*]: Now then, Demea, that's enough of your ill-temper. Your son is to be married; can't you behave properly? Try to be pleased and look happy. I'm going to call them; then I'll be back. [*He goes into* SOS-TRATA'*s house.*]

DEMEA: Ye gods, what a life! what morals! what madness! Here's a bride coming without a penny, and a girl in the house! Too much money in the home, a young man ruined by indulgence, and the old one off his head! Salvation herself might intervene, but this household's beyond saving!

[SYRUS *staggers out of* MICIO'*s house, drunk and self-satisfied. He does not see* DEMEA.]

SYRUS: Well, Syrus my lad, you've done yourself proud! Done your duty hand-some-ly. [*Hiccups*] That's better. I've had all I can take *inside*, so I just took a fancy to stretch my legs out here. . . .

DEMEA: Now look at that! A fine example of discipline in the home!

SYRUS [*lurching towards him*]: Why, here's our old man! How do? Feeling glum?

DEMEA: Scoundrel!

SYRUS: Now, now; you spouting here now, Father Wisdom?

DEMEA: If you were in my service—

SYRUS: You'd be a rich man to be sure! You'd have a fortune on a *firm* footing— [*staggers*].

DEMEA:—I would make an example of you to all.

SYRUS: Why? What have *I* done?

DEMEA: Done? Here's all this trouble and dreadful wrongdoing, and nothing properly settled yet, and all you can do is drink, you wretch, as if there was something to celebrate.

SYRUS [*somewhat dashed*]: Sorry now I came out. . . .

[DROMO *opens the door of* MICIO's *house to call* SYRUS.]

DROMO: Hey, Syrus, Ctesipho wants you.

SYRUS [*sufficiently sobered to act promptly, pushes him in again*]: Go away!

DEMEA: What's he saying about Ctesipho?

SYRUS: Nothing.

DEMEA: You brute, is Ctesipho in there?

SYRUS: No, he isn't.

DEMEA: Then why did I hear his name?

SYRUS: It's someone else, a pretty little bit of a boy who hangs around here. [*Nudging him*] Know him?

DEMEA [*grimly, as he strides towards the door*]: I shall soon find out.

SYRUS [*catching at him*]: What's this? Where are you going?

DEMEA: Let me go!

SYRUS: You're not going in there!

DEMEA: Keep your hands off me, you rascal, unless you want me to knock your brains out! [*He dashes into* MICIO's *house.*]

SYRUS: He's gone . . . and a damned unwelcome visitor he'll be, especially to Ctesipho. Now what shall *I* do? Best wait for all this to-do to settle down and find a quiet corner to sleep off this drop I've taken. That's the idea.

[*He staggers off right. Soon afterwards* MICIO *comes out of* SOSTRATA's *house.*]

MICIO: Everything's ready on our side, as I said, Sostrata. When you want. . . . Whoever is that hammering on my door?

[DEMEA *bursts out.*]

DEMEA: Good God, what can I do? How can I deal with this? Shame and sorrow, what can I say? Heaven and earth, Neptune's ocean!

MICIO: Just look at that; no wonder he's shouting, he's found it all out. We're done for, the battle's on, and I'll have to go to the rescue.

DEMEA: Here he comes! You corrupter of both our sons!

MICIO: Kindly control your temper. Calm yourself, Demea.

DEMEA: I *am* controlled, I *am* calm. I won't say another word. Let's face facts. Wasn't it agreed between us (and it was your suggestion, Micio) that you'd not worry about my boy and I'd not worry about yours? Answer me that.

MICIO: It was, I don't deny it.

DEMEA: Then why is my boy drinking in your house? Why receive him there? Why buy him a mistress? Haven't I a right to expect fair play, Micio? What do you want from me? I'm not worrying about your boy, so you leave mine alone.

MICIO: Now you're not being fair—

DEMEA: What!

MICIO: There's an old proverb that friends have everything in common.

DEMEA: Witty, aren't you. Isn't it rather late in the day for that sort of talk?

MICIO: Just listen to me a minute, Demea, if you've no objection. First of all, if it's the money the boys spend which is bothering you, please try to look at it this way. At one time you were supporting both your sons according to your means, because you thought you would have enough for two, and I suppose at the time you expected me to marry. Very well, keep to your original plan; hoard, scrape, and save to have as much as possible to leave them. You can see merit in that: all right. My money is something they didn't expect, so let them enjoy it. Your capital won't be touched, and anything I add can be counted as pure gain. If only you would be willing to see this in a true light, Demea, you'd save yourself and me and the boys a great deal of trouble.

DEMEA: I'm not talking about money. It's their morals, both of them—

MICIO: Wait. I know, I was coming to that. There are a lot of traits in people from which inferences can be drawn. Two men often do the same thing and you might say that one can safely be allowed to do it while the other might not. The difference is not in the thing done but in the doer. I can see signs in these boys which make me confident they will turn out as we want them. I see good sense, intelligence, deference when required, and mutual affection, and we can be sure they are open and generous in heart and mind. You can call them back to the right path any day you like. You may say you are anxious for them not to be so careless about money, but, my dear Demea, you must realize that in every other respect we grow wiser with increasing years, but the besetting fault of old age is simply this: we all think too much of money. Time will develop this in them well enough.

DEMEA: Be careful, Micio: these fine-sounding arguments and easy-going temperament of yours may destroy us all.

MICIO: No, no, impossible. Come along now, try to listen to me and stop frowning.

DEMEA: As things are I suppose I'll have to. . . . But tomorrow morning at crack of dawn I'm taking my boy away from here to the farm.

MICIO [*humouring him*]: *Before* dawn, I dare say. Only make yourself agreeable for today.

DEMEA: And I'm taking that girl too.

MICIO: That'll do the trick! The best way of tying him down. Only mind you keep her there.

DEMEA: I'll see to that. Once she's there I'll have her cooking and grinding corn till she's covered with ash and grime and flour, and then I'll send her out gleaning in the midday sun and make her black and burnt as a cinder!

MICIO [*ironically*]: Good! Now I find you talking sense. Go on: 'And then I'll force my son whatever he says to sleep with her—'

DEMEA: All right, laugh at me. You're lucky to be in the mood. I have my feelings. . . .

MICIO: Now don't start again—

DEMEA: No, I've done.

MICIO: Come in then, and spend this day with us in the proper way.

[*They go into* MICIO's *house. After a short interval* DEMEA *reappears, much smartened up and perhaps wearing some of* MICIO's *clothes.*]

DEMEA: A plan for life may be well worked out, but a man can still learn something new from circumstances, age and experience. You find you don't know what you thought you did, and things which seemed so important before, you reject in practice. This is what has just happened to me, for I've lived a hard life up to this very moment, and now I'm giving up when my course is almost run. And why? Hard facts have shown me that a man gains most from affability and forbearance. Look at my brother and me if you want to see the truth of this. He has always led a life of leisure, sociable, easy-going, and tolerant, with never a black look for anyone and a smile for all. He's lived for himself and spent on himself, and he's won praise and affection from everyone. I'm the country bumpkin, mannerless and surly, truculent, mean and close-fisted, and when I took a wife what troubles I brought on myself! Two sons were born—more worry. While thinking of them and struggling to make all I could for them, see how I've wasted my youth and my life in money-grubbing! Now I'm old, and what's my reward for all my trouble? They don't like me. It's my brother who enjoys the benefits of fatherhood without having lifted a finger. They love him and avoid me. He has their confidence and their affection, the two of them are always with him and I'm left all alone. They offer prayers for his long life, but you may be sure they're counting the days for me to die. I've toiled and slaved to bring them up, but he has made them his own for next to nothing, so he has all the enjoyment while the trouble's left to me. Very well then, two can play at that game; let's see now whether I can take up his challenge and show myself capable of soft answers and winning ways! *I* could also do with a bit of love and appreciation from my own children. If that comes from being generous and agreeable, I can take the lead all right. The property won't stand it, but that needn't worry me—I'm old enough for it to last *my* time.

[SYRUS *comes out of* MICIO'*s house.*]

SYRUS: Please, sir, your brother hopes you're not leaving us.

DEMEA [*genially*]: Who's that? Ah, Syrus, my man, good evening. How are you and how are things going?

SYRUS: All right, sir.

DEMEA: Splendid. [*Aside*] That's three things already which aren't like me, 'my man', 'how are you', and 'how are things going'. [*Aloud*] You may be a slave, but you have your finer points, and I should be glad to do you a good turn.

SYRUS [*incredulous*]: Thank you, sir.

DEMEA: But I mean it, Syrus, as you'll soon see.

[SYRUS *goes back into the house and* GETA *comes out of* SOSTRATA'*s.*]

GETA [*to* SOSTRATA]: I'm just going next door, madam, to see how soon they want the bride. Why, here's Demea. Good evening, sir.

DEMEA: Let me see now, what's your name?

GETA: Geta, sir.

DEMEA: Geta, today has convinced me that you are a most valuable person. Nothing recommends a slave to me so much as his care for his master's interests, such as I have seen in you. For this, if the opportunity arises, I should be glad to do you a good turn. [*Aside*] I think my affability improves with practice.

GETA [*puzzled*]: It's kind of you to think so, sir.

DEMEA [*aside*]: I've made a start, winning over the masses one by one.

[AESCHINUS *and* SYRUS *come out of* MICIO'*s.*]

AESCHINUS: They're killing me with all their fuss over wedding ceremonies! Here's a whole day wasted with preparations.

DEMEA: What's the matter, Aeschinus?

AESCHINUS: Hullo, father, are you there?

DEMEA: Father, yes, in heart and nature, your father who loves you more than his own eyes. But why don't you bring your wife home?

AESCHINUS: That's just what I *want* to do. I'm kept waiting for the flute-player and the choir for the marriage-hymn.

DEMEA: Will you take a word of advice from your old father?

AESCHINUS: What is it?

DEMEA: Scrap the lot—flutes, torches, hymn, and fuss—knock a hole in the garden wall here and now and take her across that way, join the two houses and bring the whole lot of them, mother and all, over to us!

AESCHINUS [*hugging him*]: Father darling, you're splendid!

DEMEA [*aside*]: Bravo, now I'm splendid! Micio'll have to keep open house, with all these people to entertain and no end of expense, but what do I care? I'm splendid and popular! Tell that Croesus[9] to pay out two thousand on the spot! Syrus, what are you waiting for?

SYRUS: What am I to do, sir?

DEMEA: Knock down the wall. Geta, you go and fetch them.

GETA: Heaven bless you, sir, for being so kindly disposed to us all.

DEMEA: It's no more than you deserve, [GETA *and* SYRUS *go in.*] What do you say?

AESCHINUS [*somewhat bewildered*]: I agree.

DEMEA: She's not well yet after having the baby—much better bring her that way than through the street. [*Banging and hammering are heard.*]

AESCHINUS: Nothing could be better, father.

DEMEA [*smugly*]: Ah, it's just my way. . . . But look, here's Micio.
    [MICIO *bursts out of his house.*]

MICIO: My brother's orders? Where is he? *Are* these your orders, Demea?

DEMEA [*impressively*]: They are. In this and every other way we should unite with this family to cherish and support it and make it one with ours.

AESCHINUS: Yes, please, father.

MICIO [*reluctantly*]: I suppose I have to agree.

DEMEA: Believe me, it's our duty. And now, to start with, this boy's wife has a mother.

MICIO: I know; what of it?

DEMEA: She is virtuous and discreet.

MICIO: So I'm told.

DEMEA: Not too young—

MICIO: I know.

DEMEA: But long since past the age to have children, and with no one to look after her. She's alone. . . .

MICIO: What's the point of all this?

DEMEA: The proper thing for you to do is to marry her. Aeschinus, you persuade him.

MICIO: *I* marry?

DEMEA: You.

MICIO: Did you say *I* should marry her?

DEMEA: I did.

MICIO: You're joking.

DEMEA [*to* AESCHINUS]: Talk to him as man to man and he'll do it.

AESCHINUS: Father—

MICIO: You silly ass, must you listen to him?

DEMEA: It's no good, Micio, you'll have to give in.

MICIO: You're crazy.

AESCHINUS: Do it for my sake, father.

MICIO: You're mad, leave me alone.

DEMEA: Come, do as your son asks.

MICIO: You're off your head. I'm sixty-four: should I embark on matrimony at my age with this decrepit old hag for a wife? Is that your idea?

AESCHINUS: Come on: I've promised them.

MICIO: *Promised* them? Kindly restrict your generosity to your own person, my boy.

DEMEA: But he might be asking more of you. . . .

MICIO: There couldn't be anything more.

DEMEA: Do it for him—

AESCHINUS: Don't be difficult—

DEMEA: Come, promise.

MICIO: Leave me alone, can't you!

AESCHINUS: Not until you'll give in.

MICIO: It's sheer coercion!

DEMEA: Now be generous, Micio.

MICIO: This is monstrous, crazy, ludicrous, entirely foreign to my whole way of life . . . but if you are both so set on it . . . all right.[10]

AESCHINUS: Well done! You deserve all my love now.

DEMEA: But—[*aside*] What else can I say now I've won that point?

MICIO: Now what is it?

DEMEA: There's Hegio, their closest relative, who'll be a connection of ours. He's a poor man, and we ought to do something for him.

MICIO: Well, what?

DEMEA: There's that little bit of property just outside the town which you're always letting out. We can give it to him and he'll make good use of it.

MICIO: Do you call that a 'little bit'?

DEMEA: Big or little, it's what we must do. He has been a father to the girl, he's a good man and one of us, so he ought to have it. After all, I'm only appropriating the sentiment you expressed just now, Micio: 'the besetting fault of us all is that in old age we think too much of money'.[11] Wise words and well put! We must rid ourselves of this defect, and put the truth in this saying into practice.

MICIO [*drily*]: I'm glad to hear it. Very well. Hegio shall have it when Aeschinus likes.

AESCHINUS: Oh, father!

DEMEA: Now you are my true brother, body and soul! [*Aside*] And I've got his own knife at his throat!

  [SYRUS *comes out of the house, dusting himself down.*]

SYRUS: Your orders have been carried out, sir,

DEMEA: Good man. And now I should like to propose that this very day Syrus ought to receive his freedom.

MICIO: His freedom? *Him?* Whatever for?

DEMEA: For lots of reasons.

SYRUS [*eagerly*]: Oh, master, you're a fine gentleman, sir, indeed you are. I've looked after both the young masters properly since they were boys, taught them, guided them, always given them the best advice I could. . . .

DEMEA [*drily*]: So I see. And there are other things besides—reliable shopping, procuring a girl, putting on a dinner party at all hours. It needs no ordinary man to perform services like *these*.

SYRUS: Sir, you're really splendid!

DEMEA: To crown all, it was he who helped us to buy the music-girl; in fact, he arranged it all. He ought to get something for it, and it will have a good effect on the others. . . . And then, Aeschinus wants it.

MICIO: Do you, Aeschinus?

AESCHINUS: Yes, very much.

MICIO: Well, if you really want it—Syrus, come here. [*With a blow*] Take your freedom.

SYRUS [*rubbing himself ruefully*]: You're very kind. I'm grateful to you all, especially you, sir [*to* DEMEA].

DEMEA: My congratulations.

AESCHINUS: And mine.

SYRUS: Thank you. Now there's just one thing to complete my happiness. . . .
  If only I could see my wife, Phrygia, freed as well!

DEMEA: A very fine woman.

SYRUS: And she was the first, sir, to come forward as wet-nurse for your grandson, the young master's son, this very day—

DEMEA: Ah, that's a serious reason. If she was the first, she certainly ought to have her freedom.

MICIO: Just for that?

DEMEA: Why not? I'll pay you her value to settle it.

SYRUS: Oh, sir, heaven always grant you all your wishes!

MICIO: Well, Syrus, you've done pretty well for yourself today.

DEMEA: He has, if you'll carry on with your duty and give him a little something in hand to live on. He'll soon pay you back.

MICIO [*snapping his fingers*]: That's more than he'll get.

DEMEA: He's a good fellow.

SYRUS: I'll pay it back, sir, I promise you, just give me—

AESCHINUS: Come on, father.

MICIO: I'll think about it.

DEMEA [*to* AESCHINUS]: He'll do it.

SYRUS: You're wonderful, sir!

AESCHINUS: Father, you're a darling!

MICIO: What *is* all this? Why this sudden change of heart? What's the idea? Why this sudden outburst of generosity?

DEMEA: I'll tell you. I wanted to show you, Micio, that what our boys thought was your good nature and charm didn't come from a way of living which was sincere or from anything right or good, but from your weakness, indulgence and extravagance. Now, Aeschinus, if you and your brother dislike my ways because I won't humour you in all your wishes, right or wrong, I wash my hands of you—you can spend and squander and do whatever you like. On the other hand, being young, you are short-sighted, over-eager and heedless, and you may like a word of advice or reproof from me on occasion, as well as my support at the proper time. Well, I'm here at your service.

AESCHINUS: We'd like that, father. You know best what to do. But what's going to happen to Ctesipho?

DEMEA: I've given my consent; he can keep his girl. But she must be his last.

MICIO: Well done, Demea. [*To the audience*] Now give us your applause!

[*They all go into* MICIO's *house.*]

Notes

[1] The sons of Aemilius Paullus, both aediles in the year of his death (160 B.C.). The younger was already adopted into the Scipio family and is better known as Scipio Aemilianus Africanus Numantinus. . . .

[2] According to Servius (on *Georgics* 2. 506) these are equal pipes, called after the old Latin name for Tyre.

[3] i.e. in 160 B.C.

[4] Diphilus of Sinope, a New Comedy poet of the later fourth century B.C. About sixty titles of his plays are known, and Plautus used him as a model, though this title does not appear in any list of Plautus's plays.

[5] The 'Scipionic circle'. . . .

[6] Literally, 'the wolf in the fable', a popular expression.

[7] The provision of Attic law which is the basis of the plot in *Phormio*, set out there in ll. 125 ff.

[8] Demea's sense of outrage at the head of a household dancing and singing can hardly have been in the original, as it shows Roman, not Greek prejudice.

[9] 'Croesus' as a symbol of wealth instead of *Babylon*, only found here; but Donatus implies that a Babylonian was proverbial for extravagance.

[10] Donatus comments that in Menander's play Micio did not object to the marriage, so this scene is Terence's innovation.

[11] In ll. 833–4.

from *On the Nature of the Universe*

Lucretius
Translated by R. E. Latham

Book One—Matter and Space

Mother of Aeneas and his race, delight of men and gods, life-giving Venus, it is your doing that under the wheeling constellations of the sky all nature teems with life, both the sea that buoys up our ships and the earth that yields our food. Through you all living creatures are conceived and come forth to look upon the sunlight. Before you the winds flee, and at your coming the clouds forsake the sky. For you the inventive earth flings up sweet flowers. For you the ocean levels laugh, the sky is calmed and glows with diffused radiance. When first the day puts on the aspect of spring, when in all its force the fertilizing breath of Zephyr is unleashed, then, great goddess, the birds of air give the first intimation of your entry; for yours is the power that has pierced them to the heart. Next the wild beasts and farm animals alike run wild, frisk through the lush pastures and swim the swift-flowing streams. Spellbound by your charm, they follow your lead with fierce desire. So throughout seas and uplands, rushing torrents, verdurous meadows and the leafy shelters of the birds, into the breasts of one and all you instil alluring love, so that with passionate longing they reproduce their several breeds.

Since you alone are the guiding power of the universe and without you nothing emerges into the shining sunlit world to grow in joy and loveliness, yours is the partnership I seek in striving to compose these lines *On the Nature of the Universe* for my noble Memmius. For him, great goddess, you have willed outstanding excellence in every field and everlasting fame. For his sake, therefore, endow my verse with everlasting charm.

Meanwhile, grant that this brutal business of war by sea and land may everywhere be lulled to rest. For you alone have power to bestow on mortals the blessing of quiet peace. In your bosom Mars himself, supreme commander in this business of brutality, flings himself down at times, laid low by the irremediable wound of love. Gazing upward, his neck a prostrate column, he fixes

64

hungry eyes on you, great goddess, and gluts them with love. As he lies out-stretched, his breath hangs upon your lips. Stoop, then, goddess most glorious, and enfold him at rest in your hallowed bosom and whisper with those lips sweet words of prayer, beseeching for the people of Rome untroubled peace. In this evil hour of my country's history, I cannot pursue my task with a mind at ease, as an illustrious scion of the house of Memmius cannot at such a crisis withhold his service from the common weal. ⟨I beg you for peace⟩ since it is essential to the very nature of deity that it should enjoy immortal existence in utter tranquillity, aloof and detached from our affairs. It is free from all pain and peril, strong in its own resources, exempt from any need of us, indifferent to our merits and immune from anger.

For what is to follow, my Memmius, lay aside your cares and lend undis-tracted ears and an attentive mind to true reason. Do not scornfully reject, before you have understood them, the gifts I have marshalled for you with zealous devotion. I will set out to discourse to you on the ultimate realities of heaven and the gods. I will reveal those _atoms_ from which nature creates all things and increases and feeds them and into which, when they perish, nature again resolves them. To these in my discourse I commonly give such names as the 'raw material', or 'generative bodies', or 'seeds' of things. Or I may call them 'primary particles', because they come first and everything else is com-posed of them.

When human life lay grovelling in all men's sight, crushed to the earth under the dead weight of superstition whose grim features loured menacingly upon mortals from the four quarters of the sky, a man of Greece was first to raise mortal eyes in defiance, first to stand erect and brave the challenge. Fables of the gods did not crush him, nor the lightning flash and the growling men-ace of the sky. Rather, they quickened the keen courage of his heart, so that he, first of all men, longed to smash the constraining locks of nature's doors. The vital vigour of his mind prevailed. He ventured far out beyond the flam-ing ramparts of the world and voyaged in mind throughout infinity. Returning victorious, he proclaimed to us what can be and what cannot: how the power of each thing is limited, and its boundary-stone sticks buried deep. Therefore superstition in its turn lies crushed beneath his feet, and we by his triumph are lifted level with the skies.

One thing that worries me is the fear that you may fancy yourself embarking on an impious course of philosophy, setting your feet on the path of sin. Far from it. More often it is this very superstition that is the mother of sinful and impious deeds. Remember how at Aulis the altar of the virgin goddess was foully stained with the blood of Iphigeneia by the leaders of the Greeks, the patterns of chivalry. The headband was bound about her virgin tresses and hung down evenly over both her cheeks. Suddenly she caught sight of her father standing sadly in front of the altar, the attendants beside him hiding the knife and her people bursting into tears when they saw her. Struck dumb with terror, she sank on her knees to the ground. Poor girl, at such a moment it did not help her that she had been first to give the name of father to a king. Raised by the hands of men, she was led trembling to the altar. Not for her the sacrament of marriage and the loud chant of Hymen. It was her fate in the very hour of marriage to fall a sinless victim to a sinful rite, slaughtered to her greater grief by a father's hand, so that a fleet might sail under happy auspices. Such are the heights of wickedness to which men have been driven by superstition.

You yourself, if you surrender your judgement at any time to the blood-curdling declamations of the prophets, will want to desert our ranks. Only think what phantoms they can conjure up to overturn the tenor of your life and wreck your happiness with fear. And not without cause. For, if men saw that a term was set to their troubles, they would find strength in some way to withstand the hocus-pocus and intimidations of the prophets. As it is, they have no power of resistance, because they are haunted by the fear of eternal punishment after death. They know nothing of the nature of the spirit. Is it born, or is it implanted in us at birth? Does it perish with us, dissolved by death, or does it visit the murky depths and dreary sloughs of the Underworld? Or is it transplanted by divine power into other creatures, as described in the poems of our own Ennius, who first gathered on the delectable slopes of Helicon an evergreen garland destined to win renown among the nations of Italy? Ennius indeed in his immortal verses proclaims that there is also a Hell, which is peopled not by our actual spirits or bodies but only by shadowy images, ghastly pale. It is from this realm that he pictures the ghost of Homer, of unfading memory, as appearing to him, shedding salt tears and revealing the nature of the universe.

I must therefore give an account of celestial phenomena, explaining the movements of sun and moon and also the forces that determine events on earth. Next, and no less important, we must look with keen insight into the make-up of spirit and mind: we must consider those alarming phantasms that strike upon our minds when they are awake but disordered by sickness, or when they are buried in slumber, so that we seem to see and hear before us men whose dead bones lie in the embraces of earth.

I am well aware that it is not easy to elucidate in Latin verse the obscure discoveries of the Greeks. The poverty of our language and the novelty of the theme often compel me to coin new words for the purpose. But your merit and the joy I hope to derive from our delightful friendship encourage me to face any task however hard. This it is that leads me to stay awake through the quiet of the night, studying how by choice of words and the poet's art I can display before your mind a clear light by which you can gaze into the heart of hidden things.

This dread and darkness of the mind cannot be dispelled by the sunbeams, the shining shafts of day, but only by an understanding of the outward form and inner workings of nature. In tackling this theme, our starting-point will be this principle: *Nothing is ever created by divine power out of nothing.* The reason why all mortals are so gripped by fear is that they see all sorts of things happening on the earth and in the sky with no discernible cause, and these they attribute to the will of a god. Accordingly, when we have seen that nothing can be created out of nothing, we shall then have a clearer picture of the path ahead, the problem of how things are created and occasioned without the aid of gods.

First then, if things were made out of nothing, any species could spring from any source and nothing would require seed. Men could arise from the sea and scaly fish from the earth, and birds could be hatched out of the sky. Cattle and other farm animals and every kind of wild beast, multiplying indiscriminately, would occupy cultivated and waste lands alike. The same fruits would not grow constantly on the same trees, but they would keep changing: any tree might bear any fruit. If each species were not composed of its own generative bodies, why should each be born always of the same kind of mother? Actually, since each is formed out of specific seeds, it is born and emerges into the sunlit world only from a place where there exists the right material, the right kind of atoms. This is why everything cannot be born of everything, but a specific power of generation inheres in specific objects.

Again, why do we see roses appear in spring, grain in summer's heat, grapes under the spell of autumn? Surely, because it is only after specific seeds have drifted together at their own proper time that every created thing stands revealed, when the season is favourable and the life-giving earth can safely deliver delicate growths into the sunlit world. If they were made out of nothing, they would spring up suddenly after varying lapses of time and at abnormal seasons, since there would of course be no primary bodies that could be prevented by the harshness of the season from entering into generative unions. Similarly, there would be no need of any lapse of time for the accumulation of seed in order that things might grow. Tiny tots would turn suddenly into young men, and trees would shoot up spontaneously out of the earth. But it is obvious that none of these things happens since, as is natural, everything grows gradually from a specific seed and retains its specific character. It is a fair inference that each is increased and nourished by its own raw material.

Here is a further point. Without seasonable showers the earth cannot send up gladdening growths. Lacking food, animals cannot reproduce their kind or sustain life. This points to the conclusion that many elements are common to many things, as letters are to words, rather than to the theory that anything can come into existence without atoms.

Or again, why has not nature been able to produce men on such a scale that they could ford the ocean on foot or tear down high mountains with their hands or prolong their lives over many generations? Surely because each thing requires for its birth a particular material that determines what can be produced. It must therefore be admitted that nothing can be made out of nothing, because everything must be generated from a seed before it can emerge into the unresisting air.

Lastly, we see that tilled plots are superior to untilled, and their fruits are improved by cultivation. This is because the earth contains certain atoms that we rouse to productivity by turning the fruitful clods with the ploughshare and stirring up the soil. But for these, you would see great improvements arising spontaneously without any aid from our labours.

The second great principle is this: *nature resolves everything into its component atoms and never reduces anything to nothing.* If anything were perishable in all its parts, anything might perish all of a sudden and vanish from sight. There would be no need of any force to separate its parts and loosen their links. In actual fact, since everything is composed of indestructible seeds, nature obviously does not allow anything to perish till it has encountered a force that shatters it with a blow or creeps into chinks and unknits it.

If the things that are banished from the scene by age are annihilated through the exhaustion of their material, from what source does Venus bring back the several races of animals into the light of life? And, when they are brought back, where does the inventive earth find for each the special food required for its sustenance and growth? From what fount is the sea replenished by its native springs and the streams that flow into it from afar? From where does the ether draw nutriment for the stars? For everything consisting of a mortal body must have been exhausted by the long day of time, the illimitable past. If throughout this bygone eternity there have persisted bodies from which the universe has been perpetually renewed, they must certainly be possessed of immortality. Therefore things cannot be reduced to nothing.

Again, all objects would regularly be destroyed by the same force and the same cause were it not that they are sustained by imperishable matter more or less tightly fastened together. Why, a mere touch would be enough to bring about destruction supposing there were no imperishable bodies whose union could be dissolved only by the appropriate force. Actually, because the fastenings of the atoms are of various kinds while their matter is imperishable, compound objects remain intact until one of them encounters a force that proves strong enough to break up its particular constitution. Therefore nothing returns to nothing, but everything is resolved into its constituent bodies.

Lastly, showers perish when father ether has flung them down into the lap of mother earth. But the crops spring up fresh; the branches on the trees burst into leaf; the trees themselves grow and are weighed down with fruit. Hence in turn man and beast draw nourishment. Hence we see flourishing cities blest with children and every leafy thicket loud with new broods of songsters. Hence in lush pastures cattle wearied by their bulk fling down their bodies, and the white milky juice oozes from their swollen udders. Hence a new generation frolic friskily on wobbly legs through the fresh grass, their young minds tipsy with undiluted milk. Visible objects therefore do not perish utterly, since nature repairs one thing from another and allows nothing to be born without the aid of another's death.

Well, Memmius, I have taught you that things cannot be created out of nothing nor, once born, be summoned back to nothing. Perhaps, however, you are becoming mistrustful of my words, because these atoms of mine are not visible to the eye. Consider, therefore, this further evidence of *bodies whose existence you must acknowledge though they cannot be seen.* First, wind, when its force is roused, whips up waves, founders tall ships and scatters clouds. Sometimes scouring plains with hurricane force it strews them with huge trees and batters mountain peaks with blasts that hew down forests. Such is wind in its fury, when it whoops aloud with a mad menace in its shouting. Without question, therefore, there must be invisible particles of wind that sweep sea, that sweep land, that sweep the clouds in the sky, swooping upon them and whirling them along in a headlong hurricane. In the way they flow and the havoc they spread they are no different from a torrential flood of water when it rushes down in a sudden spate from the mountain heights, swollen by heavy rains, and heaps together wreckage from the forest and entire trees. Soft though it is by nature, the sudden shock of oncoming water is more than even stout bridges can withstand, so furious is the force with which the turbid, storm-flushed torrent surges against their piers. With a mighty roar it lays them low, rolling huge rocks under its waves and brushing aside every obstacle from its course. Such, therefore, must be the movement of blasts of wind also. When they have come surging along some course like a rushing river, they push obstacles before them and buffet them with repeated blows; and sometimes, eddying round and round, they snatch them up and carry them along in a swiftly circling vortex. Here then is proof upon proof that winds have invisible bodies, since in their actions and behaviour they are found to rival great rivers, whose bodies are plain to see.

Then again, we smell the various scents of things though we never see them approaching our nostrils. Similarly, we do not look upon scorching heat nor can we grasp cold in our eyes and we do not see sounds. Yet all these must be composed of physical bodies, since they are able to impinge upon our senses. For nothing can touch or be touched except bodies.

Again, clothes hung out on a surf-beaten shore grow moist. Spread in the sun they grow dry. But we do not see how the moisture has soaked into them, nor again how it has been dispelled by the heat. It follows that the moisture is split up into minute parts which the eye cannot possibly see.

Again, in the course of many annual revolutions of the sun a ring is worn thin next to the finger with continual rubbing. Dripping water hollows a stone. A curved ploughshare, iron though it is, dwindles imperceptibly in the furrow. We see the cobblestones of the highway worn by the feet of many wayfarers. The bronze statues by the city gates show their right hands worn thin by the touch of travellers who have greeted them in passing. We see that all these are being diminished, since they are worn away. But to perceive what particles drop off at any particular time is a power grudged to us by our ungenerous sense of sight.

To sum up, whatever is added to things gradually by nature and the passage of days, causing a cumulative increase, eludes the most attentive scrutiny of our eyes. Conversely, you cannot see what objects lose by the wastage of age—sheer sea cliffs, for instance, exposed to prolonged erosion by the mordant brine—or at what time the loss occurs. It follows that nature works through the agency of invisible bodies.

On the other hand, things are not hemmed in by the pressure of solid bodies in a tight mass. This is because *there is vacuity in things*. A grasp of this fact will be helpful to you in many respects and will save you from much bewildered doubting and questioning about the universe and from mistrust of my teaching. Well then, by vacuity I mean intangible and empty space. If it did not exist, things could not move at all. For the distinctive action of matter, which is counteraction and obstruction, would be in force always and everywhere. Nothing could move forward, because nothing would give it a starting-point by receding. As it is, we see with our eyes at sea and on land and high up in the sky that all sorts of things in all sorts of ways are on the move. If there were no empty space, these things would be denied the power of restless movement—or rather, they could not possibly have come into existence, embedded as they would have been in motionless matter.

Besides, there are clear indications that things that pass for solid are in fact porous. Even in rocky caves a trickle of water seeps through, and every surface weeps with brimming drops. Food percolates to every part of an animal's body. Trees grow and pour forth their fruit in season, because their food is distributed throughout their length from the tips of the roots through the trunk and along every branch. Noises pass through walls and fly into closed buildings. Freezing cold penetrates to the bones. If there were no vacancies through which the various bodies could make their way, none of these phenomena would be possible.

Again, why do we find some things outweigh others of equal volume? If there is as much matter in a ball of wool as in one of lead, it is natural that it should weigh as heavily, since it is the function of matter to press everything downwards, while it is the function of space on the other hand to remain weightless. Accordingly, when one thing is not less bulky than another but obviously lighter, it plainly declares that there is more vacuum in it, while the heavier object proclaims that there is more matter in it and much less empty space. We have therefore reached the goal of our diligent enquiry: there is in things an admixture of what we call vacuity.

In case you should be misled on this question by the idle imagining of certain theorists, I must anticipate their argument. They maintain that water yields and opens up liquid ways to the scaly bodies of fish that push against it, because they leave spaces behind them into which the yielding water can flow together. In the same way, they suppose, other things can move by mutually changing places, although every place remains filled. This theory has been adopted utterly without warrant. For how can the fish advance till the water has given way? And how can the water retire when the fish cannot move? There are thus only two alternatives: either all bodies are devoid of movement, or you must admit that things contain an admixture of vacuity whereby each is enabled to make the first move.

Lastly, if two broad bodies suddenly spring apart from contact, all the intervening space must be void until it is occupied by air. However quickly the air rushes in all round, the entire space cannot be filled instantaneously. The air must occupy one spot after another until it has taken possession of the whole space. If anyone supposes that this consequence of such springing apart is made possible by the condensation of air, he is mistaken. For condensation implies that something that was full becomes empty, or vice versa. And I contend that air could not condense so as to produce this effect; or, at any rate, if there were no vacuum, it could not thus shrink into itself and draw its parts together.

However many pleas you may advance to prolong the argument, you must end by admitting that there is vacuity in things. There are many other proofs that I could scrape together into the pile in order to strengthen conviction; but for an acute intelligence these small clues should suffice to discover the rest for yourself. As hounds often smell out the lairs of a mountain-ranging quarry screened in thickets, when once they have got on to the right trail, so in such questions one thing will lead on to another, till you can succeed by yourself in tracking down the truth to its lurking places and dragging it forth. If you grow weary and relax from the chase, there is one thing, Memmius, that I can safely promise you: my honeyed tongue will pour from the treasury of my breast such generous draughts, drawn from inexhaustible springs, that I am afraid slow plodding age may creep through my limbs and unbolt the bars of my life before the full flood of my arguments on any single point has flowed in verse through your ears.

To pick up the thread of my discourse, all nature as it is in itself consists of two things—bodies and the vacant space in which the bodies are situated and through which they move in different directions. The existence of bodies is vouched for by the agreement of the senses. If a belief resting directly on this foundation is not valid, there will be no standard to which we can refer any doubt on obscure questions for rational confirmation. If there were no place and space, which we call vacuity, these bodies could not be situated anywhere or move in any direction whatever. This I have just demonstrated. It remains to show that *nothing exists that is distinct both from body and from vacuity* and could be ranked with the others as a third substance. For whatever *is* must also be something. If it offers resistance to touch, however light and slight, it will increase the mass of body by such amount, great or small, as it may amount to, and will rank with it. If, on the other hand, it is intangible, so that it offers no resistance whatever to anything passing through it, then it will be that empty space which we call vacuity. Besides, whatever it may be in itself, either it will act in some way, or react to other things acting upon it, or else it will be such that things can be and happen in it. But without body nothing can act or react; and nothing can afford a place except emptiness and vacancy.

Therefore, besides matter and vacuity, we cannot include in the number of things any third substance that can either affect our senses at any time or be grasped by the reasoning of our minds.

You will find that anything that can be named is either a property or an accident of these two. A *property* is something that cannot be detached or separated from a thing without destroying it, as weight is a property of rocks, heat of fire, fluidity of water, tangibility of all bodies, intangibility of vacuum. On the other hand, servitude, poverty and riches, freedom, war, peace and all other things whose advent or departure leaves the essence of a thing intact, all these it is our practice to call by their appropriate name, *accidents*.

Similarly, time by itself does not exist; but from things themselves there results a sense of what has already taken place, what is now going on and what is to ensue. It must not be claimed that anyone can sense time by itself apart from the movement of things or their restful immobility.

Again, when men say it *is* a fact that Helen was ravished or the Trojans were conquered, we must not let anyone drive us to the admission that any such factual event *exists* independently of any object, on the ground that the generations of men of whom these events were accidents have been swept away by the irrevocable lapse of time. For we could put it that whatever has taken place is an accident of a particular tract of earth or of the space it occupied. If there had been no matter and no space or place in which things could happen, no spark of love kindled by the beauty of Tyndareus' daughter would ever have glowed inside the breast of Phrygian Paris to light that dazzling blaze of pitiless war; no Wooden Horse, unmarked by the sons of Troy, would have set the towers of Ilium aflame through the midnight issue of Greeks from its womb. So you may see that events cannot be said to *be* by themselves like matter or in the same sense as space. Rather, you should describe them as accidents of matter, or of the place in which things happen.

Material objects are of two kinds, atoms and compounds of atoms. The atoms themselves cannot be swamped by any force, for they are preserved indefinitely by their absolute solidity. Admittedly, it is hard to believe that anything can exist that is absolutely solid. The lightning stroke from the sky penetrates closed buildings, as do shouts and other noises. Iron glows white-hot in the fire, and rocks crack in savage scorching heat. Hard gold is softened and melted by heat; and the ice of bronze is liquefied by flame. Both heat and piercing cold seep through silver, since we feel both alike when a cooling shower of water is poured into a goblet that we hold ceremonially in our hands. All these facts point to the conclusion that nothing is really solid. But sound reasoning and nature itself drive us to the opposite conclusion. Pay attention, therefore, while I demonstrate in a few lines that there exist certain bodies that are absolutely solid and indestructible, namely those atoms which according to our teaching are the seeds of prime units of things from which the whole universe is built up.

In the first place, we have found that nature is twofold, consisting of two totally different things, matter and the space in which things happen. Hence each of these must exist by itself without admixture of the other. For, where there is empty space (what we call vacuity), there matter is not; where matter exists, there cannot be a vacuum. Therefore the prime units of matter are solid and free from vacuity.

Again, since composite things contain some vacuum, the surrounding matter must be solid. For you cannot reasonably maintain that anything can hide vacuity and hold it within its body unless you allow that the container itself is solid. And what contains the vacuum in things can only be an accumulation of matter. Hence matter, which possesses absolute solidity, can be everlasting when other things are decomposed.

Again, if there were no empty space, everything would be one solid mass; if there were no material objects with the property of filling the space they occupy, all existing space would be utterly void. It is clear, then, that there is an alternation of matter and vacuity, mutually distinct, since the whole is neither completely full nor completely empty. There are therefore solid bodies, causing the distinction between empty space and full. And these, as I have just shown, can be neither decomposed by blows from without nor invaded and unknit from within nor destroyed by any other form of assault. For it seems that a thing without vacuum can be neither knocked to bits nor snapped nor chopped in two by cutting; nor can it let in moisture or seeping cold or piercing fire, the universal agents of destruction. The more vacuum a thing contains within it, the more readily it yields to these assailants. Hence, if the units of matter are solid and without vacuity, as I have shown, they must be everlasting.

Yet again, if the matter in things had not been everlasting, everything by now would have gone back to nothing, and the things we see would be the product of rebirth out of nothing. But, since I have already shown that nothing can be created out of nothing nor any existing thing be summoned back to nothing, the atoms must be made of imperishable stuff into which everything can be resolved in the end, so that there may be a stock of matter for building the world anew. The atoms, therefore, are absolutely solid and unalloyed. In no other way could they have survived throughout infinite time to keep the world renewed.

Furthermore, if nature had set no limit to the breaking of things, the particles of matter in the course of ages would have been ground so small that nothing could be generated from them so as to attain from them in the fullness of time to the summit of its growth. For we see that anything can be more speedily disintegrated than put together again. Hence, what the long day of time, the bygone eternity, has already shaken and loosened to fragments could never in the residue of time be reconstructed. As it is, there is evidently a limit set to breaking, since we see that everything is renewed and each according to its kind has a fixed period in which to grow to its prime.

Here is a further argument. Granted that the particles of matter are absolutely solid, we can still explain the composition and behaviour of soft things—air, water, earth, fire—by their intermixture with empty space. On the other hand, supposing the atoms to be soft, we cannot account for the origin of hard flint and iron. For there would be no foundation for nature to build on. Therefore there must be bodies strong in their unalloyed solidity by whose closer clustering things can be knit together and display unyielding toughness.

If we suppose that there is no limit set to the breaking of matter, we must still admit that material objects consist of particles which throughout eternity have resisted the forces of destruction. To say that these are breakable does not square with the fact that they have survived throughout eternity under a perpetual bombardment of innumerable blows.

Again, there is laid down for each thing a specific limit to its growth and its tenure of life, and the laws of nature ordain what each can do and what it cannot. No species is ever changed, but each remains so much itself that every kind of bird displays on its body its own specific markings. This is a further proof that their bodies are made of changeless matter. For, if the atoms could yield in any way to change, there would be no certainty as to what could arise and what could not, at what point the power of everything was limited by an immovable frontier post; nor could successive generations so regularly repeat the nature, behaviour, habits and movements of their parents.

To proceed with our argument, there is an kultimate point in visible objects that represents the smallest thing that can be seen. So also there must be anl ultimate point in objects that lie below the limit of perception by our senses. This point is without parts and is the smallest thing that can exist. It never has been and never will be able to exist by itself, but only as one primary part of something else. It is with a mass of such parts, solidly jammed together in formation, that matter is filled up. Since they cannot exist by themselves, they must needs stick together in a mass from which they cannot by any means be prized loose. The atoms, therefore, are absolutely solid and unalloyed, consisting of a mass of least parts tightly packed together. They are not compounds formed by the coalescence of their parts, but bodies of absolute and everlasting solidity. To these nature allows no loss or diminution, but guards them as seeds for things. If there are no such least parts, even the smallest bodies consist of an infinite number of parts, since they can always be halved and their halves halved again without limit. On this showing, what difference will there be between the whole universe and the very least of things? None at all. For, however endlessly infinite the universe may be, yet the smallest things will equally consist of an infinite number of parts. Since true reason cries out against this and denies that the mind can believe it, you must needs give in and admit that there are least parts which themselves are partless. Granted that these parts exist, you must needs admit that the atoms they compose are also solid and everlasting. But, if all things were compelled by all-creating nature to be broken up into these least parts, nature would lack the power to rebuild anything out of them. For partless objects cannot have the essential properties of generative matter—those varieties of attachment, weight, impetus, impact and movement on which everything depends.

For all these reasons, *those who have imagined that the raw material of things is fire and the universe consists of fire alone have evidently wandered far from the truth.* Of these the first champion to plunge into the fray was Heraclitus, illustrious for the darkness of his speech, though rather among the lighter-witted of the Greeks than among those who are earnest seekers after truth. For fools are more impressed and intrigued by what they detect under a screen of riddling words, and accept as true what pleasantly tickles their ears and all that is dyed with a smart sound. I should like to know how things can be so manifold if they are created out of nothing but sheer fire. It would not help if hot fire were condensed or rarefied, so long as the particles of fire retained the same nature that fire posesses as a whole. Its heat would simply be fiercer as its parts were more concentrated, milder as they were dispersed and dissipated. There is no further effect that you could attribute to such causes—no possibility that the infinite variety of things could result from variations in the density or rarity of fire. Even these variations in density could not occur unless we allow in things an intermixture of vacuity. But, because these theorists see that many things run counter to their theories, they dodge the issue and decline to leave any pure vacuum in things. Shunning the steep, they lose the true path. They do not see that without vacuity everything would be condensed and would become one body, which could not throw off anything at high speed from itself as blazing fire throws off light and heat, so that you can see that its parts are not solidly compacted.

If, on the other hand, they think that there is some other way in which fires in combination can be quenched and change their substance, then obviously—if they do not shrink from any implication of this view—the fieriness must be completely annihilated and whatever emerges must be a new creation out of nothing. For, if ever anything is so transformed as to overstep its own limits, this means the immediate death of what was before. It follows that they must leave something intact, or you would find everything reduced to nothing and the stock of things reborn and reinvigorated from nothing. As it is, there are certain definite bodies that always keep the same nature, and it is by the withdrawal or advent of these and their reshuffling that things change their nature and material objects are transformed. And these primary bodies cannot be fiery. So long as they possessed and retained a fiery nature, it would make no odds if some of them were detached and withdrawn and others tacked on and some were reshuffled. Whatever they created would still be simply fire. The truth, as I maintain, is this: there are certain bodies whose impacts, movements, order, position and shapes produce fires. When their order is changed, they change their nature. In themselves they do not resemble fire or anything else that can bombard our senses with particles or impinge on our organs of touch.

To say, as Heraclitus does, that everything is fire, and nothing can be numbered among things as a reality except fire, seems utterly crazy. On the basis of the senses he attacks and unsettles the senses—the foundation of all belief and the only source of his knowledge of that which he calls fire. He believes that the senses clearly perceive fire, but not the other things that are in fact no less clear. This strikes me as not only pointless but mad. For what is to be our standard of reference? What can be a surer guide to the distinction of true from false than our own senses? What grounds have we for taking everything else and leaving fire, any more than for taking away everything else and leaving some other thing? Either procedure appears equally insane.

For this reason those who have thought that fire is the raw material of things and the universe can consist of fire and those who have made *air* the starting-point for the growth of things or have supposed that *water* by itself could form everything or that *earth* could create all things and be transformed into their natures—all these have evidently wandered far from the truth.

Not less mistaken are those who make the elements two-fold, coupling air with fire and earth with water, *and those who think that everything can grow from four elements,* fire and earth and air and rain. Conspicuous among these is Empedocles of Acragas, born in the three-cornered confines of that Isle round which surges the Ionian deep, rushing far into creeks and dashing up salt spray from its grey-green billows. The sea that parts it from Aeolian shores runs headlong through its narrow channel. Here is deadly Charybdis. Here the rumbling of Etna's flames is a warning that it is rallying its wrath that once again its force may spew out fires bursting in a torrent from its throat, to bring its flashing flames back up to the sky. This great country is acknowledged to have many claims to the admiration of mankind and the attention of sight-seekers. But, for all its surfeit of good things and its ample garrison of men, it has surely held nothing more glorious than this man, nothing holier, nothing more wonderful, nothing more precious. Indeed, the songs that took shape in his divine breast proclaim in ringing tones such glorious discoveries that he scarcely seems a scion of mortal stock. Empedocles and those lesser men of whom we have spoken above, who rank far and away below him, have certainly made many excellent and divine discoveries and uttered oracles from the inner sanctuary of their hearts with more sanctity and far surer reason than those the Delphic prophetess pronounces, drugged by the laurel fumes, from Apollo's tripod. Yet among the very foundations of things they have come to grief. Great as they were, great has been their fall.

Their first error is this: they postulate movement while banishing empty space from the universe, and they admit the existence of soft and flimsy things—air, sun, water, earth, animals, vegetables—without allowing their bodies an intermixture of vacuity.

Secondly, they acknowledge no limit to the splitting of things, no rest from crumbling, no smallest unit of matter, although we see that every object has an ultimate point that seems to our senses to be the smallest, from which you may infer that the things you cannot perceive have also an ultimate point which actually is the smallest. Besides, since they rank as elements soft things that we perceive to be neither birthless nor deathless, the universe ought by now to have returned to nothing and whatever exists ought to be a new creation and growth out of nothing, both of which suppositions you already know to be false. Furthermore, these supposed elements are in many ways hurtful and lethal to one another, so that they will either be destroyed on contact or will rush apart, as when a storm has gathered we see lightning flashes, rainclouds and winds rush apart.

Again, if everything is created from four things and resolved into them, why should we say that these are the elements of things rather than the reverse—that other things are the elements of these? For one gives birth to another continually, and they interchange their colours and their entire natures throughout the whole of time. If, on the other hand, you believe that particles of fire and earth, airy wind and watery moisture, combine without changing their natures in combination, then nothing can be created from them, either animate or (like a tree) with inanimate body. For each element in a composite assemblage will betray its own nature; air will appear mixed with earth, and fire will remain side by side with moisture. But in fact the elements, in giving birth to things, must contribute a nature that is hidden and viewless, so that nothing may show that conflicts with the thing created and prevents it from being distinctively itself.

These authors trace everything back to the sky and its fires. First they make fire transform itself into the winds of air; hence is born rain, and from rain is created earth. Then the process is reversed: first from earth is born moisture, then comes air, then fire. And things never cease to interchange, migrating from heaven to earth, from earth to the starry firmament. This is something elements ought never to do. For it is essential that something should remain immutable, or everything would be reduced to nothing. For, if ever anything is so transformed that it oversteps its own limits, this means the immediate death of what was before. Therefore, since the substances just mentioned enter into interchange, they must needs consist of other substances that cannot be altered, so that you may not find everything reduced to nothing. You ought rather to postulate bodies possessed of such a nature that, if they happen to have created fire, they only need a few subtractions and additions and some change of order and movement to make gusty air. In this way we can account for any change from one thing to another.

'But,' you say, 'observation clearly shows that all growing things do grow up into the gusty air out of the earth and it is from the earth that they draw their food. And, unless an auspicious season gives free play to the rain, so that trees reel beneath the dissolving clouds, and unless the sun in turn provides fostering warmth, there can be no growth of crops, trees, or animals.' Yes, and unless we ourselves were sustained by dry food and fluid juices, our bodies would waste away till every bit of life had escaped from all our sinews and bones. There can be no doubt that we are fed and sustained by certain specific things, other things by others, and so forth. Obviously, it is because there are in things many elements common to many commingled in many ways that various things draw their food from various sources. It often makes a big difference in what combinations and positions the selfsame elements occur, and what motions they mutually pass on or take over. For the same elements compose sky, sea and lands, rivers and sun, crops, trees and animals, but they are moving differently and in different combinations. Consider how in my verses, for instance, you see many letters common to many words; yet you must admit that different verses and words differ in substance and in audible sound. So much can be accomplished by letters through mere change of order. But the elements can bring more factors into play so as to create things in all their variety.

Now let us look into the theory of Anaxagoras, which the Greeks call *homoeomeria*: the poverty of our native language will not let me translate the word, but the thing itself can be expressed readily enough. Understand, then, that in speaking of the *homoeomeria* of things Anaxagoras means that bones are formed of minute miniature bones, flesh of minute miniature morsels of flesh, blood by the coalescence of many drops of blood; gold consists of grains of gold; earth is a conglomeration of little earths, fire of fires, moisture of moistures. And he pictures everything else as formed in the same way. At the same time he does not admit any vacuum in things, or any limit to the splitting of matter, on both of which counts he seems to me guilty of the same error as the others. Add to this that he makes the elements too frail, if indeed we can allow the name of 'elements' to bodies that have the same nature as the things themselves, that suffer and decay no less than they do and are not reined in by any force in their race to destruction. For which of these things will withstand violent assault, so as to escape extinction in the very jaws of death? Will fire or water or air? Which of these? Blood or bones? Nothing, I maintain, will escape, where everything is as perishable as those objects that we see vanishing from before our eyes under stress of some force or other. In proof of the impossibility of such annihilation and regrowth from nothing, I appeal to the evidence already adduced.

Again, since food builds up and nourishes our bodies, our veins and bones and blood kand sinews must be composed of matter unlike themselves.]

Alternatively, if it is alleged that all foods are of mixed substance and contain little morsels of sinews and bones and veins and drops of blood, it must be supposed that all food, whether solid or fluid, consists of unlike matter, namely of a mixture of bones and sinews, pus and blood. Similarly, if the material of all the things that grow out of the earth occurs in the earth, earth must consist of unlike matter that rises out of it. Turn to other phenomena, and the same words will hold good. If flame, smoke and ashes lurk unseen in wood, then wood must consist of unlike matter that rises out of it. Furthermore, all the material atoms that the earth feeds and makes to grow kmust consist of things unlike themselves—and they in their turn must also contain things unlike themselves.]

Here there is left some scanty cover for escaping detection, and Anaxagoras avails himself of it. He asserts that there is in everything a mixture of everything, but all the ingredients escape detection except the one whose particles are most numerous and conspicuous and stand in the front line. This is far removed from the truth. Otherwise it would naturally happen that corn, when it is crushed by the dire force of the grindstone, would often show some trace of blood, and that blood would exude when we crush between stones any of those things that derive material from our bodies. Similarly, grass and water ought often to emit sweet drops of the same flavour as the milk in the udders of fleecy ewes. When clods of soil are crumbled, finely divided particles of different plants and grains and leaves ought to become visible, lurking among the soil. When sticks are snapped, ashes and smoke ought to be revealed, and tiny hidden fires. But observation plainly shows that none of these things happens. It is clear therefore that one sort of thing is not intermingled with another in this way, but there must be in things a mixture of invisible seeds that are common to many sorts.

'But,' you may object, 'it often happens in mountainous country that nearby tops of tall trees are rubbed together by the force of strong south winds till suddenly they blossom out into a blaze of flame.' Agreed. And yet there is no fire embedded in the wood. What it does contain is a multitude of seeds of heat, which start a conflagration in the forest only when they have been concentrated by rubbing. If there were ready-made flame concealed in the wood, the fires could not be hidden for any length of time; they would spread havoc through the woodland and burn the trees to ashes. Now do you see the point of my previous remark, that it makes a great difference in what combinations and positions the same elements occur and what motions they mutually pass on and take over, so that with a little reshuffling the same ones may produce forests and fires? This is just how the words themselves are formed, by a little reshuffling of the letters, when we pronounce 'forests' and 'fires' as two distinct utterances.

If you cannot account for what you see happen without inventing particles of matter with the same sort of nature as the whole objects, there is an end of your elements altogether; you will have to postulate particles that shake their sides with uproarious guffaws and bedew their cheeks with salt tears.

And now pay special attention to what follows and listen more intently. I am well aware how full it is of obscurity. But high hope of fame has struck my heart with its holy staff and in so doing has implanted in my breast the sweet love of the Muses. That is the spur that lends my spirit strength to pioneer through pathless tracts of their Pierian realm where no foot has ever trod before. What joy it is to light upon virgin springs and drink their waters. What joy to pluck new flowers and gather for my brow a glorious garland from fields whose blossoms were never yet wreathed by the Muses round any head. This is my reward for teaching on these lofty topics, for struggling to loose men's minds from the tight knots of superstition and shedding on dark material the bright beams of my song that irradiate everything with the sparkle of the Muses. My art is not without a purpose. Physicians, when they wish to treat children with a nasty dose of wormwood, first smear the rim of the cup with the sweet yellow fluid of honey. The children, too young as yet for foresight, are lured by the sweetness at their lips into swallowing the bitter draught. So they are tricked but not trapped, for the treatment restores them to health. In the same way our doctrine often seems unpalatable to those who have not handled it, and the masses shrink from it. That is why I have tried to administer my philosophy to you in the dulcet strains of poesy, to touch it with the sweet honey of the Muses. My object has been to engage your mind with my verses while you gain insight into the nature of the universe and the pattern of its architecture.

Well then, since I have shown that there are completely solid indestructible particles of matter flying about through all eternity, let us unroll whether or not there is any limit to their number. Similarly, as we have found that there is a vacuum, the place or space in which things happen, let us see whether its whole extent is limited or whether it stretches far and wide into immeasurable depths.

Learn, therefore, that *the universe is not bounded in any direction*. If it were, it would necessarily have a limit somewhere. But clearly a thing cannot have a limit unless there is something outside to limit it, so that the eye can follow it up to a certain point but not beyond. Since you must admit that there is nothing outside the universe, it can have no limit and is accordingly without end or measure. It makes no odds in which part of it you may take your stand: whatever spot anyone may occupy, the universe stretches away from him just the same in all directions without limit. Suppose for a moment that the whole of space were bounded and that someone made his way to its uttermost boundary and threw a flying dart. Do you choose to suppose that the missile, hurled with might and main, would speed along the course on which it was aimed? Or do you think something would block the way and stop it? You must assume one alternative or the other. But neither of them leaves you a loophole. Both force you to admit that the universe continues without end. Whether there is some obstacle lying on the boundary line that prevents the dart from going farther on its course or whether it flies on beyond, it cannot in fact have started from the boundary. With this argument I will pursue you. Wherever you may place the ultimate limit of things, I will ask you: 'Well then, what does happen to the dart?' The upshot is that the boundary cannot stand firm anywhere, and final escape from this conclusion is precluded by the limitless possibility of running away from it.

Further, if all the space in the universe were shut in and confined on every side by definite boundaries, the supply of matter would already have accumulated by its own weight at the bottom, and nothing could happen under the dome of the sky—indeed, there would be no sky and no sunlight, since all the available matter would have settled down and would be lying in a heap throughout eternity. As it is, no rest is given to the atoms, because there is no bottom where they can accumulate and take up their abode. Things go on happening all the time through ceaseless movement in every direction; and atoms of matter bouncing up from below are supplied out of the infinite. Lastly it is a matter of observation that one thing is limited by another. The hills are demarcated by air, and air by the hills. Land sets bounds to sea, and sea to every land. But the universe has nothing outside to limit it. There is therefore a limitless abyss of space, such that even the dazzling flashes of the lightning cannot traverse it in their course, racing through an interminable tract of time, nor can they even shorten the distance still to be covered. So vast is the scope that lies open to things far and wide without limit in any dimension.

The universe is restrained from setting any limit to itself by nature, which compels body to be bounded by vacuum and vacuum by body. Thus nature either makes them both infinite in alternation, or else one of them, if it is not bounded by the other, must extend in a pure state without limit. kSpace, however, being infinite, so must matter be. Otherwisel neither sea nor land nor the bright zones of the sky nor mortal beings nor the holy bodies of the gods could endure for one brief hour of time. The supply of matter would be shaken loose from combination and swept through the vastness of the void in isolated particles; or rather, it would never have coalesced to form anything, since its scattered particles could never have been driven into union.

Certainly the atoms did not post themselves purposefully in due order by an act of intelligence, nor did they stipulate what movements each should perform. As they have been rushing everlastingly throughout all space in their myriads, undergoing a myriad changes under the disturbing impact of collisions, they have experienced every variety of movement and conjunction till they have fallen into the particular pattern by which this world of ours is constituted. This world has persisted many a long year, having once been set going in the appropriate motions. From these everything else follows. The rivers replenish the thirsty sea with profuse streams of water. Incubated by the sun's heat, the earth renews its fruits, and the brood of animals that springs from it grows lustily. The gliding fires of ether sustain their life. None of these results would be possible if there were not an ample supply of matter to bounce up out of infinite space in replacement of all that is lost. Just as animals deprived of food waste away through loss of body, so everything must decay as soon as its supply of matter goes astray and is cut off.

Whatever world the atoms have combined to form, impacts from without cannot preserve it at every point. By continual battering they can hold back part of it till others come along to make good the deficiency. But they are compelled now and then to bounce back and in so doing to leave ample space and time for the atoms to break free from combination. It is thus essential that there should be great numbers of atoms coming up. Indeed, the impacts themselves could not be maintained without an unlimited supply of matter from all quarters.

There is one belief, Memmius, that you must beware of entertaining— *the theory that everything tends towards what they call 'the centre of the universe'.* On this theory, the world stands fast without any impacts from without, and top and bottom cannot be parted in any direction, because everything has been tending towards the centre—if you can believe that anything rests upon itself. Whatever heavy bodies there may be under the earth must then tend upwards and rest against the surface upside down, like the images of things which we now see reflected in water. In the same way they would have it that animals walk about topsy-turvy and cannot fall off the earth into the nether quarters of the sky any more than our bodies can soar up spontaneously into the heavenly regions. When they are looking at the sun, we see the stars of night; so they share the hours with us alternately and experience nights corresponding to our days. But this is an idle fancy of fools who have got hold of the wrong end of the stick. There can be no centre in infinity. And, even if there were, nothing could stand fast there rather than flee from it. For all place or space, at the centre no less than elsewhere, must give way to heavy bodies, no matter in what direction they are moving. There is no place to which bodies can come where they lose the property of weight and stand still in the void. And vacuum cannot support anything but rather must allow it free passage, as its own nature demands. Therefore things cannot be held in combination by this means through surrender to a craving for the centre.

Besides, they do not claim that all bodies have this tendency towards the centre, but only those of moisture and earth—the waters of the deep and the floods that pour down from the hills and in general whatever is composed of a more or less earthy body. But according to their teaching the light breaths of air and hot fires are simultaneously wafted outwards away from the centre. The reason why the encircling ether twinkles with stars and the sun feeds its flames in the blue pastures of the sky is supposed to be that fire all congregates there in its flight from the centre. Similarly, the topmost branches of trees could not break into leaf unless their food had this same upward urge. kBut, if you allow matter to escape from the world in this way,l you are leaving the ramparts of the world at liberty to crumble of a sudden and take flight with the speed of flame into the boundless void. The rest will follow. The thunder-breeding quarters of the sky will rush down from aloft. The ground will fall away from our feet, its particles dissolved amid the mingled wreckage of heaven and earth. The whole world will vanish into the abyss, and in the twinkling of an eye no remnant will be left but empty space and invisible atoms. At whatever point you first allow matter to fall short, this will be the gateway to perdition. Through this gate the whole concourse of matter will come streaming out.

If you take a little trouble, you will attain to a thorough understanding of these truths. For one thing will be illumined by another, and eyeless night will not rob you of your road till you have looked into the heart of nature's darkest mysteries. So surely will facts throw light upon facts.

Book Two—Movements and Shapes of Atoms

What joy it is, when out at sea the stormwinds are lashing the waters, to gaze from the shore at the heavy stress some other man is enduring! Not that anyone's afflictions are in themselves a source of delight; but to realize from what troubles you yourself are free is joy indeed. What joy, again, to watch opposing hosts marshalled on the field of battle when you have yourself no part in their peril! But this is the greatest joy of all: to possess a quiet sanctuary, stoutly fortified by the teaching of the wise, and to gaze down from that elevation on others wandering aimlessly in search of a way of life, pitting their wits one against another, disputing for precedence, struggling night and day with unstinted effort to scale the pinnacles of wealth and power. O joyless hearts of men! O minds without vision! How dark and dangerous the life in which this tiny span is lived away! Do you not see that nature is barking for two things only, a body free from pain, a mind released from worry and fear for the enjoyment of pleasurable sensations?

So we find that the requirements of our bodily nature are few indeed, no more than is necessary to banish pain, and also to spread out many pleasures for ourselves. Nature does not periodically seek anything more gratifying than this, not complaining if there are no golden images of youths about the house, holding flaming torches in their right hands to illumine banquets prolonged into the night. What matter if the hall does not sparkle with silver and gleam with gold, and no carved and gilded rafters ring to the music of the lute? Nature does not miss these luxuries when men recline in company on the soft grass by a running stream under the branches of a tall tree and refresh their bodies pleasurably at small expense. Better still if the weather smiles upon them, and the season of the year stipples the green herbage with flowers. Burning fevers flee no swifter from your body if you toss under figured counterpanes and coverlets of crimson than if you must lie in rude homespun.

If our bodies are not profited by treasures or titles or the majesty of kingship, we must go on to admit that neither are our minds. Or tell me, Memmius, when you see your legions thronging the Campus Martius in the ardour of

mimic warfare, supported by ample auxiliaries and a force of cavalry, magnifi-
cently armed and fired by a common purpose, does that sight scare the terrors
of superstition from your mind? Does the fear of death retire from your breast
and leave it carefree? Or do we not find such resources absurdly ineffective?
The fears and anxieties that dog the human breast do not shrink from the clash
of arms or the fierce rain of missiles. They stalk unabashed among princes and
potentates. They are not awestruck by the gleam of gold or the bright sheen of
purple robes.

Can you doubt then that this power rests with reason alone? All life is a
struggle in the dark. As children in blank darkness tremble and start at everything, so we in broad daylight are oppressed at times by fears as baseless as
those horrors which children imagine coming upon them in the dark. This
dread and darkness of the mind cannot be dispelled by the sunbeams, the shining shafts of day, but only by an understanding of the outward form and inner
workings of nature.

And now to business. I will explain *the motion by which the generative bodies of matter give birth to various things*, and, after they are born, dissolve them
once more; the force that compels them to do this; and the power of movement through the boundless void with which they are endowed. It is for you
to devote yourself attentively to my words.

Be sure that matter does not stick together in a solid mass. For we see that
everything grows less and seems to melt away with the lapse of time and with-
draw its old age from our eyes. And yet we see no diminution in the sum of
things. This is because the bodies that are shed lessen the thing they leave but
enlarge the thing they join; here they bring decay, there full bloom, but they do
not settle. So the sum of things is perpetually renewed. Mortals live by mutual
interchange. One race increases by another's decrease. The generations of living
things pass in swift succession and like runners hand on the torch of life.

If you think that the atoms can stop and by their stopping generate new
motions in things, you are wandering far from the path of truth. Since the
atoms are moving freely through the void, they must all be kept in motion
either by their own weight or on occasion by the impact of another atom. For
it must often happen that two of them in their course knock together and
immediately bounce apart in opposite directions, a natural consequence of
their hardness and solidity and the absence of anything behind to stop them.

As a further indication that all particles of matter are on the move,
remember that the universe is bottomless: there is no place where the atoms
could come to rest. As I have already shown by various arguments and proved

conclusively, space is without end or limit and spreads out immeasurably in all directions alike.

It clearly follows that no rest is given to the atoms in their course through the depths of space. Driven along in an incessant but variable movement, some of them bounce far apart after a collision while others recoil only a short distance from the impact. From those that do not recoil far, being driven into a closer union and held there by the entanglement of their interlocking shapes, are composed firmly rooted rock, the stubborn strength of steel and the like. Those others that move freely through larger tracts of space—few and far between, springing far apart and carried far by the rebound—these provide for us thin air and blazing sunlight. Besides these, there are many other atoms at large in empty space that have been thrown out of compound bodies and have nowhere even been granted admittance so as to bring their motions into harmony.

This process, as I might point out, is illustrated by an image of it that is continually taking place before our very eyes. Observe what happens when sunbeams are admitted into a building and shed light on its shadowy places. You will see a multitude of tiny particles mingling in a multitude of ways in the empty space within the actual light of the beam, as though contending in everlasting conflict, rushing into battle rank upon rank with never a moment's pause in a rapid sequence of unions and disunions. From this you may picture what it is for the atoms to be perpetually tossed about in the illimitable void. To some extent a small thing may afford an illustration and an imperfect image of great things. Besides, there is a further reason why you should give your mind to these particles that are seen dancing in a sunbeam: their dancing is an actual indication of underlying movements of matter that are hidden from sight. There you will see many particles under the impact of invisible blows changing their course and driven back upon their tracks, this way and that, in all directions. You must understand that they all derive this restlessness from the atoms. It originates with the atoms, which move of themselves. Then those small compound bodies that are least removed from the impetus of the atoms are set in motion by the impact of their invisible blows and in turn cannon against slightly larger blows. So the movement mounts up from the atoms and gradually emerges to the level of our senses, so that those bodies are in motion that we see in sunbeams, moved by blows that remain invisible.

And now, Memmius, as to the rate at which the atoms move, you may gauge this readily from these few indications. First, when dawn sprays the earth with new-born light and the birds, flitting through pathless thickets, fill the neighbourhood according to their kind with liquid notes that glide through the thin air, it is plain and palpable for all to see how suddenly the sun at the moment of his rising drenches and clothes the world with his radiance. But the heat and the bright light that the sun emits do not travel through empty space. Therefore they are forced to move more slowly, cleaving their way as it were through waves of air. And the atoms that compose this radiance do not travel as isolated individuals but linked and massed together. Thus their pace is retarded by one dragging back another as well as by external obstacles. But, when separate atoms are travelling in solitary solidity through empty space, they encounter no obstruction from without and move as single units, being composed of their own parts, on the course on which they have embarked. Obviously therefore they must far outstrip the sunlight in speed of movement and traverse an extent of space many times as great in the time it takes for the sun's rays to flash across the sky . . . [No wonder that men] cannot follow the individual atoms, so as to discern the agency by which everything is brought about.

In the face of these truths, some people who know nothing of matter believe that nature without the guidance of the gods could not bring round the changing seasons in such perfect conformity to human needs, creating the crops and those other blessings that mortals are led to enjoy by the guide of life, divine pleasure, which coaxes them through the arts of Venus to reproduce their kind, lest the human race should perish. Obviously, in imagining that the gods established everything for the sake of men, they have stumbled in all respects far from the path of truth. Even if I knew nothing of the atoms, I would venture to assert on the evidence of the celestial phenomena themselves, supported by many other arguments, that the universe was certainly not created for us by divine power: it is so full of imperfections. All this, Memmius, I will elucidate for you at a later stage. Now let me complete my account of atomic movements.

Now, I should judge, is the place to insert a demonstration that *no material thing can be uplifted or travel upwards by its own power.* Do not be misled by the particles that compose flame. The fact that all weights taken by themselves tend downwards does not prevent lusty crops and trees from being born with an upward thrust and from growing and increasing upwards. Similarly, when fires leap up to the housetops and lick beams and rafters with rapid flame, it must not be supposed that they do this of their own accord with no force to fling them up. Their behavior is like that of blood released from our body when it spouts forth and springs aloft in a gory fountain. Observe also with what force beams and rafters are heaved up by water. The more we have shoved them down into the depths, many of us struggling strenuously together to push them under, the more eagerly the water spews and ejects them back again, so that more than half their bulk shoots up above the surface. And yet, I should judge, we have no doubt that all these, taken by themselves, would move downwards through empty space. It must be just the same with flames: under pressure they can shoot up through the gusty air, although their weight, taken by itself, strives to tug them down. Do you observe how the nocturnal torches of the sky in their lofty flight draw in their wake long trails of flame in whatever direction nature has set their course? Do you see how stars and meteors fall upon the earth? The sun from the summit of the sky scatters heat in all directions and sows the fields with light. The sun's radiance therefore tends also towards the earth. Note again how the lightning flies through the rain-storms aslant. The fires that break out of the clouds rush together, now this way, now that; often enough the fiery force falls upon the earth.

In this connection there is another fact that I want you to grasp. *When the atoms are travelling straight down through empty space by their own weight, at quite indeterminate times and places they swerve ever so little from their course,* just so much that you can call it a change of direction. If it were not for this swerve, everything would fall downwards like raindrops through the abyss of space. No collision would take place and no impact of atom upon atom would be created. Thus nature would never have created anything.

If anyone supposes that heavier atoms on a straight course through empty space could outstrip lighter ones and fall on them from above, thus causing impacts that might give rise to generative motions, he is going far astray from the path of truth. The reason why objects falling through water or thin air must accelerate their fall in proportion to their weight is simply that the matter composing water or air cannot obstruct all objects equally, but is forced to give way more speedily to heavier ones. But empty space can offer no resistance to any object in any quarter at any time, so as not to yield free passage as its own nature demands. Therefore, through undisturbed vacuum all bodies must travel at equal speed though impelled by unequal weights. The heavier will never be able to fall on the lighter from above or generate of themselves impacts leading to that variety of motions out of which nature can produce things. We are thus forced back to the conclusion that the atoms swerve a little—but only by a minimum, or we shall be caught imagining slantwise movements, and the facts will prove us wrong. For we see plainly and indisputably that weights, when they come tumbling down, have no power of their own to move aslant, so far as meets the eye. But who can possibly perceive that they do not diverge in the very least from a vertical course?

Again, if all movement is always interconnected, the new arising from the old in a determinate order—if the atoms never swerve so as to originate some new movement that will snap the bonds of fate, the everlasting sequence of cause and effect—what is the source of the free will possessed by living things throughout the earth? What, I repeat, is the source of that willpower snatched from the fates, whereby we follow the path along which we are severally led by pleasure, swerving from our course at no set time or place but at the bidding of our own hearts? There is no doubt that on these occasions the will of the individual originates the movements that trickle through his limbs. Observe, when the starting-barriers are flung back, how the racehorses in the eagerness of their strength cannot break away as suddenly as their hearts desire. For the whole supply of matter must first be mobilized throughout every member of the body: only then, when it is mustered in a continuous array, can it respond to the prompting of the heart. So you may see that the beginning of movement is generated by the heart; starting from the voluntary action of the mind, it is then transmitted throughout the body and the limbs. Quite different is our experience when we are shoved along by a blow inflicted with compulsive force by someone else. In that case it is obvious that all the matter of our body is set going and pushed along against our will, till a check is imposed through the limbs by the will. Do you see the difference? Although many men are driven by an external force and often constrained involuntarily to advance or to rush headlong, yet there is within the human breast something that can fight against this force and resist it. At its command the supply of matter is forced at times to take a new course through our limbs and joints or is checked in its course and brought once more to a halt. So also in the atoms you must recognize the same possibility: besides weight and impact there must be a third cause of movement, the source of this inborn power of ours, since we see that nothing can come out of nothing. For the weight of an atom prevents its movements from being completely determined by the impact of other atoms. But the fact that the mind itself has no internal necessity to determine its every act and compel it to suffer in helpless passivity—this is due to the slight swerve of the atoms at no determinate time or place.

The supply of matter in the universe was never more tightly packed than it is now, or more widely spaced out. For nothing is ever added to it or subtracted from it. It follows that the movement of atoms today is no different from what it was in bygone ages and always will be. So the things that have regularly come into being will continue to come into being in the same manner; they will be and grow and flourish so far as each is allowed by the laws of nature. The sum of things cannot be changed by any force. For there is no place into which any kind of matter might escape out of the universe or out of which some newly risen force could break into the universe and transform the whole nature of things and reverse their movements.

In this connection there is one fact that need occasion no surprise. _Although all the atoms are in motion, their totality appears to stand totally motionless,_ except for such movements as particular objects may make with their own bodies. This is because the atoms all lie far below the range of our senses. Since they are themselves invisible, their movements must also elude observation. Indeed, even visible objects, when set at a distance, often disguise their movements. Often on a hillside fleecy sheep, as they crop their lush pasture, creep slowly onward, lured this way or that by grass that sparkles with fresh dew, while the full-fed lambs gaily frisk and butt. And yet, when we gaze from a distance, we see only a blur—a white patch stationary on the green hillside. Take another example. Mighty legions, waging mimic war, are thronging the plain with their manoeuvres. The dazzling sheen flashes to the sky and all around the earth is ablaze with bronze. Down below there sounds the tramp of mighty marching men's feet. A noise of shouting strikes upon the hills and reverberates to the celestial vault. Wheeling horsemen gallop hotfoot across the midst of the plain, till it quakes under the fury of their charge. And yet there is a vantage-ground high among the hills from which all these appear immobile—a blaze of light stationary upon the plain. . . .

Give your mind now to the true reasoning I have to unfold. A new fact is battling strenuously for access to your ears. A new aspect of the universe is striving to reveal itself. But no fact is so simple that it is not harder to believe than to doubt at the first presentation. Equally, there is nothing so mighty or so marvellous that the wonder it evokes does not tend to diminish in time. Take first the pure and undimmed lustre of the sky and all that it enshrines: the stars that roam across its surface, the moon and the surpassing splendour of the sunlight. If all these sights were now displayed to mortal view for the first time by a swift unforeseen revelation, what miracle could be recounted greater than this? What would men before the revelation have been less prone to conceive as possible? Nothing, surely. So marvellous would have been that sight—a sight which no one now, you will admit, thinks worthy of an upward glance into the luminous regions of the sky. So has satiety blunted the appetite of our eyes. Desist, therefore, from thrusting out reasoning from your mind because of its disconcerting novelty. Weigh it, rather, with discerning judgement. Then, if it seems to you true, give in. If it is false, gird yourself to oppose it. For the mind wants to discover by reasoning what exists in the infinity of space that lies out there, beyond the ramparts of this world—that region into which the intellect longs to peer and into which the free projection of the mind does actually extend its flight.

Here, then, is my first point. In all directions alike, on this side or that, upward or downward through the universe, there is no end. This I have shown, and indeed the fact proclaims itself aloud and the nature of space makes it crystal clear. Granted, then, that empty space extends without limit in every direction and that seeds innumerable in number are rushing on countless courses through an unfathomable universe under the impulse of perpetual motion, *it is in the highest degree unlikely that this earth and sky is the only one to have been created* and that all those particles of matter outside are accomplishing nothing. This follows from the fact that our world has been made by nature through the spontaneous and casual collision and the multifarious, accidental, random and purposeless congregation and coalescence of atoms whose suddenly formed combinations could serve on each occasion as the starting-point of substantial fabrics—earth and sea and sky and the races of living creatures. On every ground, therefore, you must admit that there exist elsewhere other clusters of matter similar to this one which the ether clasps in ardent embrace.

When there is plenty of matter in readiness, when space is available and no cause or circumstance impedes, then surely things must be wrought and effected. You have a store of atoms that could not be counted out by the whole population of living creatures throughout history. You have the same natural force to congregate them in any place precisely as they have been congregated here. You are bound therefore to acknowledge that in other regions there are other earths and various tribes of men and breeds of beasts.

Add to this the fact that nothing in the universe is the only one of its kind, unique and solitary in its birth and growth; everything is a member of a species comprising many individuals. Turn your mind first to the animals. You will find the rule applies to the brutes that prowl the mountains, to the double-breed of men, the voiceless scaly fish and all the forms of flying things. So you must admit that sky, earth, sun, moon, sea and the rest are not solitary, but rather numberless. For a firmly established limit is set to their lives also and their bodies also are a product of birth, no less than that of any creature that flourishes here according to its kind.

Bear this well in mind, and you will immediately perceive that *nature is free and uncontrolled by proud masters* and runs the universe by herself without the aid of gods. For who—by the sacred hearts of the gods who pass their unruffled lives, their placid aeon, in calm and peace!—who can rule the sum total of the measureless? Who can hold in coercive hand the strong reins of the unfathomable? Who can spin all the firmaments alike and foment with the fires of ether all the fruitful earths? Who can be in all places at all times, ready to darken the clear sky with clouds and rock it with a thunderclap— to launch bolts that may often wreck his own temples, or retire and spend his fury letting fly at deserts with that missile which often passes by the guilty and slays the innocent and blameless?

After the natal season of the world, the birthday of sea and lands and the uprising of the sun, many atoms have been added from without, many seeds contributed on every side by bombardment from the universe at large. From these the sea and land could gather increase: the dome of heaven could gain more room and lift its rafters high above the earth, and the air could climb upwards. From every corner of the universe atoms are being chipped and circulated to each thing according to its own kind: water goes to water, earth swells with earthy matter; fire is forged by fires, ether by ether. At length everything is brought to its utmost limit of growth by nature, the creatress and perfectress. This is reached when what is poured into the veins of life is no more than what flows and drains away. Here the growing-time of everything must halt. Here nature checks the increase of her own strength. The things you see growing merrily in stature and climbing the stairs of maturity step by step— these are gaining more atoms than they lose. The food is easily introduced into all their veins; and they themselves are not so widely expanded as to shed much matter and squander more than their age absorbs as nourishment. It must, of course, be conceded that many particles ebb and drain away from things. But more particles must accrue, until they have touched the topmost peak of growth. Thereafter the strength and vigour of maturity is gradually broken, and age slides down the path of decay. Obviously the bulkier anything is and the more expanded when it begins to wane, the more particles it sheds and gives off from every surface. The food is not easily distributed through all its veins, or supplied in sufficient quantities to make good the copious effluences it exudes. It is natural, therefore, that everything should perish when it is thinned out by the ebbing out of matter and succumbs to blows from without. The food supply is no longer adequate for its aged frame, and the deadly bombardment of particles from without never pauses in the work of dissolution and subdual.

In this way the ramparts of the great world also will be breached and collapse in crumbling ruin about us. For everything must be restored and renewed by food, and by food buttressed and sustained. And the process is doomed to failure, because the veins do not admit enough and nature does not supply all that is needed. Already the life-force is broken. The earth, which generated every living species and once brought forth from its womb the bodies of huge beasts, has now scarcely strength to generate tiny creatures. For I assume that the races of mortal creatures were not let down into the fields from heaven by a golden cord, nor generated from the sea or the rock-beating surf, but born of the same earth that now provides their nurture. The same earth in her prime spontaneously generated for mortals smiling crops and lusty vines, sweet fruits and gladsome pastures, which now can scarcely be made to grow by our toil. We wear down the oxen and wear out the strength of farmers, we wear out the ploughshare and find ourselves scarcely supplied by the fields that grudge their fruits and multiply our toil. Already the ploughman of ripe years shakes his head with many a sigh that his heavy labours have gone for nothing: and, when he compares the present with the past, he often applauds his father's luck. In the same despondent vein, the cultivator of old and wilted vines decries the trend of the times and rails at heaven. He grumbles that past generations, when men were old-fashioned and god-fearing, supported life easily enough on their small farms, though one man's holding was then far less than now. He does not realize that everything is gradually decaying and going aground onto the rocks, worn out by old age.

from *The Georgics*: Book IV

Virgil
Translated by A. S. Kline

1–7 Introduction

Next I'll speak about the celestial gift of honey from the air.
Maecenas, give this section too your regard.
I'll tell you in proper sequence about the greatest spectacle
of the slightest things, and of brave generals,
and a whole nation's customs and efforts, tribes and battles.
Labour, over little: but no little glory, if favourable powers
allow, and Apollo listens to my prayer.

8–66 Location and Maintenance of the Apiary

First look for a site and position for your apiary,
where no wind can enter (since the winds prevent them
carrying home their food) and where no sheep or butting kids
leap about among the flowers, or wandering cattle brush
the dew from the field, and wear away the growing grass.
Let the bright-coloured lizard with scaly back, and the bee-eater
and other birds, and Procne, her breast marked
by her blood-stained hands, keep away from the rich hives:
since they all lay waste on every side, and while the bees are flying,
take them in their beaks, a sweet titbit for their pitiless chicks.
But let there be clear springs nearby, and pools green with moss,
and a little stream sliding through the grass,
and let a palm tree or a large wild-olive shade the entrance,
so that when the new leaders command the early swarms
in their springtime, and the young enjoy freedom from the combs,
a neighbouring bank may tempt them to leave the heat,
and a tree in the way hold them in its sheltering leaves.
Whether the water flows or remains still, throw willows

across the centre, and large stones, so that it's full
of bridges where they can rest, and spread their wings
to the summer sun, if by chance a swift Easterly
has wet the lingerers or dipped them in the stream.
Let green rosemary, and wild thyme with far-flung fragrance,
and a wealth of strongly-scented savory, flower around them,
and let beds of violets drink from the trickling spring.
Let the hives themselves have narrow entrances,
whether they're seamed from hollow bark,
or woven from pliant osiers: since winter congeals
the honey with cold, and heat loosens it with melting.
Either problem's equally to be feared with bees:
it's not for nothing that they emulate each other in lining
the thin cells of their hives with wax, and filling the crevices
with glue made from the flowers, and keep a store of it
for this use, stickier than bird lime or pitch from Phrygian Ida.
If rumour's true they also like homes in tunnelled hiding-places
underground, and are often found deep in the hollows
of pumice, and the caverns of decaying trees.
You keep them warm too, with clay smoothed by your fingers
round their cracked hives, and a few leaves on top.
Don't let yew too near their homes, or roast
blushing crabs on your hearth, or trust a deep marsh
or where there's a strong smell of mud, or where hollow rock
rings when struck, and an echoed voice rebounds on impact.
As for the rest, when the golden sun has driven winter
under the earth, and unlocked the heavens with summer light,
from the first they wander through glades and forests,
grazing the bright flowers, and sipping the surface of the streams.
With this, with a delightful sweetness, they cherish their hive
and young: with it, with art, they form
fresh wax and produce their sticky honey.
So, when you look up at the swarm released from the hive,
floating towards the radiant sky through the clear summer air,
and marvel at the dark cloud drawn along by the wind,
take note: they are continually searching for sweet waters
and leafy canopies. Scatter the scents I demanded,
bruised balm and corn parsley's humble herb, and make
a tinkling sound, and shake Cybele's cymbals around:

they'll settle themselves on the soporific rest sites:
they'll bury themselves, as they do, in their deepest cradle.

67–102 The Fighting Swarms

But if on the other hand they've gone out to fight—
because often discord, with great turmoil, seizes two leaders:
and immediately you may know in advance the will of the masses
and, from far off, how their hearts are stirred by war:
since the martial sound of the harsh brass rebukes the lingerers,
and an intermittent noise is heard, like a trumpet blast—
then they gather together restlessly, and their wings quiver,
and they sharpen their stings with their mouths, and flex their legs.
And they swarm round their leader, and the high command,
in crowds, and call out to the enemy with loud cries:
So, when they've found a clear spring day, and an open field,
they burst out of the gates: there's a clash, the noise rises high
in the air, they're gathered together, mingled in one great ball,
and fall headlong: hail from the sky's no thicker,
nor is the rain of acorns from a shaken oak-tree.
The leaders themselves in the middle of their ranks,
conspicuous by their wings, have great hearts in tiny breasts,
determined not to give way until the victor's might has forced
these here, or those there, to turn their backs in flight.
The tossing of a little dust restrains and calms
these fits of passion and these mighty battles.
When you've recalled both generals from the fight,
give death to the one that appears weaker, to avoid waste:
and let the stronger one hold power alone.
That one will shine with rough blotches of gold,
since there are two kinds: the better is distinguished in looks,
and bright with reddish armour: the other's shaggy from sloth,
and ingloriously drags a swollen belly.
As the features of the leaders are twofold, so their subjects' bodies.
Since some are ugly and bristling, like a parched traveller who
comes out of the deep dust, and spits the dirt from his dry mouth:
others gleam and sparkle with brightness, their bodies
glowing and specked with regular drops of gold.
These are the stronger offspring: in heaven's due season,

you'll take sweet honey from these, and no sweeter than it is clear,
and needed to tame the strong flavour of wine.

103–148 The Surrounding Garden

But when the swarms fly aimlessly, and swirl in the air,
neglecting their cells, and leaving the hive cold,
you should prevent their wandering spirits from idle play.
It's no great effort to stop them: tear the wings
from the leaders: while they linger no one will dare
to fly high or take the standards from the camp.
Let gardens fragrant with saffron flowers tempt them,
and let watchful Priapus, lord of the Hellespont, the guard
against thieves and birds, protect them with his willow hook.
He whose concerns are these, let him bring thyme and wild-bay,
himself, from the high hills, and plant them widely round his house:
let him toughen his hands himself with hard labour, let him set
fruitful plants in the ground himself, and sprinkle kind showers.
And for my part, if I were not at the furthest end of my toil,
furling my sails, and hurrying to turn my prow towards shore,
perhaps I too would be singing how careful cultivation ornaments
rich gardens, and of the twice-flowering rose-beds of Paestum,
how the endive delights in the streams it drinks,
and the green banks in parsley, and how the gourd, twisting
over the ground, swells its belly: nor would I be silent about
the late-flowering narcissi, or the curling stem of acanthus,
the pale ivy, and the myrtle that loves the shore.
Since I recall how I saw an old Corycian, under Tarentum's towers,
where the dark Galaesus waters the yellow fields,
who owned a few acres of abandoned soil,
not fertile enough for bullocks to plough,
not suited to flocks, or fit for the grape harvest:
yet as he planted herbs here and there among the bushes,
and white lilies round them, and vervain, and slender poppies,
it equalled in his opinion the riches of kings, and returning home
late at night it loaded his table with un-bought supplies.
He was the first to gather roses in spring and fruit in autumn:
and when wretched winter was still splitting rocks
with cold, and freezing the water courses with ice,
he was already cutting the sweet hyacinth flowers,

complaining at the slow summer and the late zephyrs.
So was he also first to overflow with young bees,
and a heavy swarm, and collect frothing honey
from the squeezed combs: his limes and wild-bays were the richest,
and as many as the new blossoms that set on his fertile fruit trees
as many were the ones they kept in autumn's ripeness.
He planted advanced elms in rows as well, hardy pears,
blackthorns bearing sloes, and plane-trees
already offering their shade to drinkers.
But I pass on from this theme, confined within narrow limits,
and leave it for others to speak of after me.

149–227 The Nature and Qualities of Bees

Come now and I'll impart the qualities Jupiter himself
gave bees, for which reward they followed after
the melodious sounds and clashing bronze of the Curetes,
and fed Heaven's king in the Dictean cave.
They alone hold children in common: own the roofs
of their city as one: and pass their life under the might of the law.
They alone know a country, and a settled home,
and in summer, remembering the winter to come,
undergo labour, storing their gains for all.
For some supervise the gathering of food, and work
in the fields to an agreed rule: some, walled in their homes,
lay the first foundations of the comb, with drops of gum
taken from narcissi, and sticky glue from tree-bark,
then hang the clinging wax: others lead the mature young,
their nation's hope, others pack purest honey together,
and swell the cells with liquid nectar:
there are those whose lot is to guard the gates,
and in turn they watch out for rain and clouds in the sky,
or accept the incoming loads, or, forming ranks,
they keep the idle crowd of drones away from the hive.
The work glows, and the fragrant honey is sweet with thyme.
And like the Cyclopes when they forge lightning bolts
quickly, from tough ore, and some make the air come and go
with ox-hide bellows, others dip hissing bronze
in the water: Etna groans with the anvils set on her:
and they lift their arms together with great and measured force,

and turn the metal with tenacious tongs:
so, if we may compare small things with great,
an innate love of creation spurs the Attic bees on,
each in its own way. The older ones take care of the hive,
and building the comb, and the cleverly fashioned cells.
But at night the weary young carry back sacs filled with thyme:
they graze far and wide on the blossom of strawberry-trees,
and pale-grey willows, and rosemary and bright saffron,
on rich lime-trees and on purple hyacinths.
All have one rest from work: all have one labour:
they rush from the gates at dawn: no delay: when the evening star
has warned them to leave their grazing in the fields again,
then they seek the hive, then they refresh their bodies:
there's a buzzing, a hum around the entrances and thresholds.
Then when they've settled to rest in their cells, there's silence
in the night, and sleep seizes their weary limbs.
If rain's threatening they don't go far from their hives,
or trust the sky when Easterlies are nearing,
but fetch water from nearby, in the safety of their city wall,
and try brief flights, and often lift little stones,
as unstable ships take up ballast in a choppy sea,
and balance themselves with these in the vaporous clouds.
And you'll wonder at this habit that pleases the bees,
that they don't indulge in sexual union, or lazily relax
their bodies in love, or produce young in labour,
but collect their children in their mouths themselves from leaves,
and sweet herbs, provide a new leader and tiny citizens themselves,
and remake their palaces and waxen kingdoms.
Often too as they wander among harsh flints they bruise
their wings, and breathe their lives away beneath their burden.
so great is their love of flowers, and glory in creating honey.
And though the end of a brief life awaits the bees themselves
(since it never extends beyond the seventh summer)
the species remains immortal, and the fortune of the hive
is good for many years, and grandfathers' grandfathers are counted.
Besides, Egypt and mighty Lydia and the Parthian tribes,
and the Median Hydaspes do not pay such homage to their leader.
With the leader safe all are of the same mind:
if the leader's lost they break faith, and tear down the honey
they've made, themselves, and dissolve the latticed combs.

The leader is the guardian of their labours: to the leader
they do reverence, and all sit round the leader in a noisy throng,
and crowd round in large numbers, and often
they lift the leader on their shoulders and expose their bodies
in war, and, among wounds, seek a glorious death.
Noting these tokens and examples some have said
that a share of divine intelligence is in bees,
and a draught of *aether*: since there is a god in everything,
earth and the expanse of sea and the sky's depths:
from this source the flocks and herds, men, and every species
of creature, each derive their little life, at birth:
to it surely all then return, and dissolved, are remade,
and there is no room for death, but still living
they fly to the ranks of the stars, and climb the high heavens.

228–250 Gathering the Honey

Whenever you would unseal their noble home, and the honey
they keep in store, first bathe the entrance, moistening it
with a draught of water, and follow it with smoke held out
in your hand. Their anger knows no bounds, and when hurt
they suck venom into their stings, and leave their hidden lances
fixed in the vein, laying down their lives in the wound they make.
Twice men gather the rich produce: there are two seasons
for harvest, as soon as Taygete the Pleiad has shown
her lovely face to Earth and spurned the Ocean stream
with scornful foot, and when that same star fleeing watery Pisces
sinks more sadly from the sky into the wintry waves.
But if you fear a harsh winter, and would spare their future,
and pity their bruised spirits, and shattered fortunes,
who would then hesitate to fumigate them with thyme
and cut away the empty wax? For often a newt has nibbled
the combs unseen, cockroaches, light-averse, fill the cells,
and the useless drone sits down to another's food:
or the fierce hornet has attacked with unequal weapons,
or the dread race of moths, or the spider, hated by Minerva,
hangs her loose webs in the entrances.
The more is taken, the more eagerly they devote themselves
to repairing the damage to their troubled species,
and filling the cells, and building their stores from flowers.

251–280 Disease in Bees

Since life has brought the same misfortunes to bees as ourselves,
if their bodies are weakened with wretched disease,
you can recognise it straight away by clear signs:
as they sicken their colour immediately changes: a rough
leanness mars their appearance: then they carry outdoors
the bodies of those without life, and lead the sad funeral procession:
or else they hang from the threshold linked by their feet, or linger
indoors, all listless with hunger and dull with depressing cold.
Then a deeper sound is heard, a drawn out murmur,
as the cold Southerly sighs in the woods sometimes,
as the troubled sea hisses on an ebb tide,
as the rapacious fire whistles in a sealed furnace.
Then I'd urge you to burn fragrant resin, right away,
and give them honey through reed pipes, freely calling them
and exhorting the weary insects to eat their familiar food.
It's good too to blend a taste of pounded oak-apples
with dry rose petals, or rich new wine boiled down
over a strong flame, or dried grapes from Psithian vines,
with Attic thyme and strong-smelling centaury.
There's a meadow flower also, the Italian starwort,
that farmers call *amellus*, easy for searchers to find:
since it lifts a large cluster of stems from a single root,
yellow-centred, but in the wealth of surrounding petals
there's a purple gleam in the dark blue: often the gods' altars
have been decorated with it in woven garlands:
its flavour is bitter to taste: the shepherd's collect it
in valleys that are grazed, and by Mella's winding streams.
Boil the plant's roots in fragrant wine, and place it
as food at their entrances in full wicker baskets.

281–314 Autogenesis of Bees

But if someone's whole brood has suddenly failed,
and he has no stock from which to recreate a new line,
then it's time to reveal the famous invention of Aristaeus,
the Arcadian master, and the method by which in the past
the adulterated blood of dead bullocks has generated bees.
I will tell the whole story in depth, tracing it from its first origins.
Where the fortunate peoples of Pellaean Canopus live

by the overflowing waters of the flooded Nile,
and sail around their fields in painted boats,
where the closeness of the Persian bowmen oppresses them,
and where the river's flow splits, in seven distinct mouths,
enriching green Egypt with its black silt,
the river that has flowed down from the dark Ethiopians,
all in that country depend on this sure stratagem.
First they choose a narrow place, small enough for this purpose:
they enclose it with a confined roof of tiles, walls close together,
and add four slanting window lights facing the four winds.
Then they search out a bullock, just jutting his horns out
of a two year olds forehead: the breath from both its nostrils
and its mouth is stifled despite its struggles: it's beaten to death,
and its flesh pounded to a pulp through the intact hide.
They leave it lying like this in prison, and strew broken branches
under its flanks, thyme and fresh rosemary.
This is done when the Westerlies begin to stir the waves
before the meadows brighten with their new colours,
before the twittering swallow hangs her nest from the eaves.
Meanwhile the moisture, warming in the softened bone, ferments,
and creatures, of a type marvellous to see, swarm together,
without feet at first, but soon with whirring wings as well,
and more and more try the clear air, until they burst out,
like rain pouring from summer clouds,
or arrows from the twanging bows,
whenever the lightly-armed Parthians first join battle.

315–386 Aristaeus and His Mother Cyrene

Muses, what god produced this art for us?
How did this new practice of men begin?
Aristaeus the shepherd, so the tale goes, having lost his bees,
through disease and hunger, leaving Tempe along the River Peneus,
stopped sadly by the stream's sacred source,
and called to his mother, with many groans, saying:
'O mother, Cyrene, you who live here in the stream's depths,
why did you bear me, of a god's noble line,
(if Thymbrean Apollo's my father, indeed, as you say)
to be hated by fate? Or why is your love taken from me?
Why did you tell me to set my hopes on the heavens?

See how, though you are my mother, I even relinquish
this glory of mortal life itself, that skilful care
for the crops and herds hardly achieved for all my efforts.
Come and tear down my fruitful trees, with your own hands,
set destructive fire to my stalls, and destroy my harvest,
burn my seed, and set the tough axe to my vines,
if such loathing for my honour has seized you.'
But his mother felt the cry from her chamber in the river's depths,
Around her the Nymphs were carding fleeces
from Miletus, dyed with deep glassy colours:
Drymo and Xantho, Phyllodoce, Ligea,
their bright hair flowing over their snowy necks,
Cydippe and golden-haired Lycorias, one a virgin,
the other having known the pangs of first childbirth,
Clio and her sister Beroe, both daughters of Ocean,
both ornamented with gold, clothed in dappled skins:
Ephyre and Opis, and Asian Deiopea,
and swift Arethusa, her arrows at last set aside.
Among them Clymene was telling of Vulcan's
baffled watch, and Mars's tricks and stolen sweetness,
and recounting the endless loves of the gods, from Chaos on.
And while they unwound the soft thread from the spindles,
captivated by the song, Aristaeus's cry again struck
his mother's ear, and all were startled, sitting on their crystal seats:
But Arethusa, before all her other sisters, lifted her golden hair
above the wave's surface and, looking out, called from far off:
'O Cyrene, sister, your fear at such loud groaning is not idle,
it is your own Aristaeus, your chief care, standing weeping
by the waters of father Peneus, calling, and naming you as cruel.'
His mother, her heart trembling with fresh fear, calls to her:
Bring him, bring him to me: it's lawful for him to touch
the divine threshold': at that she ordered the river to split apart
so the youth could enter. And the wave arched above him like a hill
and, receiving him in its vast folds, carried him below the stream.
Now, marvelling at his mother's home, and the watery regions,
at the lakes enclosed by caves, and the echoing glades,
he passed along, and, dazed by the great rushing of water,
gazed at all the rivers as, each in its separate course, they slide
beneath the mighty earth, Phasis and Lycus
and the source from which deep Enipeus first rises,

the source of father Tiber, and that of Anio's streams,
and rock-filled sounding Hypanis, and Mysian Caicus,
and Eridanus, with twin golden horns on his forehead,
than whom no more forceful river flows
through the rich fields to the dark blue sea.
As soon as he had reached her chamber, with its roof
of hanging stone, and Cyrene knew of her son's useless tears,
the sisters bathed his hands with spring water, and, in turn,
brought him smooth towels: some of them set a banquet
on the tables and placed brimming cups: the altars
blazed with incense-bearing flames. Then his mother said:
'Take the cup of Maeonian wine: let us pour
a libation to Ocean.' And with that she prayed
to Ocean, the father of things, and her sister Nymphs
who tend a hundred forests, a hundred streams.
Three times she sprinkled the glowing hearth with nectar,
three times the flame flared, shooting towards the roof.
With this omen to strengthen his spirit, she herself began:

387–452 The Capture of Proteus

'A seer, Proteus, lives in Neptune's Carpathian waters,
who, sea-green, travels the vast ocean in a chariot
drawn by fishes and two-footed horses.
Even now he's revisiting the harbours of Thessaly,
and his native Pallene. We nymphs venerate him,
and aged Nereus himself: since the seer knows all things,
what is, what has been, what is soon about to be:
since it's seen by Neptune, whose monstrous sea-cows
and ugly seals he grazes in the deep.
You must first capture and chain him, my son, so that he
might explain the cause of the disease, and favour the outcome.
For he'll give you no wisdom unless you use force, nor will you
make him relent by prayer: capture him with brute force and chains:
only with these around him will his tricks fail uselessly.
When the sun has gathered his midday heat, when the grass thirsts,
and the shade's welcome now to the flock, I'll guide you myself
to the old man's hiding place, where he retreats from the waves
when he's weary, so you can easily approach him when he's asleep.
When you seize him in your grip, with chains and hands,

then varied forms, and the masks of wild beasts, will baffle you.
Suddenly he'll become a bristling boar, a malicious tiger,
a scaly serpent, or a lioness with tawny mane,
or he'll give out the fierce roar of flames, and so slip his bonds,
or he'll dissolve into tenuous water, and be gone.
But the more he changes himself into every form,
the more you, my son, tighten the stubborn chains,
until, having altered his shape, he becomes such as you saw
when he closed his eyes at the start of his sleep.
She spoke, and spread about him liquid perfume of ambrosia,
with which she drenched her son's whole body:
and a sweet fragrance breathed from his ordered hair,
and strength entered his supple limbs. There's a vast cave
carved in a mountain side, from which many a wave
is driven by the wind, and separates into secluded bays,
safest of harbours at times for unwary sailors:
Proteus hides himself in there behind a huge barrier of rock.
Here the Nymph placed the youth, hidden from the light,
she herself stood far off, veiled in mist.
Now the Dog Star blazed in the sky, fiercely parching
the thirsty Indians, and the fiery sun had consumed
half his course: the grass withered, and deep rivers were heated
and baked, by the rays at their parched sources, down to the mud,
when Proteus came from the sea, to find his customary cave.
Round him the moist race of the vast sea frolicked,
scattering the salt spray far and wide.
The seals lay down to sleep here and there on the shore:
he himself sat on the rock in the middle, as the guardian
of a sheepfold on the hills sometimes sits, when Vesper brings
the calves home from pasture, and the bleating of lambs rouses
the wolf, hearing them, and the shepherd counts his flock.
As soon as chance offered itself, Aristaeus,
hardly allowed the old man to settle his weary limbs
before he rushed on him, with a great shout, and fettered him
as he lay there. The seer does not forget his magic arts,
but transforms himself into every marvellous thing,
fire, and hideous creature, and flowing river.
but when no trickery achieves escape, he returns
to his own shape, beaten, and speaks at last with human voice:

'Now who has told you to invade my home, boldest of youths?
What do you look for here?' he said, but Aristaeus replied:
'You know, yourself, Proteus, you know: you are deceived
by nothing: but let yourself cease. Following divine counsel,
I come to seek the oracle here regarding my weary tale.'
So he spoke. At that the seer, twisting in his grip, eyes blazing
with grey-green light, and grimly gnashing his teeth,
opened his lips at last, and spoke this fate:

453–527 Orpheus and Eurydice

'Not for nothing does divine anger harass you:
you atone for a heavy crime: it is Orpheus, wretched man,
who brings this punishment on you, no less than you deserve
if the fates did not oppose it: he raves madly for his lost wife.
She, doomed girl, running headlong along the stream,
so as to escape you, did not see the fierce snake, that kept
to the riverbank, in the deep grass under her feet.
But her crowd of Dryad friends filled the mountaintops
with their cry: the towers of Rhodope wept, and the heights
of Pangaea, and Thrace, the warlike land of Rhesus,
and the Getae, the Hebrus, and Orythia, Acte's child.
Orpheus, consoling love's anguish, with his hollow lyre,
sang of you, sweet wife, you, alone on the empty shore,
of you as day neared, of you as day departed.
He even entered the jaws of Taenarus, the high gates
of Dis, and the grove dim with dark fear,
and came to the spirits, and their dread king, and hearts
that do not know how to soften at human prayer.
The insubstantial shadows, and the phantoms of those without light,
came from the lowest depths of Erebus, startled by his song,
as many as the thousand birds that hide among the leaves,
when Vesper, or wintry rain, drives them from the hills,
mothers and husbands, and the bodies of noble heroes
bereft of life, boys and unmarried girls, and young men
placed on the pyre before their father's eyes:
round them are the black mud and foul reeds
of Cocytus, the vile marsh, holding them with its sluggish waters,
and Styx, confining them in its nine-fold ditches.
The House of the Dead itself was stupefied, and innermost

Tartarus, and the Furies, with dark snakes twined in their hair,
and Cerberus held his three mouths gaping wide,
and the whirling of Ixion's wheel stopped in the wind.
And now, retracing his steps, he evaded all mischance,
and Eurydice, regained, approached the upper air,
he following behind (since Proserpine had ordained it),
when a sudden madness seized the incautious lover,
one to be forgiven, if the spirits knew how to forgive:
he stopped, and forgetful, alas, on the edge of light,
his will conquered, he looked back, now, at his Eurydice.
In that instant, all his effort was wasted, and his pact
with the cruel tyrant was broken, and three times a crash
was heard by the waters of Avernus. 'Orpheus,' she cried,
'what madness has destroyed my wretched self, and you?
See, the cruel Fates recall me, and sleep hides my swimming eyes,
Farewell, now: I am taken, wrapped round by vast night,
stretching out to you, alas, hands no longer yours.'
She spoke, and suddenly fled, far from his eyes,
like smoke vanishing in thin air, and never saw him more,
though he grasped in vain at shadows, and longed
to speak further: nor did Charon, the ferryman of Orcus,
let him cross the barrier of that marsh again.
What could he do? Where could he turn, twice robbed of his wife?
With what tears could he move the spirits, with what voice
move their powers? Cold now, she floated in the Stygian boat.
They say he wept for seven whole months,
beneath an airy cliff, by the waters of desolate Strymon,
and told his tale, in the icy caves, softening the tigers' mood,
and gathering the oak-trees to his song:
as the nightingale grieving in the poplar's shadows
laments the loss of her chicks, that a rough ploughman saw
snatching them, featherless, from the nest:
but she weeps all night, and repeats her sad song perched
among the branches, filling the place around with mournful cries.
No love, no wedding-song could move Orpheus's heart.
He wandered the Northern ice, and snowy Tanais,
and the fields that are never free of Rhipaean frost,
mourning his lost Eurydice, and Dis's vain gift:
the Ciconian women, spurned by his devotion,
tore the youth apart, in their divine rites and midnight

Bacchic revels, and scattered him over the fields.
Even then, when Oeagrian Hebros rolled the head onwards,
torn from its marble neck, carrying it mid-stream,
the voice alone, the ice-cold tongue, with ebbing breath,
cried out: 'Eurydice, ah poor Eurydice!'
'Eurydice' the riverbanks echoed, all along the stream.

528–558 Aristaeus Sacrifices to Orpheus

So Proteus spoke, and gave a leap into the deep sea,
and where he leapt the waves whirled with foam, under the vortex.
But not Cyrene: speaking unasked to the startled youth:
'Son, set aside these sad sorrows from your mind.
This is the cause of the whole disease, because of it the Nymphs,
with whom that poor girl danced in the deep groves,
sent ruin to your bees. Offer the gifts of a suppliant,
asking grace, and worship the gentle girls of the woods,
since they'll grant forgiveness to prayer, and abate their anger.
But first I'll tell you in order the method of worship.
Choose four bulls of outstanding physique,
that graze on your summits of green Lycaeus,
and as many heifers, with necks free of the yoke.
Set up four altars for them by the high shrines of the goddesses,
and drain the sacred blood from their throats
leaving the bodies of the steers in the leafy grove.
Then when the ninth dawn shows her light
send funeral gifts of Lethean poppies to Orpheus,
and sacrifice a black ewe, and revisit the grove:
worship Eurydice, placate her with the death of a calf.'
Without delay he immediately does as his mother ordered:
he comes to the shrines, raises the altars as required,
and leads four chosen bulls there of outstanding physique,
and as many heifers with necks free of the yoke.
Then when the ninth dawn brings her light,
he sends funeral gifts to Orpheus, and revisits the grove.
Here a sudden wonder appears, marvellous to tell,
bees buzzing and swarming from the broken flanks
among the liquefied flesh of the cattle,
and trailing along in vast clouds, and flowing together
on a tree top, and hanging in a cluster from the bowed branches.

559–566 Virgil's Envoi

So I sang, above, of the care of fields, and herds,
and trees besides, while mighty Caesar thundered in battle,
by the wide Euphrates, and gave a victor's laws
to willing nations, and took the path towards the heavens.
Then was I, Virgil, nursed by sweet Parthenope,
joyous in the pursuits of obscure retirement,
I who toyed with shepherds' songs, and, in youth's boldness,
sang of you, Tityrus, in the spreading beech-tree's shade.

Luke 15:11–32

New American Bible (NAB)

The Prodigal Son

11 **15** Then he said, "A man had two sons,

12 and the younger son said to his father, 'Father, give me the share of your estate that should come to me.' So the father divided the property between them.

13 After a few days, the younger son collected all his belongings and set off to a distant country where he squandered his inheritance on a life of dissipation.

14 When he had freely spent everything, a severe famine struck that country, and he found himself in dire need.

15 So he hired himself out to one of the local citizens who sent him to his farm to tend the swine.

16 And he longed to eat his fill of the pods on which the swine fed, but nobody gave him any.

17 Coming to his senses he thought, 'How many of my father's hired workers have more than enough food to eat, but here am I, dying from hunger.

18 I shall get up and go to my father and I shall say to him, "Father, I have sinned against heaven and against you.

19 I no longer deserve to be called your son; treat me as you would treat one of your hired workers."'

20 So he got up and went back to his father. While he was still a long way off, his father caught sight of him, and was filled with compassion. He ran to his son, embraced him and kissed him.

21 His son said to him, 'Father, I have sinned against heaven and against you; I no longer deserve to be called your son.'

22 But his father ordered his servants, 'Quickly bring the finest robe and put it on him; put a ring on his finger and sandals on his feet.

23 Take the fattened calf and slaughter it. Then let us celebrate with a feast,

24 because this son of mine was dead, and has come to life again; he was lost, and has been found.' Then the celebration began.

25   Now the older son had been out in the field and, on his way back, as he neared the house, he heard the sound of music and dancing.

26   He called one of the servants and asked what this might mean.

27   The servant said to him, 'Your brother has returned and your father has slaughtered the fattened calf because he has him back safe and sound.'

28   He became angry, and when he refused to enter the house, his father came out and pleaded with him.

29   He said to his father in reply, 'Look, all these years I served you and not once did I disobey your orders; yet you never gave me even a young goat to feast on with my friends.

30   But when your son returns who swallowed up your property with prostitutes, for him you slaughter the fattened calf.'

31   He said to him, 'My son, you are here with me always; everything I have is yours.

32   But now we must celebrate and rejoice, because your brother was dead and has come to life again; he was lost and has been found.'"

Luke 10:25–37

New American Bible (NAB)

The Good Samaritan

25 **10** There was a scholar of the law who stood up to test him and said, "Teacher, what must I do to inherit eternal life?"

26 Jesus said to him, "What is written in the law? How do you read it?"

27 He said in reply, "You shall love the Lord, your God, with all your heart, with all your being, with all your strength, and with all your mind, and your neighbor as yourself."

28 He replied to him, "You have answered correctly; do this and you will live."

29 But because he wished to justify himself, he said to Jesus, "And who is my neighbor?"

30 Jesus replied, "A man fell victim to robbers as he went down from Jerusalem to Jericho. They stripped and beat him and went off leaving him half-dead.

31 A priest happened to be going down that road, but when he saw him, he passed by on the opposite side.

32 Likewise a Levite came to the place, and when he saw him, he passed by on the opposite side.

33 But a Samaritan traveler who came upon him was moved with compassion at the sight.

34 He approached the victim, poured oil and wine over his wounds and bandaged them. Then he lifted him up on his own animal, took him to an inn and cared for him.

35 The next day he took out two silver coins and gave them to the innkeeper with the instruction, 'Take care of him. If you spend more than what I have given you, I shall repay you on my way back.'

36 Which of these three, in your opinion, was neighbor to the robbers' victim?"

37 He answered, "The one who treated him with mercy." Jesus said to him, "Go and do likewise."

Matthew 20:1–15

New American Bible (NAB)

Workers in the Vineyard ("Day Laborers")

1 **20** "The kingdom of heaven is like a landowner who went out at dawn to hire laborers for his vineyard.

2 After agreeing with them for the usual daily wage, he sent them into his vineyard.

3 Going out about nine o'clock, he saw others standing idle in the marketplace,

4 and he said to them, 'You too go into my vineyard, and I will give you what is just.'

5 So they went off. (And) he went out again around noon, and around three o'clock, and did likewise.

6 Going out about five o'clock, he found others standing around, and said to them, 'Why do you stand here idle all day?'

7 They answered, 'Because no one has hired us.' He said to them, 'You too go into my vineyard.'

8 When it was evening the owner of the vineyard said to his foreman, 'Summon the laborers and give them their pay, beginning with the last and ending with the first.'

9 When those who had started about five o'clock came, each received the usual daily wage.

10 So when the first came, they thought that they would receive more, but each of them also got the usual wage.

11 And on receiving it they grumbled against the landowner,

12 saying, 'These last ones worked only one hour, and you have made them equal to us, who bore the day's burden and the heat.'

13 He said to one of them in reply, 'My friend, I am not cheating you. Did you not agree with me for the usual daily wage?

14   Take what is yours and go. What if I wish to give this last one the same as you?

15   (Or) am I not free to do as I wish with my own money? Are you envious because I am generous?'

Does philosophy's efforts to try and comfort Boethius seem more effective than the Muses' strategy?

from *The Consolation of Philosophy*, Book I

Boethius
Translated by R. H. Green

Poem 1

who is she?

I who once wrote songs with keen delight am now by sorrow driven to take up melancholy measures. Wounded Muses tell me what I must write, and elegiac verses bathe my face with real tears. Not even terror could drive from me these faithful companions of my long journey. Poetry, which was once the glory of my happy and flourishing youth, is still my comfort in this misery of my old age.

Old age has come too soon with its evils, and sorrow has commanded me to enter the age which is hers. My hair is prematurely gray, and slack skin shakes on my exhausted body. Death, happy to men when she does not intrude in the sweet years, but comes when often called in sorrow, turns a deaf ear to the wretched and cruelly refuses to close weeping eyes.

The sad hour that has nearly drowned me came just at the time that faithless Fortune favored me with her worthless gifts. Now that she has clouded her deceitful face, my accursed life seems to go on endlessly. My friends, why did you so often think me happy? Any man who has fallen never stood securely.

Prose 1

Lady Philosophy appears to him and drives away the Muses of poetry.

While I silently pondered these things, and decided to write down my wretched complaint, there appeared standing above me a woman of majestic countenance whose flashing eyes seemed wise beyond the ordinary wisdom of men. Her color was bright, suggesting boundless vigor, and yet she seemed so old that she could not be thought of as belonging to our age. Her height seemed to vary: sometimes she seemed of ordinary human stature, then again her head seemed to touch the top of the heavens. And when she raised herself

could she be philosophy

to her full height she penetrated heaven itself, beyond the vision of human eyes. Her clothing was made of the most delicate threads, and by the most exquisite workmanship; it had—as she afterwards told me—been woven by her own hands into an everlasting fabric. Her clothes had been darkened in color somewhat by neglect and the passage of time, as happens to pictures exposed to smoke. At the lower edge of her robe was woven a Greek π, at the top the letter Θ, and between them were seen clearly marked stages, like stairs, ascending from the lowest level to the highest.[1] This robe had been torn, however, by the hands of violent men, who had ripped away what they could. In her right hand, the woman held certain books; in her left hand, a scepter.

When she saw the Muses of poetry standing beside my bed and consoling me with their words, she was momentarily upset and glared at them with burning eyes.[2] "Who let these whores from the theater come to the bedside of this sick man?" she said. "They cannot offer medicine for his sorrows; they will nourish him only with their sweet poison. They kill the fruitful harvest of reason with the sterile thorns of the passions; they do not liberate the minds of men from disease, but merely accustom them to it. I would find it easier to bear if your flattery had, as it usually does, seduced some ordinary dull-witted man; in that case, it would have been no concern of mine. But this man has been educated in the philosophical schools of the Eleatics and the Academy.[3] Get out, you Sirens; your sweetness leads to death. Leave him to be cured and made strong by my Muses."

And so the defeated Muses, shamefaced and with downcast eyes, went sadly away. My sight was so dimmed by tears that I could not tell who this woman of imperious authority might be, and I lay there astonished, my eyes staring at the earth, silently waiting to see what she would do. She came nearer and sat at the foot of my bed. When she noticed my grief-stricken, downcast face, she reproved my anxiety with this song.

Poem 2

"Alas! how this mind is dulled, drowned in the overwhelming depths. It wanders in outer darkness, deprived of its natural light. Sick anxiety, inflated by worldly winds, swells his thoughts to bursting.

"Once this man was free beneath the open heaven, and he used to run along heavenly paths. He saw the splendor of the red sun, the heaven of the cold moon. And any star that pursued its vagrant paths, returning through various spheres, this master understood by his computations.

instead of teaching something he does why? *and observing now*

"Beyond all this, he sought the causes of things: why the sighing winds vex the seawaves; what spirit turns the stable world; and why the sun rises out of the red east to fall beneath the western ocean. He sought to know what tempers the gentle hours of spring and makes them adorn the earth with rosy flowers; what causes fertile autumn to flow with bursting grapes in a good year.

"This man used to explore and reveal Nature's secret causes. Now he lies here, bound down by heavy chains, the light of his mind gone out; his head is bowed down and he is forced to stare at the dull earth.

Prose 2

jail

Seeing his desperate condition, Philosophy speaks more gently and promises to cure him.

"But," she said, "it is time for medicine rather than complaint." Fixing me with her eyes, she said: "Are you not he who once was nourished by my milk and brought up on my food; who emerged from weakness to the strength of a virile soul? I gave you weapons that would have protected you with invincible power, if you had not thrown them away. Don't you recognize me? Why don't you speak? Is it shame or astonishment that makes you silent? I'd rather it were shame, but I see that you are overcome by shock." When she saw that I was not only silent but struck dumb, she gently laid her hand on my breast and said: "There is no danger. You are suffering merely from lethargy, the common illness of deceived minds. You have forgotten yourself a little, but you will quickly be yourself again when you recognize me. To bring you to your senses, I shall quickly wipe the dark cloud of mortal things from your eyes." Then, she dried my tear-filled eyes with a fold of her robe.

Poem 3

Then, when the night was over, darkness left me and my eyes regained their former strength; just as when the stars are covered by swift Corus, and the sky is darkened by storm clouds, the sun hides and the stars do not shine; night comes down to envelop the earth. But if Boreas, blowing from his Thracian cave, beats and lays open the hiding day, then Phoebus shines forth, glittering with sudden light, and strikes our astonished eyes with his rays.[4]

Prose 3

Boethius recognizes Lady Philosophy. She promises to help him as she has always helped those who love and serve her.

In a similar way, I too was able to see the heavens again when the clouds of my sorrow were swept away; I recovered my judgment and recognized the face of my physician. When I looked at her closely, I saw that she was Philosophy, my nurse, in whose house I had lived from my youth. "Mistress of all virtues," I said, "why have you come, leaving the arc of heaven, to this lonely desert of our exile? Are you a prisoner, too, charged as I am with false accusations?"

She answered, "How could I desert my child, and not share with you the burden of sorrow you carry, a burden caused by hatred of my name? Philosophy has never thought it right to leave the innocent man alone on his journey. Should I fear to face my accusers, as though their enmity were something new? Do you suppose that this is the first time wisdom has been attacked and endangered by wicked men? We fought against such rashness and folly long ago, even before the time of our disciple Plato. And in Plato's own time, his master Socrates, with my help, merited the victory of an unjust death.[5] Afterwards, the inept schools of Epicureans, Stoics, and others, each seeking its own interests, tried to steal the inheritance of Socrates and to possess me (in spite of my protests and struggles), as though I were the spoils of their quarreling. They tore this robe which I had woven with my own hands and, having ripped off some little pieces of it, went away supposing that they possessed me wholly.[6] Then, when traces of my garments were seen on some of them, they were rashly thought to be my friends, and they were therefore condemned by the error of the profane mob.

"Perhaps you have not heard of the banishment of Anaxagoras, the poisoning of Socrates, the torments of Zeno,[7] for these men were strange to you. But you probably know about Canius, Seneca, and Soranus,[8] for their fame is recent and widely known. They were disgraced only because they had been trained in my studies and therefore seemed obnoxious to wicked men. You should not be surprised, then, if we are blown about by stormy winds in the voyage of this life, since our main duty is to oppose the wicked. But, even though our enemies are numerous, we should spurn them because they are without leadership and are driven frantically this way and that by error. And if they sometimes attack us with extraordinary force, our leader withdraws her followers into a fortress, leaving our enemies to waste their energies on worthless spoils. While they fight over things of no value, we laugh at them from above, safe from their fury and defended by a strength against which their aggressive folly cannot prevail.

Poem 4

"The serene man who has ordered his life stands above menacing fate and unflinchingly faces good and bad fortune. This virtuous man can hold up his head unconquered. The threatening and raging ocean storms which churn the waves cannot shake him; nor can the bursting furnace of Vesuvius, aimlessly throwing out its smoky fire; nor the fiery bolts of lightning which can topple the highest towers. Why then are we wretched, frightened by fierce tyrants who rage without the power to harm us? He who hopes for nothing and fears nothing can disarm the fury of these impotent men; but he who is burdened by fears and desires is not master of himself. He throws away his shield and retreats; he fastens the chain by which he will be drawn."

Prose 4

Boethius gives an account of his public career and especially of the causes of his present misery.[9]

"Do you understand what I have told you," Philosophy asked; "have my words impressed you at all, or are you 'like the ass which cannot hear the lyre'?[10] Why are you crying? Speak out, don't hide what troubles you. If you want a doctor's help, you must uncover your wound."[11]

I pulled myself together and answered: "Do I have to explain; isn't the misery of my misfortune evident enough? I should think this place alone would make you pity me. Compare this prison with my library at home which you chose as your own and in which you often discussed with me the knowledge of human and divine things. Did I look like this? Was I dressed this way when I studied nature's mysteries with you, when you mapped the courses of the stars for me with your geometer's rod, when you formed my moral standards and my whole view of life according to the norm of the heavenly order?[12] Are these miseries the rewards your servants should expect? You yourself proposed the course I have followed when you made Plato say that civil governments would be good if wise men were appointed rulers, or if those appointed to rule would study wisdom.[13] Further, you decreed in the words of the same philosopher that government of the commonwealth ought to be in the hands of wise men; that if it should be left to unscrupulous and wicked men, they would bring about the ruin of the good.[14]

"On this authority, I decided to apply to public administration the principles I had learned privately from you. You, and God who gave you to the minds of wise men, know that I became a magistrate only because of the unanimous wish of all good men. For these reasons I have become involved in grave and hopeless trouble with dishonest men; and, as always happens to the administrator of independent conscience, I have had to be willing to make powerful enemies in the interest of safeguarding justice.

"I have often opposed the greed of Conigastus in his swindling of the poor. I have condemned the crimes of Triguilla, Provost of the King's house, both in their beginnings and after they had been committed. At grave risk to my position I have protected the weak from the lies and avarice of cruel men in power. No man ever corrupted my administration of justice. I was as depressed as those who suffered the losses when I saw the wealth of our citizens dissipated either by private fraud or oppressive taxation. At the time of the severe famine, when prices were set so exorbitantly high that the province of Campania seemed about to starve, I carried on the people's fight against the Praetorian Prefect himself and, with the King's approval, I won—the fixed prices were not enforced.

"I saved Paulinus, the former Consul, from the howling dogs of the court who hoped to devour his wealth. In order to save Albinus, another former Consul, from unjust punishment, I risked the hatred of his accuser, Cyprian. One would think I had stirred up enough opposition. But I ought to have been defended by others, especially since, through devotion to justice, I had given up the favor of the courtiers who might have saved me. But who were the accusers who overthrew me? One of them was Basil who had earlier been expelled from the King's service and was now forced by his debts to testify against me. My other accusers were Opilio and Gaudentius, also men banished by royal decree for their many corrupt practices. They tried to avoid exile by taking sanctuary, but when the King heard of it he decreed that, if they did not leave Ravenna by a certain day, they should be branded on the forehead and forcibly expelled. How could the King's judgment have been more severe? And yet on that very day their testimony against me was accepted. Why should this have happened? Did I deserve it? Did their criminal records make them just accusers? Fortune ought to have been shamed, if not by the innocence of the accused, then at least by the villainy of the accusers.

"Finally, what am I accused of? They say I desired the safety of the Senate. But how? I am convicted of having hindered their accuser from giving evidence that the Senate is guilty of treason. What is your judgment, my teacher?

Shall I deny the charge in order to avoid shaming you? But I did desire to protect the Senate, and I always will. And how can I confess, since I have already stopped hindering their accuser? Shall I consider it a crime to have supported the integrity of the Senate? It is true that the Senate itself, by its decrees against me, has made my position a crime. But folly, driven by self-deception, cannot change the merits of the case; nor, following the rule of Socrates, can I think it right either to hide the truth or concede a lie.[15] I leave it to you, and to the judgment of the wise, whether my course of action is right. I have put this in writing so that posterity may know the truth and have a record of these events.

"Why should I even mention the spurious letters in which I am charged with having hoped for Roman liberty? That fraud would have been exposed had I been permitted to use the confession of my accusers, the strongest evidence in any case. But there is now no hope for freedom of any kind—I only wish there were. I should have answered in the words of Canius when Gaius Caesar, son of Germanicus,[16] accused Canius of having known of a conspiracy against him: 'If I had known of it,' Canius said, 'you would never have known." But I am not so discouraged by what has happened to me that I complain now of the attacks of wicked men against virtue; the reason for my surprise is that they have accomplished what they set out to do. The desire to do evil may be due to human weakness; but for the wicked to overcome the innocent in the sight of God—that is monstrous. I cannot blame that friend of yours who said, 'If there is a God, why is there evil? And if there is no God, how can there be good?'[17] It is not surprising that evil men, who want to destroy all just men, and the Senate too, should try to overthrow one who stood up for justice and the Senate. But surely I did not deserve the same treatment from the Senators themselves.

"You remember well that you always directed me in everything I said and everything I tried to do or say. You recall, for example, the time at Verona when the King wanted to overturn the government and tried to involve the whole Senate in the treason of which Albinus was accused; then, at great risk to my personal safety I defended the innocence of the whole Senate. You know that this is true, and that I have never acted out of a desire for praise; for integrity of conscience is somehow spoiled when a man advertises what he has done and receives the reward of public recognition. But you see where my innocence has brought me; instead of being rewarded for true virtue, I am falsely punished as a criminal. Even the full confession of a crime does not usually make all the judges in the case equally severe; some, at least, temper their severity by recognizing the errors of human judgment and the uncertain conditions of fortune to which all mortals are subject. If I had been accused of plotting the burning of churches, the murder of priests, even the murder of all good men, even then

I would have been sentenced only after I had confessed and been convicted, and when I was present before the court. But now, five hundred miles away, mute and defenseless, I am condemned to proscription and death because of my concern for the safety of the Senate. The Senate deserves that no one should ever again be convicted for such a 'crime'!

"Even my accusers understood the honor implicit in the charges they brought against me, and, in order to confuse the issue by the appearance of some crime, they falsely alleged that I had corrupted my conscience with sacrilege out of a desire for advancement. But your spirit, alive within me, had driven from my soul all sordid desire for earthly success, and those whom you protect do not commit sacrilege. You have daily reminded me of Pythagoras' saying: 'Follow God.'[18] It is not likely that I would have sought the protection of evil spirits at a time when you were forming in me that excellence which makes man like God. Moreover, the innocence of my family, the honesty of my closest friends, the goodness of my father-in-law,[19] who is as worthy of honor as yourself—all these ought to have shielded me from any suspicion of this crime. But the worst is that my enemies readily believe that wisdom itself is capable of the crime of ambition, and so they associate me with such misconduct because I am imbued with your knowledge and endowed with your virtues. So, my reverence for you is no help; their hatred of me leads them to dishonor you.

"Finally, and this is the last straw, the judgment of most people is based not on the merits of a case but on the fortune of its outcome; they think that only things which turn out happily are good. As a result, the first thing an unfortunate man loses is his good reputation. I cannot bear to think of the rumors and various opinions that are now going around; I can only say that the final misery of adverse fortune is that when some poor man is accused of a crime, it is thought that he deserves whatever punishment he has to suffer. Well, here am I, stripped of my possessions and honors, my reputation ruined, punished because I tried to do good.

"It seems to me that I can see wicked men everywhere celebrating my fall with great pleasure, and all the criminally depraved concocting new false charges. I see good men terrorized into helplessness by my danger, and evil men encouraged to risk any crime with impunity and able to get away with it by bribery. The innocent are deprived not only of their safety, but even of any defense. Now hear my appeal.

Poem 5

Boethius concludes with a prayer.

"Creator of the star-filled universe, seated upon your eternal throne You move the heavens in their swift orbits. You hold the stars in their assigned paths, so that sometimes the shining moon is full in the light of her brother sun and hides the lesser stars; sometimes, nearer the sun she wanes and loses her glory. You ordain that Hesperus, after rising at nightfall to drive the cold stars before him, should change his role and, as Lucifer, grow pale before the rising sun.[20]

"When the cold of winter makes the trees bare, You shorten the day to a briefer span; but when warm summer comes, You make the night hours go swiftly. Your power governs the changing year: in spring, Zephyrus renews the delicate leaves[21] that Boreas, the wind of winter, had destroyed; and Sirius burns the high corn in autumn that Arcturus had seen in seed.[22]

"Nothing escapes Your ancient law; nothing can avoid the work of its proper station. You govern all things, each according to its destined purpose. Human acts alone, O Ruler of All, You refuse to restrain within just bounds. Why should uncertain Fortune control our lives?

"Harsh punishment, deserved by the criminal, afflicts the innocent. Immoral scoundrels now occupy positions of power and unjustly trample the rights of good men. Virtue, which ought to shine forth, is covered up and hides in darkness, while good men must suffer for the crimes of the wicked. Perjury and deceit are not held blameworthy as long as they are covered by the color of lies. When these scoundrels choose to use their power they can intimidate even powerful kings, because the masses fear them.

"O God, whoever you are who joins all things in perfect harmony, look down upon this miserable earth! We men are no small part of Your great work, yet we wallow here in the stormy sea of fortune. Ruler of all things, calm the roiling waves and, as You rule the immense heavens, rule also the earth in stable concord."

Prose 5

Philosophy suggests that the source of the prisoner's trouble is within himself and begins to reassure him.

While I poured out my long sad story, Philosophy looked on amiably, quite undismayed by my complaints. Then she said: "When I first saw you downcast and crying, I knew you were in misery and exile. But without your story I would not have known how desperate your exile is. You have not been driven out of your homeland; you have willfully wandered away. Or, if you prefer to think that you have been driven into exile, you yourself have done the driving, since no one else could do it. For if you can remember your true country you know that it is not, as Athens once was, ruled by many persons; rather 'it has one ruler and one king,' [23] who rejoices in the presence of citizens, not in their expulsion. To be governed by his power and subject to his laws is the greatest liberty. Surely you know the oldest law of your true city, that the citizen who has chosen to establish his home there has a sacred right not to be driven away.[24] The man who lives within the walls of that city need not fear banishment; but if he loses his desire to live there, he loses also the assurance of safety. And so, I am not so much disturbed by this prison as by your attitude. I do not need your library with its glass walls and ivory decoration, but I do need my place in your mind. For there I have placed not books but that which gives value to books, the ideas which are found in my writings.

"What you have said about your merits in the commonwealth is true; your many services deserve even more than you claim. And what you have said about the truth or falsity of the accusations against you is well known to everyone. You were right to speak sparingly of the crimes and deceit of your enemies; such things are better talked about by the man in the street who hears about them. You have sharply protested the injustice done you by the Senate; and you have expressed sorrow for the accusations against me and the weakening of my place in the public esteem. Finally, you protested against Fortune in sorrow and anger, and complained that rewards are not distributed equally on the grounds of merit. At the end of your bitter poem, you expressed the hope that the same peace which rules the heavens might also rule the earth. But because you are so upset by sorrow and anger, and so blown about by the tumult of your feelings, you are not now in the right frame of mind to take strong medicine. For the time being, then, I shall use more gentle treatment, so that your hardened and excited condition may be softened by gentle handling and thus prepared for more potent remedies.

Poem 6

"The fool who plants his seed in the hard ground when summer burns with the sun's heat[25] must feed on acorns in the fall, because his hope of harvest is in vain. Do not look for violets in purple meadows when fields are blasted by winter winds. And do not cut your vine branches in the spring if you want to enjoy the grapes, for Bacchus brings his fruit in autumn.[26]

"God assigns to every season its proper office; and He does not permit the condition He has set to be altered. Every violent effort to upset His established order will fail in the end."

Prose 6

Philosophy begins to remind Boethius of certain basic truths which will place his misfortunes in proper perspective.

"First," Philosophy said, "will you let me test your present attitude with a few questions, so that I can decide on a way to cure you?"

"Ask whatever you like," I replied, "and I will try to answer."

"Do you think," she began, "that this world is subject to random chance, or do you believe that it is governed by some rational principle?"

"I cannot suppose that its regular operation can be the result of mere chance; indeed, I know that God the Creator governs his work, and the day will never come when I can be shaken from the truth of this judgment."

"That is true," Philosophy answered, "and you said as much in your poem a while ago when you deplored the fact that only men were outside God's care. You did not doubt that all other things were ruled by reason. Strange, isn't it, that one who has so healthy an attitude should be so sick with despair. We must search further, because obviously something is missing. Tell me, since you have no doubt that the world is ruled by God, do you know *how* it is governed?"

"I don't quite get the point of your question, so I am unable to answer."

"You see, I was right in thinking that you had some weakness, like a breach in the wall of a fort, through which the sickness of anxiety found its way into your soul.

"But tell me, do you remember what the end, or goal, of all things is—the goal toward which all nature is directed?"

"I heard it once," I answered, "but grief has dulled my memory."

"Well, do you know where all things come from?"

I answered that I knew all things came from God.

"How then," she went on, "is it possible that you can know the origin of all things and still be ignorant of their purpose? But this is the usual result of anxiety; it can change a man, but it cannot break him and cannot destroy him.

"I want you to answer this, too: do you remember that you are a man?"

"How could I forget that," I answered.

"Well then, what is a man? Can you give me a definition?"

"Do you mean that I am a rational animal, and mortal? I know that, and I admit that I am such a creature."

"Do you know nothing else about what you are?"

"No, nothing."

"Now, I know another cause of your sickness, and the most important: you have forgotten what you are. And so I am fully aware of the reason for your sickness and the remedy for it too. You are confused because you have forgotten what you are, and, therefore, you are upset because you are in exile and stripped of all your possessions. Because you are ignorant of the purpose of things, you think that stupid and evil men are powerful and happy. And, because you have forgotten how the world is governed, you suppose that these changes of your fortune came about without purpose. Such notions are enough to cause not only sickness but death. But be grateful to the Giver of health that nature has not entirely forsaken you. For you have the best medicine for your health in your grasp of the truth about the way the world is governed. You believe that the world is not subject to the accidents of chance, but to divine reason. Therefore, you have nothing to fear. From this tiny spark, the living fire can be rekindled. But the time has not yet come for stronger remedies. It is the nature of men's minds that when they throw away the truth they embrace false ideas, and from these comes the cloud of anxiety which obscures their vision of truth. I shall try to dispel this cloud by gentle treatment, so that when the darkness of deceptive feeling is removed you may recognize the splendor of true light.

Poem 7

"Stars hidden by black clouds send down no light. If the wild south wind[27] churns up the sea, the waves which once were clear as glass, as clear as the bright days, seem muddy and filthy to the beholder. The flowing stream, tumbling down from the high mountain, is often blocked by the stone broken off from the rocky cliff.

"So it is with you. If you want to see the truth in clear light, and follow the right road, you must cast off all joy and fear. Fly from hope and sorrow. When these things rule, the mind is clouded and bound to the earth."

Notes

[1] π and Θ are the first letters of the Greek words for the two divisions of philosophy, theoretical and practical. Boethius wrote (*In Porph. Dial.* I. 3): ". . . for philosophy is a genus of which there are two species, one of which is called theoretical, the other practical, that is, speculative and active."

[2] Boethius' condemnation of the Muses provided the enemies of poetry in the later Middle Ages with a powerful, if specious, argument. In his authoritative and influential *Genealogy of the Gods*, Boccaccio argues that Boethius is here condemning only a certain kind of obscene theatrical poetry; he cites Boethius' extensive use of ancient poetry and myth as evidence of a high regard for poetry. See *Boccaccio on Poetry*, tr. C. G. Osgood. "Library of Liberal Arts," No. 82 (New York, 1956). pp. 94–96.

[3] The Eleatics represent a school of Greek philosophy at Elia in Italy. Zeno, one of its members in the fifth century b.c, was thought to be the inventor of dialectic, the art of reasoning about matters of opinion. The Academy is the traditional name for Plato's school of philosophy.

[4] Corus, the north-west wind; Boreas, the north wind. Thrace, part of modern Turkey, was regarded by the ancients as an extreme northern place. Phoebus is the sun.

[5] Socrates was accused of corrupting youth and ridiculing the gods. In 309 B.C., the Athenian state condemned him to death (by drinking poison). For a description of the death scene of Socrates, see Plato, *Phædo* 115a–118.

[6] Boethius, and most other medieval thinkers until the late thirteenth century, regarded Plato as the greatest of the ancient philosophers. Philosophy's robe is the figure of the unity of true philosophy; this unity was, in Boethius' opinion, shattered by such limited philosophies as Epicureanism, based on the principle of pleasure, and Stoicism, based on the principle that whatever happens must be accepted without grief or joy. Epicurus founded his school in Greece late in the fourth century B.C. The Stoic school was founded by Zeno of Athens at about the same time.

[7] Anaxagoras, a Greek astronomer and philosopher, was banished from Athens when his theory of the heavens led to his being accused of impiety. He was exiled about 450 B.C. Zeno of Elea . . . was tortured by Nearchus from whose tyranny he had sought to deliver his country. Boethius is comparing his own predicament to those of earlier philosophers who were punished for honoring their principles.

[8] Julius Canius was executed about A.D. 40 for reproaching the Roman Emperor Caligula. Seneca, the great Roman poet and philosopher of the first century, and a high public official under Nero, was accused of conspiracy by the emperor and forced to commit suicide. Soranus was also a victim of Nero's tyranny; he was condemned to death in A.D. 66.

[9] For a discussion of the historical circumstances of Boethius' imprisonment and death, see Introduction, pp. xii–xiv.

[10] Boethius here cites the Greek proverb: ὄνος λύρας.

[11] Cf. Homer, *Iliad* I. 363.

[12] Cf. Plato, *Republic* 592b.

[13] Cf. Plato, *Republic* 473d, 487e.

[14] Cf. Plato, *Epistle X* 350b; *Republic* 347c.

[15] Plato, *Theaetetus* 151d and *Republic* 485c.

[16] Gaius Caesar is the Emperor Caligula. (See above, note 8.)

[17] The friend is Epicurus; the quotation is from Lactantius, *De ira Dei* 13. 21.

[18] Boethius gives the Greek ἕπου θεῷ. This saying of Pythagoras is quoted frequently in classical literature, e.g., Iamblichus, *Vita Pyth.* 18 (86), and Seneca, *De vita beata* 15. 5.

[19] Symmachus, also executed by Theodoric. See Introduction, p. x.

[20] Evening Star (Hesperus) and Morning Star (Lucifer) both signify the planet Venus. Literally the poet says that Hespeius changes his customary reins (i.e., his chariot) to become Lucifer.

[21] Zephyrus, the west wind, was said to produce fruits and flowers by his breath.

[22] Sirius. the dog-star, supposedly supplied great heat to cause crops to ripen. Arcturus was the brightest star in the constellation Boötes.

[23] Homer, *Iliad* II. 204.

[24] Boethius compares the inner security of the philosopher with the civil rights provided by Roman law.

[25] Literally, "when the sign of Cancer, heavy with the rays of Apollo, burns down."

[26] Bacchus, god of wine.

[27] In the text the south wind is called Auster.

from Hildegard of Bingen's *Scivias*

Translated by Bruce Hozeski

The Fourth Vision of the First Part

Next I saw a very great and peaceful brightness which was similar to a flame. This brightness had a lot of eyes in it, and it had four corners turned to the four parts of the world. This brightness, indicating the mystery of the heavenly creator, was shown to me in a very great mystery. Inside this brightness, there was another brightness which was similar to the dawn. This second brightness had the clearness of purple lightning inside itself. I also saw the earth with people on it. The people were carrying some milk in their vessels, and they were making cheese from this milk. Some of the milk was thick, from which strong cheese was being made; some of the milk was thin, from which mild cheese was being curdled; and some of the milk was spoiling, from which bitter cheese was being produced. With the people, I saw a woman who had the complete form of a person in her womb. And behold by means of the hidden plan of the heavenly creator, this second brightness set itself in motion with the movement of life. This burning sphere did not have the outline of a human body in it, but it did possess a heart. It touched the mind of the complete form of the person in the woman's womb, and it poured itself throughout all the limbs of that person.

After that, the form of the person, now that it had life, passed out of the womb of the woman. This was the result of the second brightness having set itself in motion with the movement of life. Accordingly, this brightness even changed its color.

Finally, I saw many storms approach the earth. These storms tried to bend the burning sphere that was in the body of the person, but that sphere worked vigorously to renew the person. It resisted these storms strongly. Then with a sigh, the person spoke.

Vision Four: 1

Where am I, a stranger? In *the shadow of death. (Luke 1:79)* And which way am I going? In the way of error. And what consolation do I have? That which strangers have. I ought to have a tent the size of five square stones. My tent ought to be decorated with the sun and with bright stars. The setting sun and the setting stars should not be bright in my tent, but angelic glory should be. The foundation of my tent ought to be made of topaz, and its structure should be made all of gems. Its stairs ought to be made of crystal and its floor should be gold. I ought to be a companion of the angels since I am the living breath which God sent into dry dust. I ought to know and understand God.

But alas! My tent is full of eyes which are able to see everywhere, and it placed itself in the north. Ach, ach! In the north, I have been attacked and plundered with the eyes and with the joy of knowledge, with my garment completely torn. I was removed from my rightful place, and I was led into another place which lacked any beauty and honor where I was subjected to the worst servitude. Those who had seized me, struck me with blows and they made me eat with the pigs. Having taken me into this forsaken place, they made me eat the bitterest of herbs that had been dipped in honey. Later they placed me upon a press and tortured me. Then they stripped me of my garments and chased me. They sent many plagues to me, and they made poisonous snakes seize me. Scorpions, adders, and other similar snakes spat their poison upon me. After that, those who were mocking me said: "Where is your honor now?" I trembled violently and with a great sigh of grief, I quietly said:

O where am I? Ach, how did I get here? And whom will I seek to console me? How will I break these chains? O whose eye will be able to see my wounds? And whose nose will be able to endure the stink of these sick ones? Or whose hands will anoint these with oil? Ach, who will weigh out mercy for my pain?

Therefore let heaven hear my voice clearly and let the earth tremble from my grief. Let everything that lives bend itself over with pity of my captivity because the bitterest pain pressed me down. I am a stranger without any consolation and without any to help me. O who will console me? Even my mother has deserted me since I strayed from the way of salvation. Who will help me unless it be God? When, however, I think of you—o mother of Zion—with whom I ought to dwell, I end up thinking about the very bitter slavery in which I find myself. And when I remember all the different types of music which is in you, I notice my wounds more. But when I think of the joy and delight of your glory, I then pray for deliverance from all the poisons which pollute my wounds. O where should I turn? And where will I flee to? For my sorrow is immeasurable. If I persevere in these evils, I will become a partner of those with whom I live dishonorably in the land of Babylon. And where are you, o mother of Zion? Ach to me because I brought myself back to you. If I had remained ignorant of you, I might have suffered my pain more lightly! Now, however, I will flee from my very bad companions. Unhappily Babylon placed me in a leaden restraint and pressed me down with heavy wooden beams so that I was not able to take a deep breath, except with difficulty. But when I pour out my tears and sighs to you, o mother of mine, Babylon pours out a great crashing of waters so that you cannot hear my voice. Therefore I will very carefully seek the narrow ways by which I may flee my very bad companions and my unhappy captivity.

After I had said these things, I entered a narrow footpath. I hid myself in a little cave, protected against the north. I wept most bitterly because I had harmed my mother. I also thought about my suffering and all my wounds while I was in that cave. I wept and wept so much that all my suffering and all my wounds were covered with my tears.

And behold a very sweet odor—as smooth as gold—touched my nose. It had been sent by my mother. O I poured out so many sighs and tears because she had sent me that tiny consolation! I wailed and wept so much on account of my joy that the very mountain where I hid in the cave even shook. And I said:

O mother, o mother of Zion, what will come of me? And where is your noble daughter now? O how very long I longed for your motherly pleasantness!

And so I was delighted in my tears as I saw my mother. But my enemies hearing my shouting, said:

Where is she whom we had up to this point as a companion? She did our every wish, according to our will. Behold, see where she calls upon those in heaven. Let us stir up our skills and surrounded her so carefully that she will not be able to flee from us—this one who had previously subjected herself to ourselves so completely. Once we have done this, she will follow us again.

Having stepped out of the cave where I had been hiding myself secretly, I wanted to climb up to a certain height where my enemies would not be able to reach me. But they had placed a foaming sea before me which I was not able to cross in any way. There was a small and narrow bridge there, but I was not strong enough to go across it. At the edge of this sea, there were mountains with such high peaks that I was not able to walk there either. And I said:

O what will I, such a miserable one, do now? I had felt the pleasantness of my mother for a little while, and I thought she would take me back to herself. But ach! She will not leave me behind again, will she? Ach! Where will I turn to then? For if go back to my previous captivity, my enemies will mock me even more than before since I had cried out tearfully to my mother. I had felt her sweet pleasantness for a little while, but I have been forsaken by her again.

But because of the pleasantness which I had previously felt coming from my mother, I had enough strength that I turned to the east and once again I began to go along those very narrow footpaths. However, these footpaths were so full of thorns and thorny plants and other hindrances of this type that I was hardly able to take any footsteps on these footpaths. But nevertheless I went along these paths with the greatest of toil and sweat. I became so tired from this hard work that I could hardly take a deep breath.

Eventually I reached the top of the mountain where I had hid myself, and I turned toward the valley where I ought to descend. But behold there were adders, scorpions, dragons, and other serpents of this type blocking my way. They were all hissing at me. Terrified, I shrieked loudly, saying:

O mother, where are you? My pain would be less if had not felt the pleasantness of your presence earlier. I am going to fall back into that captivity where I had been hurled some time ago. Where is your help now?

Vision Four: 2

O daughter, hurry, because the strongest giver has given you wings to fly with. Nothing can stop these wings. Therefore, fly over these obstacles quickly.

Comforted by this consolation, I took up these wings and I quickly flew over all those poisonous and deadly beasts.

Vision Four: 3

I came to a tent which had very strong steel all over its inside. Entering it, I performed works of light, when previously I had performed only works of darkness. However, I placed a rod of unpolished iron to the north inside the tent. On it, I hung various wings and other moving things. Then I saw a hand coming into that tent. To the east, I built a fortress out of square stones. I had a fire burning in the fortress, and I drank myrrh wine with new wine near the fire. To the south, I built a tower out of square stones. I hung red-colored shields in the tower, and I placed trumpets that were made from ivory in its windows. In the middle of the tower, I poured out some honey and added other aromatic things in order to make a most precious perfume. I dispersed this perfume throughout the tent. To the west, I did not build anything since that part had been turned over to time.

In the meantime, while I had been busy with my work, my enemies grabbed their quivers and approached my tent with their arrows. But because I had done my work carefully, I did not pay attention to their madness for very long, even though the door of my tent was filled all over with their arrows. None of their arrows pierced my door or the steel inside of my tent. So I was not struck by any of them. Seeing that, my enemies sent forth a great flood of water. They wanted to wash away both myself and my tent, but they gained nothing from their wickedness. Therefore I boldly mocked them by saying:

The worker who made this tent was wiser and stronger than you are. Collect your arrows and put them down because they cannot win a victory of your will over mine. Behold, do any wounds show? I fought many wars against you with much suffering and hard work. You wanted to hand me over to death, but you were not able to. Fortified with the strongest of weapons, I shook sharpened swords against you, and I was able to actively defend myself from you. Go back therefore, go back, because you will not be able to take anything behind me.

Vision Four: 9

Now in order that you, o people, may receive more deeply and you may reveal more openly what you have received, I will explain. I saw a very great and peaceful brightness which was similar to a flame. This brightness had a lot of eyes in it, and it had four corners turned to the four parts of the world. This signifies the vast knowledge of God in the various mysteries and the pureness of the knowledge of God as it is shown to the world, extending itself as a brightness with great clearness and crispness to the four corners of the world. This brightness, indicating the mystery of the heavenly creator, was shown to me in a very great mystery. This knowledge of God foresees most keenly those who will be hurled away from God and those who will be united to the divinity. Inside this brightness, there was another brightness which was similar to the dawn. This second brightness had the clearness of purple lightning inside itself. This means that the knowledge of God has the Only-Begotten of God in itself. This Only-Begotten took flesh from the Virgin and eventually poured out the divine blood for the salvation of humanity. This knowledge of God is not covered over in any way; therefore it knows both good and evil. But you, o person, say: "What will a person do since God is able to foresee everything that the person is about to do?" And to you, o person, I respond as follows.

Vision Four: 10

O foolish one, you imitate the devil in the worthlessness of your heart. The devil refused the way of truth and put falsehood in opposition to truth when the devil wished to be similar to the highest goodness. Who will be able to darken both the beginning and the end of all things? The one who is, was, and will remain. But who are you, o ashes of ashes? And what did you know before you existed as a human? You, having a lamentable beginning and a miserable end, contradict the excellence of the justice of God where no unworthy injustice is found, has been found, or will be found. O foolish one, where do you expect to find the father of evil whom you imitate? Where? When you are puffed up with pride, you want to be lifted up above the stars, above other creatures and above the angels. The angels fulfilled all the commands of God, but you will fall just as the devil fell. For the devil chose falsehood and became involved with death, thereby falling down into the abyss. Therefore, o person, be careful. When you do not look back to God's charity which made you free, when you do not notice the good things God weighed out for you, or when you do not pay attention when God calls you back from the death of sin, then you choose death rather than life. If you would call back to mind the

Scriptures and the doctrines which the ancient and faithful fathers gave to you, you would avoid evil and do good. You should say in the depth of your heart:

I have sinned seriously, so it moves me to go back with worthy repentance to the one who created me. (Luke 15:18)

Then God would support you with kindness and would place you in God's bosom, embracing you sweetly. Now, however, you despise the blessedness given to you by God, and you refuse to hear about or do to the justice of God. If you acted justly, you would not think of the judgment of God as unjust, would you? You would think of it as true. If you had not been redeemed by the blood of the Word of God, you—o wretched one—would lie in destruction. But the judgment of God is just and true. Therefore, o wretched one, what purpose does it serve you to pluck yourself away from my judgment as God? The choir of angels and the ones in my chosen vineyard praise me, saying: "Glory to you, Lord!" (Luke 2:14) My judgment does not go against them because they are just. But what did it benefit the devil to be opposed to me? The devil wished to be very bright and to be elevated above all things. The other proud spirits agreed with the devil. My divine power with the strength of righteousness cast them all out together. So likewise God casts out all those who prize evil rather than justice. God did not in any way establish injustice, but God did ordain everything that is right in the fairness of goodness.

Vision Four: 11

Those people who cast God away with their unfaithfulness made carved images which the devil entered into. This was vanity on their part. They ignored that Adam and Eve had told them that they had been made in the likeness of God, and they ignored when Adam and Eve told them how they had been cast out of paradise. Other people followed those people and paid more attention to the creatures God created rather than to God. They wanted to divide up those things which do not have life. Nevertheless, all these unfaithful ones may give up their foolishness and may turn back to God. They would then put down the oldness of ignorance and take up the newness of life. My servant Ezekiel encourages this.

Vision Four: 12

Throw away from you all your collusions in which you have walked crookedly, and make a new heart and a new spirit for yourselves. (Ezekiel 18:31)

What does this mean? You who wish to be righteous, as blessed sheep are, throw out of your heart all those things which are useless in comparison to your original wisdom. You have been in a deep lake where no honor dwells. And when you have thrown those things out, follow the path of truth for your salvation. There you will find the newness of heaven—shining with a reddish gleam—in your heart and the newness of life—giving the breath of life—in your sight.

Vision Four: 13

I also saw the earth with people in it. The people were carrying some milk in their vessels, and they were making cheese from this milk. This signifies the men and women of the world who have human seed in their bodies for the procreation of the human race. Some of the milk was thick, from which strong cheese was being made. This means the seed which, assembled and tempered usefully and well in its strength, brings forth strong people. This seed brings spiritual and fleshly gifts to great and high-born persons, so that these persons have the prosperity of prudence, discretion, and usefulness in their works which are done both in the presence of God and in the presence of other people. The devil cannot enter such people. Some of the milk was thin, from which mild cheese was being curdled. This means the seed which, half-assembled and half-tempered uselessly in its softness, brings forth delicate people. These people are foolish, lukewarm, and useless in their works before God and before other people. They do not seek God very strongly. And some of the milk was spoiling, from which bitter cheese was being produced. This means the seed, worthless and useless in the weakness of its mixture, brings forth deformed people. These people are often unpleasant, difficult and oppressed-in-heart. They do not lift up their mind to higher things. However, some of these do become useful because they suffer many storms and much restlessness in their hearts and in their wills. They become victorious. If they rested in peace, they would remain lukewarm and useless. Because they become victorious, God embraces them and leads them to the way of salvation. It has been written accordingly.

Vision Four: 14

I may strike down and I may make to live, and I will heal the wound, and there is not anyone who may be able to tear anything from my hand. (Deuteronomy 32:39) What does this mean? I who am, have neither a beginning nor an end. I slay shameful people who have been weakened, having faults because of the filth of the devil, and who have been deceived, having begotten unhappily through the devil. O how crafty is the mouth of the serpent which puffs them up with pride so that death tries to enter them! I take their prosperity away from them, and they become struck down with hardships which they cannot overcome. But they are always tested fairly. I, however, am not cast aside. Instead, I wondrously cause them to change the direction of their lives because when I live in them, I draw them up from the wastefulness of earthly things. Sometimes I fill those with suffering who are so proud that they think that they are so strong that they cannot be cast down by anyone. But when I am present in those again, I lift them up to sound health. As a result, they are not consumed by their false pride. But among all these people, there is not one of them who is able to tear out my works in any way through craftiness or pride. There is no one nor anything strong enough to resist my fairness and my will.

Vision Four: 15

Many times they forgot me. They mock me by conceiving with a mixture of the devil's sea water and a woman, thereby giving birth to a deformed child. When they have been tormented enough by this child, they return to me with repentance. Many times I allow this wonder in creation to be born for my glory and the glory of my holy ones. The deformed can be restored through the help of my holy ones. Let my name be glorified by people for this! Those, however, who have grasped the beauty of virginity, will ascend at dawn to the heavenly mysteries since they have restrained themselves from the delights of their bodies because of their love from my Word.

Vision Four: 16

With the people, I saw a woman who had the complete form of a person in her womb. This means that after a woman has taken in human seed, a whole infant with all its members is formed in her womb. And behold by means of the hidden plan of the heavenly creator, this second brightness set itself in motion with the movement of life. This means that—according to the secret and hidden order and will of God—when an infant has been conceived in its mother's womb, it will receive a spirit at the right time and will move its body. This is just like the earth when it uncovers itself and brings forth flowers and fruit after the dew and rain have fallen on it. This burning sphere did not have the outline of a human body in it, but it did possess a heart. This signifies that the soul, burning with the fire of understanding, comprehends various things in its understanding. Since it does not have flesh and has not fallen like the human race, the soul comforts the heart of the person. It serves as the foundation of the body and rules the entire body, just as the firmament of heaven contains heavenly things and covers earthly things. This burning sphere touched the mind of the complete form of the person in the woman's womb. This means that the soul has not only earthly but also heavenly powers when it knows God wisely. And this burning sphere poured itself throughout all the limbs of that person. This means that the soul gives life to the heart and its veins and to all the members of the entire body, just as the sap from the root of a tree gives greenness to all of its branches. After that, the form of the person, now that it had life, passed out of the womb of the woman. This was the result of the second brightness having set itself in motion with the movement of life. Accordingly, this brightness even changed its color. This means that after the infant in the womb of its mother received its living spirit, it was then born. The infant moved, which the soul does to the body. It covers itself with brightness from good things and darkness from evil things, according to the merits of both.

Vision Four: 17

The soul also shows its strength in relation to the strength of the body. It shows simplicity in the infancy of a person, it shows strength at the time of youth, and it shows its strongest powers in wisdom when all the veins of the person are full in the fullness of age. This is just like the tree—tender in its first bud, but producing fruit after that. The soul leads the person to full usefulness. After this, at the time of the old age of the person when the heart and its veins are beginning to get feeble, the soul shows softer strength in the weariness of the knowledge of the person. Again, this is just like the tree. When winter begins to set in, the tree collects its sap from its leaves and branches. The tree also does this when it begins to be attacked in its old age.

Vision Four: 18

A person has three footpaths. What are they? The soul, the body, and the senses. These make the person strong. How do they do this? The soul makes the body alive, and it breathes forth the senses. The body, however, attracts the soul to itself, and it uncovers the senses. The senses truly touch the soul, and they draw the body to themselves. For the soul provides life to the body, just as fire pours its light into the darkness. The soul has the strength of two branches, namely the understanding and the will. The soul does not have a branch for moving itself, but it shows its strength just like the sun shows its brightness. Wherefore, o person, since you are not all heart, pay attention to the knowledge found in Scriptures.

Vision Four: 19

Understanding has been attached to the soul just like an arm to the body. And just as an arm, to which a hand with fingers has been attached, is extended from the body, so also understanding, attached to the various powers of the soul in order to understand all the works of people, comes forth most certainly from the soul. Because of the various powers of the soul, understanding can discern whether the works of people are good or evil. All things are understood through the soul as through a master. The soul investigates things in the same way that wheat is separated from the chaff. It inquires whether things are useful or useless, or lovable or hateful, or whether they relate to life or to death. Likewise, just as food is tasteless without salt, so also the various powers of the soul are weak and unintelligible without understanding. Further, understanding is present in the soul just as the back is in the body—it exists as the heart of the various powers of the soul. It is like a strong shoulder with an arm that can bend—it understands the divinity and the humanity of God. Like the movement of the hand, it has true faith in its work; and like the fingers on the hand, it discerns various works with discretion. However; understanding does not function this way with all the powers of the soul. What does this mean?

Vision Four: 20

The will warms the work, the soul supports it, and the power of reason brings it forth. Understanding, however, understands the work—understanding good and evil just like the Angels have understanding in order to choose good and to avoid evil. And as the body has a heart, so the soul has understanding which exercises its power in the soul. Similarly, the will is in other powers of the soul. How does this work? The will has great power in the soul. The will supports the heart of the soul. It stands in the corner of the house, just like the man who stands in the corner of his house—seeing the whole house. This man rules the house and points to the useful things in it by raising his right arm as a signal. This man then turns to the east. The soul does the same thing. It looks back toward the rising sun through the plains of the entire body. For the soul places the will inside itself as if it were a person's right arm, supporting veins and the heart and the movement of the entire human body. The will performs each work, whether it is good or evil.

Vision Four: 21

The will is like a fire, cooking each work as if it were in a furnace. Bread is cooked and fed to people so that they are comfortable and may live. Similarly, the will is the fortitude of the entire work. In the beginning, the soul grinds the grain; then it strengthens the flour by putting in the yeast; next it prepares the dough as bread through its contemplation; and finally it cooks it to perfection with its heat—which is the will. And actually the soul and the will make better food for people than even bread is. But food eventually stops working in people. The work of the will, however, continues to work in a person right up to the time that the person dies and the soul is separated from the body. The will works with great diversity from infancy and youth until the fullness of age and into infirmity. And the will shows its perfection in all these stages.

Vision Four: 22

The will has a tent in the breast of people. This tent is clearly the soul. Understanding, the will, and other strengths flow into this tent. All of these are warmed in the tent, and they join themselves together. How does this work? If anger springs up, bitterness is enkindled and sends smoke into the tent in order to complete the anger. If false joy lifts itself up, the fire of desire is lit so that wantonness—leading to sin—is raised up and helped into the tent. But actually, true joy is enkindled in the tent by the Holy Spirit. And the Holy Spirit supports the happy soul faithfully and helps the soul to complete its good works with heavenly desires. There is, however, a certain sadness in the tent which comes from bitterness and leads to numbness. This causes indignation, hard-heartedness, and stubbornness in people, and it depresses the soul unless it is quickly rescued by the helping grace of God.

But sometimes contradictory forces attack the soul so that it hates and does other terrible things. This slaughters the soul, and it prepares it for great destruction. If these contradictory forces are in the soul, it will cook its food accordingly and then give it to people to taste. As a result, a great turmoil is raised between good and evil. This is the same as when another person is helped in another place. When the leader has arrived, if he likes what is going on, he will support the activity. If he does not like what is going on, he will order it stopped. The will acts the same way. If good or evil has sprung up in the heart of a person, the will either helps the good or neglects the evil.

Vision Four: 23

Similar to understanding and the will, reason is like a sound in the soul. It brings forth whatever work of God or of people that may exist. Sound carries a word up high just as the wind carries an eagle up high so that it may fly. Likewise, the soul sends forth the sound of reason to the hearing and to the understanding of people. In proportion to their ability to understand, they are able to complete their work with perfection. The body is like the tent and supports all the powers of the soul. While the soul remains in the body, the soul and the body work with each other, whether for good or for evil.

Vision Four: 24

The work of the inner powers of the soul cling truthfully to the senses. These powers are understood through the senses and through the fruits of their work. The senses have been subjected to these powers, because these powers lead the soul to work. The soul, however, does not put work on the senses since it is only a shadow of these senses which do only what pleases them. Similarly, an unborn child senses the outer world through the womb of its mother— some of the powers of the soul are hidden at this time. What does this mean? The dawn announces the light of the day; the senses together with reason show forth all the powers of the soul. And as the law and the prophets are judged according to the two commandments of God, so also the senses flourish in the soul and in its powers. What does this mean?

The law was made for the salvation of humanity. And the prophets made manifest the hidden things of God. Similarly, the senses drive harmful things away from people, and they uncover the innermost things of the soul. For the soul breathes the senses forth. How does it do this? The soul makes a person alive, and it is glorified by the person's use of sight, hearing, taste, smell, and touch. A person with the sense of touch is always watchful for danger. The senses are a sign of the powers of the soul, just as the body is the vessel for the soul. How is this? The senses shut all the powers of the soul inside the person. What does this mean? A person is known in a certain shape. And the person sees with eyes, hears with ears, opens his mouth for talking, touches gently with hands, and walks with feet. Therefore, the senses are like precious stones in a person. And they are like a precious treasure in the vessel of the will. But just as the vessel can be seen and its treasure known, so also certain powers of the soul are known through the senses.

Vision Four: 25

The soul, however, is a mistress, and the body is truly a maid-servant. What does this mean? The soul rules the entire body by making it living. The body, however, supports the life from the soul, since if the soul did not make the body living, the body might melt away into a liquid. When a person does something evil, this is as bitter to the soul as poison is to the body—especially when the body welcomes the evil knowingly. On the other hand, the soul rejoices in good, just as the body is delighted by pleasant food. For the soul passes through the body just as sap passes through a tree. What does this mean? It is through the sap that a tree is green, produces flowers, and then fruit. And how does that fruit come to maturity? By the mildness of the air. The sun warms it, the rain waters it, and it is perfected by the mildness of the air. What is the significance of this? The mercy of the grace of God will make a person bright as the sun, the breadth of the Holy Spirit will water the person just as the rain, and thus discretion will lead the person to the perfection of good fruits just like the mildness of the air does for the tree.

Vision Four: 26

The soul is in the body just like sap is in a tree. And the powers of the soul are like the shape of the tree. How is this? Understanding is in the soul just like the greenness of the branches and of the leaves is in the tree. The will, however, is like the flowers on the tree. The soul is truly like the power of the tree bursting forth its fruit. Reason, however, is like the fruit—perfected in maturity. The senses are truly like the height and the width of the tree. Accordingly, the body of a person is made solid and is sustained by the soul. Therefore, o person, you who trust your understanding as good and you who wish to compare yourself to a sheep, understand what you are in your soul.

Vision Four: 27

You, o person, reflect upon these things which you see. I saw many storms approach the earth. These storms tried to bend the burning sphere that was in the body of the person. This signifies that as long as a person lives in soul and body, many invisible trials will disturb the soul. Through the pleasure of the body, these trials will bend the soul many times toward the sins of earthly concupiscence. But that sphere worked vigorously to renew the person. It resisted these storms strongly. This signifies that a faithful person who has been disturbed by sin, is often urged on by a gift from God. As a result, the person forsakes sin and comes to hope in God. The person hurls away the deceits of the devil and seeks the creator faithfully. This is like the soul shown earlier which conquered its miseries and perfected itself faithfully.

Vision Four: 28

Why do you see these many storms rushing into another sphere, wishing to hurl it down even though they are not strong enough to do so? Because the many snares of the devil try to entice the soul to sinning with many evil deeds, but these snares are not strong enough with their deceitfulness. The soul, resisting strongly, does not give way to these raging storms. Guarding itself with heavenly inspiration, the soul drives the darts of false deceptions away from itself, and it rushes back to its savior. This was shown earlier in the words of the complaint of the soul, just as it was prophesied.

Vision Four: 29

Then truly you see another sphere, drawing itself together out of the lines of its form and loosening its knots. This signifies the soul forsaking the members of its fleshly dwelling place. It leaves behind its relationship to the body when the time of the dissolution of the body has come. The soul extracts itself from the body with a groan. Grieving, it shatters its seat. By removing itself from the body with distress, it allows the place of its dwelling to fall away with much trembling. It will then know the merits of its works by the just judgment of God. This was shown earlier in the complaint of the soul. When the soul unties itself in this way, various spirits of both light and darkness come. These spirits are companions of the conversation that takes place in the dwelling place of the soul. At the time of the resolution of the conversation—when the soul of the person leaves its dwelling—the angelic spirits of both good and evil are present according to the just and true plan of God. They are like inspectors for the work of the person, checking to see what was performed with the body while the soul was in the body. They expect the resolution, and after the soul has untied itself from the body, they will lead the soul away with themselves. They pay attention to the knowledge of the just judge concerning the soul as it is separated from its body. The heavenly judge will judge according to the merits of the works of that person. This was also faithfully prophesied to you.

Whence whoever has knowledge in the Holy Spirit and wings in faith, let that person not pass over my warning, but let that person lay hold of it by embracing it in the enjoyment of the soul.

from *The Lais of Marie de France*

Translated by Robert Manning and Joan Ferrante

Prologue

Whoever has received knowledge
and eloquence in speech from God
should not be silent or secretive
but demonstrate it willingly.
When a great good is widely heard of,   5
then, and only then, does it bloom,
and when that good is praised by many,
it has spread its blossoms.
The custom among the ancients—
as Priscian testifies—   10
was to speak quite obscurely
in the books they wrote,
so that those who were to come after
and study them
might gloss the letter   15
and supply its significance from their own wisdom.
Philosophers knew this,
they understood among themselves
that the more time they spent,
the more subtle their minds would become   20
and the better they would know how to keep themselves
from whatever was to be avoided.
He who would guard himself from vice
should study and understand
and begin a weighty work   25
by which he might keep vice at a distance,
and free himself from great sorrow.
That's why I began to think
about composing some good stories
and translating from Latin to Romance;   30

146

but that was not to bring me fame:
too many others have done it.
Then I thought of the *lais* I'd heard.
I did not doubt, indeed I knew well,
that those who first began them   35
and sent them forth
composed them in order to preserve
adventures they had heard.
I have heard many told;
and I don't want to neglect or forget them.   40
To put them into word and rhyme
I've often stayed awake.

In your honor, noble King,
who are so brave and courteous,
repository of all joys   45
in whose heart all goodness takes root,
I undertook to assemble these *lais*
to compose and recount them in rhyme.
In my heart I thought and determined,
sire, that I would present them to you.   50
If it pleases you to receive them,
you will give me great joy;
I shall be happy forever.
Do not think me presumptuous
if I dare present them to you.   55
Now hear how they begin.

Guigemar

Whoever deals with good material
feels pain if it's treated improperly.
Listen, my lords, to the words of Marie,
who does not forget her responsibilities when her turn comes.

People should praise anyone   5
who wins admiring comments for herself.
But anywhere there is

a man or a woman of great worth,
people who envy their good fortune
often say evil things about them;   10
they want to ruin their reputations.
Thus they act like
vicious, cowardly dogs
who bite people treacherously.
I don't propose to give up because of that;   15
if spiteful critics or slanderers
wish to turn my accomplishments against me,
they have a right to their evil talk.
　　　The tales—and I know they're true—
from which the Bretons made their *lais*   20
I'll now recount for you briefly;
and at the very beginning of this enterprise,
just the way it was written down,
I'll relate an adventure
that took place in Brittany,   25
in the old days.
　　　At that time, Hoel ruled Brittany,
sometimes peacefully, sometimes at war.
The king had a vassal
who was lord of Leonnais;   30
his name was Oridial
and he was on very intimate terms with his lord.
A worthy and valiant knight,
he had, by his wife, two children,
a son and a beautiful daughter.   35
The girl's name was Noguent;
they called the boy Guigemar.
There wasn't a more handsome youngster in the kingdom.
His mother had a wonderful love for him,
and his father a great devotion;   40
when he could bring himself to part with the boy,
his father sent him to serve the king.
The boy was intelligent and brave,
and made himself loved by all.
When his time of probation was at an end,   45
and he was mature in body and mind,

people are jealous

the king dubbed him knight,
giving him luxurious armor, which was exactly what he desired.
Guigemar left the court,
but not before dispensing many rich gifts.　　　　　　　　　50
　　　He journeyed to Flanders to seek his fame;
there was always a war, or a battle raging there.
Neither in Lorraine nor in Burgundy,
in Anjou nor in Gascony,
could one find, in those days,　　　　　　　　　　　　55
Guigemar's equal as a fine knight.
But in forming him nature had so badly erred
that he never gave any thought to love.
There wasn't a lady or a maid on earth,
no matter how noble, or how beautiful,　　　　　　　　60
who wouldn't have willingly granted him her love,
had he asked her for it.
Many maids asked him,
but he wasn't interested in such things;
no one could discover in him　　　　　　　　　　　65
the slightest desire to love.
Therefore both friends and strangers
gave him up for lost.
　　　At the height of his fame,
this baron, Guigemar, returned to his own land　　　　70
to visit his father and his lord,
his good mother and his sister,
all of whom were most eager to see him.
Guigemar stayed with them,
I believe, an entire month.　　　　　　　　　　　75
Then he was seized by a desire to hunt;
that night he summoned his companions in arms,
his huntsmen, and his beaters;
next morning he set out for the woods
to indulge in the sport that gave him much pleasure.　　80
They gathered in pursuit of a great stag;
the dogs were unleashed.
The hunters ran ahead
while the young man lingered behind;
a squire carried his bow,　　　　　　　　　　　85

his hunting knife, and his quiver.
He wanted to fire some arrows, if he had the opportunity,
before he left the spot.
In the thickest part of a great bush
Guigemar saw a hind with a fawn;   90
a completely white beast,
with deer's antlers on her head.
Spurred by the barking of the dogs, she sprang into the open.
Guigemar took his bow and shot at her,
striking her in the breastbone.   95
She fell at once,
but the arrow rebounded,
gave Guigemar such a wound—
it went through his thigh right into the horse's flank—
that he had to dismount.   100
He collapsed on the thick grass
beside the hind he'd struck.
The hind, wounded as she was,
suffered pain and groaned.
Then she spoke, in this fashion: 105
"Alas! I'm dying!
And you, vassal, who wounded me,
this be your destiny:
may you never get medicine for your wound!
Neither herb nor root,   110
neither physician nor potion,
will cure you
of that wound in your thigh,
until a woman heals you,
one who will suffer, out of love for you,   115
pain and grief
such as no woman ever suffered before.
And out of love for her, you'll suffer as much;
the affair will be a marvel
to lovers, past and present,   120
and to all those yet to come.
Now go away, leave me in peace!"
     Guigemar was badly wounded;
what he had heard dismayed him.

He began to consider carefully   125
what land he might set out for
to have his wound healed.
He didn't want to remain there and die.
He knew, he reminded himself,
that he'd never seen a woman   130
to whom he wanted to offer his love,
nor one who could cure his pain.
He called his squire to him;
"Friend," he said, "go quickly!
Bring my companions back here;   135
I want to talk to them."
The squire rode off and Guigemar remained;
he complained bitterly to himself.
Making his shirt into a bandage,
he bound his wound tightly;   140
Then he mounted his horse and left that spot.
He was anxious to get far away;
he didn't want any of his men to come along,
who might interfere, or try to detain him.
Through the woods he followed   145
a grassy path, which led him
out into open country; there, at the edge of the plain,
he saw a cliff and a steep bank
overlooking a body of water below:
a bay that formed a harbor.   150
There was a solitary ship in the harbor;
Guigemar saw its sail.
It was fit and ready to go,
calked outside and in—
no one could discover a seam in its hull.   155
Every deck rail and peg
was solid ebony;
no gold under the sun could be worth more.
The sail was pure silk;
it would look beautiful when unfurled.   160
      The knight was troubled;
he had never heard it said
anywhere in that region

that ships could land there.
He went down to the harbor   165
and, in great pain, boarded the ship.
He expected to discover men inside,
guarding the vessel,
but he saw no one, no one at all.
Amidships he found a bed   170
whose posts and frame
were wrought in the fashion of Solomon,
of cypress and ivory,
with designs in inlaid gold.
The quilt on the bed was made   175
of silken cloth, woven with gold.
I don't know how to estimate the value of the other bedclothes,
but I'll tell you this much about the pillow:
whoever rested his head on it
would never have white hair.   180
The sable bedspread
was lined with Alexandrian silk.
Two candelabra of fine gold—
the lesser of the two worth a fortune—
were placed at the head of the cabin,   185
lighted tapers placed in them.
        Guigemar, astonished by all this,
reclined on the bed
and rested; his wound hurt.
Then he rose and tried to leave the ship,   190
but he couldn't return to land.
The vessel was already on the high seas,
carrying him swiftly with it.
A good, gentle wind was blowing,
so turning back now was out of the question.   195
Guigemar was very upset; he didn't know what to do.
It's no wonder he was frightened,
especially as his wound was paining him a great deal.
Still, he had to see the adventure through.
He prayed to God to watch over him,   *god? again?*   200
to use his power to bring him back to land,
and to protect him from death.

He lay down on the bed, and fell asleep.
That day he'd survived the worst;
before sundown he would arrive   205
at the place where he'd be cured—
near an ancient city,
the capital of its realm.
    The lord who ruled over that city
was a very aged man who had a wife,   210
a woman of high lineage,
noble, courteous, beautiful, intelligent;
he was extremely jealous,
which accorded with his nature.
(All old folk are jealous;   215
every one of them hates the thought of being cuckolded,
such is the perversity of age.)
The watch he kept over her was no joke.
The grove beneath the tower
was enclosed all around   220
with walls of green marble,
very high and thick.
There was only one entrance,
and it was guarded day and night.
On the other side, the sea enclosed it;   225
no one could enter, no one leave,
except by means of a boat,
as the castle might require it.
Inside the castle walls,
the lord had built a chamber—   230
none more beautiful anywhere—to keep his wife under guard—
And its entrance was a chapel.
The room was painted with images all around;
Venus the goddess of love
was skillfully depicted in the painting,   235
her nature and her traits were illustrated,
whereby men might learn how to behave in love,
and to serve love loyally.
Ovid's book, the one in which he instructs
lovers how to control their love,   240
was being thrown by Venus into a fire,

and she was excommunicating all those
who ever perused this book
or followed its teachings.
That's where the wife was locked up.   245
Her husband had given her
a girl to serve her,
one who was noble and well educated—
she was his niece, the daughter of his sister.
There was great affection between the two women.   250
She stayed with her mistress when he went off,
remaining with her until he returned.
No one else came there, man or woman,
nor could the wife leave the walls of the enclosure.
An old priest, hoary with age,   255
kept the gate key;
he'd lost his nether member
or he wouldn't have been trusted.
He said mass for her
and served her her food.   260
        That same day, as soon as she rose from a nap,
the wife went into the grove;
she had slept after dinner,
and now she set out to amuse herself,
taking her maid with her.   265
Looking out to sea,
they saw the ship on the rising tide
come sailing into the harbor.
They could see nothing guiding it.
The lady started to flee—   270
it's not surprising if she was afraid;
her face grew red from fear.
But the girl, who was wise   *thema?*.
and more courageous,
comforted and reassured her,   275
and they went toward the water, fast as they could.
The damsel removed her cloak,
and boarded the beautiful ship.
She found no living thing
except the sleeping knight.   280

She saw how pale he was and thought him dead;
she stopped and looked at him.
Then she went back
quickly, and called her mistress,
told her what she'd found,   285
and lamented the dead man she'd seen.
The lady answered, "Let's go see him!
If he's dead, we'll bury him;
the priest will help us.
If I find that he's alive, he'll tell us all about this."   290
        Without tarrying any longer, they returned together,
the lady first, then the girl.
When the lady entered the ship,
she stopped in front of the bed.
She examined the knight,   295
lamenting his beauty and fine body;
she was full of sorrow on his account,
and said it was a shame he'd died so young.
She put her hand on his breast,
and felt that it was warm, and his heart healthy,   300
beating beneath his ribs.
The knight, who was only asleep,
now woke up and saw her;
he was delighted, and greeted her—
he realized he'd come to land.   305
The lady, upset and weeping,
answered him politely
and asked him how
he got there, what country he came from,
if he'd been exiled because of war.   310
"My lady," he said, "not at all.
But if you'd like me to tell you
the truth, I'll do so;
I'll hide nothing from you.
        I come from Brittany.   315
Today I went out hunting in the woods,
and shot a white hind;
the arrow rebounded,
giving me such a wound in the thigh

that I've given up hope of being cured.   320
The hind complained and spoke to me,
cursed me, swore
that I'd never be healed
except by a girl;
I don't know where she might be found.   325
        When I heard my destiny,
I quickly left the woods:
I found this boat in a harbor,
and made a big mistake: I went on board.
The boat raced off to sea with me on it;   330
I don't know where I've arrived,
or what this city's called.
Beautiful one, I beg you, for God's sake,
please advise me!
I don't know where to go   335
and I can't even steer this ship!"
        She answered him, "My dear lord,
I'll be happy to advise you;
this is my husband's city,
and so is the region around it.   340
He is a rich man of high lineage,
but extremely old;
he's also terribly jealous.
On my word of honor,
he has locked me up in this stronghold.   345
There's only one entrance,
and an old priest guards the gate:
may God let him burn in hell!
I'm shut in here night and day.
I'd never dare   350
to leave except at his command,
when my lord asks for me.
Here I have my room and my chapel,
and this girl lives with me.
If it pleases you to stay here   355
until you're better able to travel,
we'll be happy to put you up,
we'll serve you willingly."

When he hears this,
Guigemar thanks the lady warmly,   360
and says he'll stay with her.
He rose from the bed;
with some difficulty they supported him,
and the lady brought him to her chamber.
The young man lay down   365
on the girl's bed,
behind a drape that was hung
across her room like a curtain.
They brought him water in a golden basin,
washed his thigh,   370
and with a fine, white silk cloth
they wiped the blood from his wound.
Then they bound it tightly.
They treated him very kindly.
When their evening meal came,   375
the girl left enough of hers
for the knight to have some;
he ate and drank quite well.
     But now love struck him to the quick;
great strife was in his heart   380
because the lady had wounded him so badly
that he forgot his homeland.
His other wound no longer bothered him,
but he sighed with new anguish.
He begged the girl, who was assigned to take care of him,   385
to let him sleep.
She left him and went away,
since he had requested it,
returning to her mistress,
who was also feeling somewhat scorched   390
by the same fire Guigemar felt
igniting and consuming his heart.
     The knight was alone now,
preoccupied and in distress.
He didn't yet know what was wrong,   395
but this much he could tell:
if the lady didn't cure him,

he was sure to die.
"Alas!" he said, "what shall I do?
I'll go to her and tell her   400
that she should have mercy and pity
on a poor, disconsolate wretch like me.
If she refuses my plea,
shows herself so proud and scornful,
then I'll have to die of grief,   405
languishing forever in this pain."
He sighed; but a little later
formed a new resolution,
and said to himself he'd have to keep suffering;
you have to endure what you can't change.   410
He lay awake all night,
sighing in distress.
He turned over in his mind
her words and appearance,
the bright eyes, the fair mouth   415
whose sweetness had touched his heart.
Under his breath he cried for mercy;
he almost called her his beloved.
If he only knew what she was feeling—
how love was torturing her—   420
I think he would have been very happy;
that little bit of consolation
would have diminished the pain
that drained him of his color.
If he was suffering from love of her,   425
she had nothing to gloat about, either.
Next morning, before dawn,
the lady arose.
She'd been awake all night, that was her complaint.
It was the fault of love, pressing her hard.   430
The damsel, who was with her,
noticed from the appearance of her lady
that she was in love
with the knight who was staying
in her chamber until he was healed;   435
but her mistress didn't know whether or not he loved her.

The lady went off to church
and the girl went off to the knight.
    She sat down by the bed;
he spoke to her, saying,   440
"My dear friend, where has my lady gone?
Why did she rise so early?"
He paused, and sighed.
The girl spoke frankly:
"My lord," she said, "you're in love;   445
take care not to hide it too well!
The love you offer
may in fact be well received.
Anyone whom my lady chooses to love
certainly ought to think well of her.   450
This love would be suitable
if both of you were constant:
you're handsome and she's beautiful."
He answered the girl,
"I'm so in love with her   455
that if I don't get relief soon
I'll be in a very bad way.
Advise me, dear friend!
What should I do about my passion?"
The girl very sweetly   460
comforted the knight,
promised to help him
in every way she could;
she was very good-hearted and well bred.
    When the lady had heard mass   465
she returned; she was anything but neglectful:
she wanted to know whether the man
whom she couldn't help loving
was awake or asleep.
The girl called her   470
and brought her to the knight;
now she'll have all the time she needs
to tell him what she's feeling,
for better or for worse.
He greeted her and she him;   475

they were both very scared now.
He didn't dare ask anything from her,
for he was a foreigner
and was afraid, if he told her what he felt,
she'd hate him for it, send him away.   480
But he who hides his sickness
can hardly be brought back to health;
love is a wound in the body,
and yet nothing appears on the outside.
It's a sickness that lasts a long time,   485
because it comes from nature.
Many people treat it lightly,
like these false courtiers
who have affairs everywhere they go,
then boast about their conquests;   490
that's not love but folly,
evil and lechery.
If you can find a loyal love,
you should love and serve it faithfully,
be at its command.   495
Guigemar was deeply in love;
he must either get help quickly
or live in misery.
So love inspires bravery in him:
he reveals his desires to the lady.   500
  "Lady," he said, "I'm dying because of you;
my heart is full of anguish.
if you won't cure me,
I'll have to perish sooner or later.
I beg you to love me—   505
fair one, don't deny me!"
When she had heard him out,
she gave a fitting answer.
She laughed, and said, "My love,
I'd be ill advised to act too quickly   510
in granting your prayer.
I'm not accustomed to such a request."
"My lady," he replied, "for God's sake, have mercy!
Don't be annoyed if I speak like this to you.

It's appropriate for an inconstant woman   515
to make some one plead with her a long time
to enhance her worth; that way he won't think
she's used to such sport.
But a woman of good character,
sensible as well as virtuous,   520
if she finds a man to her liking,
oughtn't to treat him too disdainfully.
Rather she should love and enjoy him;
this way, before anyone knows or hears of it,
they'll have done a lot that's to their advantage.   525
Now, dear lady, let's end this discussion."
The lady realized he was telling the truth,
and immediately granted him
her love; then he kissed her.
From now on, Guigemar is at ease.   530
They lie down together and converse,
kissing and embracing often.
I hope they also enjoy whatever else
others do on such occasions.
        It appears to me that Guigemar   535
stayed with her a year and a half.
Their life was full of pleasure.
But fortune, who never forgets her duty,
turns her wheel suddenly,
raising one person up while casting another down;   540
and so it happened with the lovers,
because suddenly they were discovered.
        One summer morning,
the lady was lying beside her young lover;
she kissed his mouth and eyes,   545
and said to him, "Dear, sweet love,
my heart tells me I'm going to lose you.
We're going to be found out.
If you die, I want to die, too,
but if you can escape,   550
you'll go find another love
while I stay here in misery."
"Lady," he said, "don't say such a thing!

I would never have any joy or peace
if I turned to another woman.   555
You needn't be afraid of that!"
"Beloved, I need your promise.
Give me your shirt;
I'll make a knot in the tail.
You have my leave to love the woman,   560
whoever she may be,
who will be able to undo it."
He gave her the shirt, and his promise;
she made the knot in such a way
that no woman could untie it   565
except with scissors or knife.
She gave him back the shirt,
and he took it on condition
that she should make a similar pledge to him,
by means of a belt   570
that she would wear next to her bare flesh,
tightened about her flanks.
Whoever could open the buckle
without breaking it or severing it from the belt,
would be the one he would urge her to love.   575
He kissed her, and left it at that.
     That day they were discovered—
spied upon and found out
by an evil, cunning chamberlain,
sent by the husband.   580
He wanted to speak with the lady,
and couldn't get into her chamber;
he looked in a window and saw the lovers,
he went and told his lord.
When he heard about it,   585
the lord was sorrier than he'd ever been before.
He called for three of his henchmen
and straightaway went to the wife's chamber;
he had the door broken down.
Inside he found the knight.   590
He was so furious
that he gave orders to kill the stranger.

Guigemar got up,
not at all afraid.
He grabbed a wooden rod   595
on which clothes were usually hung,
and waited for his assailants.
Guigemar will make some of them suffer for this;
before they get close to him,
he'll have maimed them all.   600
      The lord stared at him for a long time,
and finally asked him
who he was, where he came from,
how he'd gotten in there.
Guigemar told him how he'd come there   605
and how the lady had received him;
he told him all about the adventure
of the wounded hind,
about his wound and the ship;
now he is entirely in the other's power.   610
The lord replied that he didn't believe him,
but if it really was the way he had told it
and if he could find the ship,
he'd send Guigemar back out to sea.
If he survived, that would be a shame;   615
he'd be happier if Guigemar drowned.
      When he had made this pledge,
they went together to the harbor,
and found the ship; they put Guigemar on it—
it will take him back to his own land.   620
The ship got under way without waiting.
The knight sighed and cried,
often lamenting his lady
and praying to almighty God
to grant him a quick death,   625
and never let him come to port
if he couldn't regain his mistress,
whom he desired more than his own life.
He persisted in his grief
until the ship came to the port   630
where he'd first found it;

he was now very near his native land.
He left the ship as quickly as he could.
    A boy whom Guigemar had raised
came by, following a knight,   635
and leading a war-horse.
Guigemar recognized him and called to him;
the squire looked at him,
recognized his lord, dismounted,
and presented the charger to him.   640
Guigemar went off with him; all his friends
rejoiced that they had found him again.
He was highly honored in his land,
but through it all he was sad and distracted.
His friends wanted him to take a wife,   645
but he refused them altogether;
he'll never have to do with a woman,
for love or money,
if she can't untie
his knotted shirt without tearing it.   650
The news traveled throughout Brittany;
all the women and girls
came to try their luck,
but none could untie the knot.
    Now I want to tell you about the lady   655
whom Guigemar loved so dearly.
On the advice of one of his barons,
her husband had her imprisoned
in a dark marble tower.
There she passed bad days, worse nights.   660
No one in the world could describe
the pain, the suffering,
the anguish and the grief,
that she endured in that tower.
She remained there two years and more, I believe,   665
without ever having a moment of pleasure.
Often, she mourned for her lover:
"Guigemar, my lord, why did I ever lay eyes on you?
I'd rather die quickly
than suffer this lingering torture.   670

My love, if I could escape,
I'd go to where you put out to sea
and drown myself." Then she got up;
in astonishment she went to the door
and found it unlocked;   675
by good fortune, she got outside—
no one bothered her.
She came to the harbor, and found the boat.
It was tied to the rock
where she had intended to drown herself.   680
When she saw it there, she went aboard;
she could think of only one thing—
that this was where her lover had perished.
Suddenly, she couldn't stand up.
If she could have gotten back up on deck,   685
she would have thrown herself overboard,
so great was her suffering.
The boat set out, taking her with it.
It came to port in Brittany,
beneath a strong, well-built castle.   690
      The lord of the castle
was named Meriaduc.
He was fighting a war with a neighbor,
and had risen early that morning
because he wanted to dispatch his troops   695
to attack his enemy.
Standing at a window,
he saw the ship arrive.
He went downstairs
and called his chamberlain;   700
quickly they went to the ship,
climbed up its ladder;
inside they found the woman
who had a fairylike beauty.
He took her by the cloak   705
and brought her with him to his castle.
He was delighted with his discovery,
for she was incredibly beautiful;
whoever had put her on the boat,

he could tell she came from high lineage.   710
He felt for her a love
as great as he'd ever had for a woman.
          He had a young sister,
a beautiful maiden, in his care;
he commended the lady to her attention.   715
So she was waited on and made much of;
the damsel dressed her richly.
But she remained constantly sad and preoccupied.
The lord often came to speak with her,
since he wanted to love her with all his heart.   720
He pleaded for her love; she didn't want it,
instead she showed him her belt:
she would never love any man
except the one who could open the belt
without breaking it. When he heard that,   725
Meriaduc replied angrily,
"There's another one like you in this land,
a very worthy knight,
who avoids, in a similar manner, taking a wife
by means of a shirt   730
the right tail of which is knotted;
it can't be untied
except by using scissors or a knife.
I think you must have made that knot!"
          When the lady heard this, she sighed,   735
and almost fainted.
He took her in his arms,
cut the laces of her tunic,
and tried to open the belt.
But he didn't succeed.   740
There wasn't a knight in the region
whom he didn't summon to try his luck.
          Things went on like this for quite a while,
up to the time of a tournament
that Meriaduc had proclaimed   745
against the lord he was fighting.
He sent for knights and enlisted them in his service,
knowing very well that Guigemar would come.

He asked him as a special favor,
as his friend and companion,   750
not to let him down in this hour of need,
but to come help him.
So Guigemar set out, richly supplied,
leading more than one hundred knights.
Meriaduc entertained him   755
as an honored guest in his stronghold.
He then sent two knights to his sister,
and commanded her
to prepare herself and come to him,
bringing with her the woman he so much loved.   760
The girl obeyed his order.
Lavishly outfitted,
they came hand in hand into the great hall.
The lady was pale and upset;
she heard Guigemar's name   765
and couldn't stand up.
If the damsel hadn't supported her,
she'd have fallen to the ground.
Guigemar arose when the women entered;
he looked at the lady and noticed   770
her appearance and behavior;
involuntarily, he shrank back a bit.
"Is this," he said, "my dear love,
my hope, my heart, and my life—
my beautiful lady who loved me?   775
Where did she come from? Who brought her here?
Now, that was a foolish thought!
I know it can't be she;
women often look alike—
I got all excited for no reason.   780
But because she looks like the one
for whom my heart aches and sighs,
I'll gladly speak to her."
Then the knight came forward,
he kissed her and sat her down beside him;   785
he didn't say another word,
except that he asked her to sit down.

Meriaduc looked at them closely,
upset by the sight of them together.
He called Guigemar cheerfully: 790
"My lord," he said, "please
let this girl try
to untie your shirt,
to see if she can manage to do it."
Guigemar answered, "Certainly."   795
        He summoned a chamberlain
who was in charge of the shirt
and commanded him to bring it.
It was given to the girl,
but she couldn't untie it at all.   800
The lady knew the knot very well;
her heart is greatly agitated,
for she would love to try to untie it,
if she dared and could.
Meriaduc saw this clearly;   805
he was as sorry as he could be.
"My lady," he said, "now try
to untie it, if you can."
When she heard his order,
she took the shirttail   810
and easily untied the knot.
Guigemar was thunderstruck;
he knew her very well, and yet
he couldn't bring himself to believe firmly it was she.
So he spoke to her in this way: 815
"Beloved, sweet creature,
is that you? Tell me truly!
Let me see your body,
and the belt I put on you."
He put his hands on her hips,   820
and found the belt.
"My beautiful one," he said, "what a lucky adventure
that I've found you like this!
Who brought you here?"
She told him about the grief,   825
the great pains, the monotony

of the prison where she was held captive,
and everything that had happened to her—
how she escaped,
how she wished to drown, but found the ship instead,   830
and how she entered it and was brought to this port;
and how the lord of the castle kept her in custody,
guarding her in luxury
but constantly asking for her love.
Now her joy has returned: 835
"My love, take back your beloved!"
    Guigemar got up.
"My lords," he said, "listen to me!
Here I have the mistress
I thought I had lost forever.   840
Now I ask and implore Meriaduc
to give her back to me out of kindness.
I will become his vassal,
serve him two or three years,
with one hundred knights, or more!"   845
Meriaduc answered,
"Guigemar," he said, "my handsome friend,
I'm not so harried
or so afflicted by any war
that you can bargain with me about this.   850
I found this woman and I propose to take care of her
and defend her against you."
    When Guigemar heard that, he quickly
commanded his men to mount.
He galloped away, defying Meriaduc.   855
It upset him to leave his beloved behind.
Guigemar took with him
every knight who had come
to the town for the tournament.
Each declared his loyalty to Guigemar;   860
they'll accompany him wherever he goes.
Whoever fails him now will truly be dishonored!
That night they came to the castle
of Meriaduc's opponent.
The lord of the castle put them up;   865

he was joyful and delighted
that Guigemar came over to his side, bringing help with him.
Now he's sure the war's as good as over.
    The next morning they arose,
and equipped themselves at their lodgings.   870
They departed from the village, noisily;
Guigemar came first, leading them.
Arriving at Meriaduc's castle, they assaulted it;
but it was very strong and they failed to take it.
Guigemar besieged the town;   875
he won't leave until it has fallen.
His friends and other troops increased so greatly
that he was able to starve everyone inside.
He captured and destroyed the castle,
killed its lord.   880
Guigemar led away his mistress with great rejoicing;
all his pain was now at an end.
    From this story that you have heard
the *lai* of Guigemar was composed,
which is now recited to the harp and rote;   885
the music is a pleasure to hear.

Equitan

Most noble barons
were those Bretons of Brittany.
In the old days they were accustomed, out of bravery,
courtliness, and nobility,
to create *lais* from the adventures they heard,   5
adventures that had befallen all sorts of people;
they did this as a memorial,
so that men should not forget them.
They made one that I heard—
it should never be forgotten—   10
about Equitan, a most courtly man,
the lord of Nauns, a magistrate and king.

Equitan was a man of great worth,
dearly loved in his own land.

He loved sport and lovemaking;   15
and so he kept a body of knights in his service.
Whoever indulges in love without sense or moderation
recklessly endangers his life;
such is the nature of love
that no one involved with it can keep his head.   20
Equitan had a seneschal,
a good knight, brave and loyal,
who took care of his land for him,
governed and administered it.
Unless the king was making war,   25
he would never, no matter what the emergency,
neglect his hunting,
his hawking, or his other amusements.
      This seneschal took a wife
through whom great harm later came to the land.   30
She was a beautiful woman
of fine breeding,
with an attractive form and figure.
Nature took pains in putting her together:
bright eyes in a lovely face,   35
a pretty mouth and a well-shaped nose.
She hadn't an equal in the entire kingdom.
The king often heard her praised.
He frequently sent his greetings to her,
presents as well;   40
without having seen her, he wanted her,
so he spoke to her as soon as he could.
      For his private amusement
he went hunting in the countryside
where the seneschal dwelt;   45
in the castle, where the lady also lived,
the king took lodging for the night
after he had finished the day's sport.
He now had a good chance to speak to the wife,
to reveal to her his worth, his desires.   50
He found her refined and clever,
with a beautiful body and face,
and a pleasing, cheerful demeanor.

Love drafted him into his service:
he shot an arrow at the king   55
that opened a great wound in the heart,
where Love had aimed and fixed it.
Neither good sense nor understanding were of use to the king now;
love for the woman so overcame him
that he became sad and depressed.   60
Now he has to give in to love completely;
he can't defend himself at all.
That night he can't sleep or even rest,
instead he blames and scolds himself:
"Alas," he says, "what destiny   65
led me to these parts?
Because I have seen this woman
pain has struck at my heart,
my whole body shivers.
I think I have no choice but to love her—   70
yet if I love her, I'm doing wrong;
she's the wife of my seneschal.
I owe him the same faith and love
that I want him to give me.
If, by some means, he found out about this   75
I know how much it would upset him.
Still, it would be a lot worse
if I went mad out of concern for him.
It would be a shame for such a beautiful woman
not to have a lover!   80
What would become of her finer qualities
if she didn't nourish them by a secret love?
There isn't a man in the world
who wouldn't be vastly improved if she loved him.
And if the seneschal should hear of the affair,   85
he oughtn't be too crushed by it;
he certainly can't hold her all by himself,
and I'm happy to share the burden with him!"
When he had said all that, he sighed,
and lay in bed thinking.   90
After a while, he spoke again: "Why
am I so distressed and frightened?

I still don't even know
if she will take me as her lover;
but I'll know soon!   95
If she should feel the way I do,
I'd soon be free of this agony.
God! It's still so long till morning!
I can't get any rest,
it's been forever since I went to bed."   100
        The king stayed awake until daybreak;
he could hardly wait for it.
He rose and went hunting,
but he soon turned back
saying that he was worn out.   105
He returns to his room and lies down.
The seneschal is saddened by this;
he doesn't know what's bothering the king,
what's making him shiver;
in fact, his wife is the reason for it.   110
The king, to get some relief and some pleasure,
sends for the wife to come speak with him.
He revealed his desire to her,
letting her know that he was dying because of her;
that it lay in her power to comfort him   115
or to let him die.
"My lord," the woman said to him,
"I must have some time to think;
this is so new to me,
I have no idea what to say.   120
You're a king of high nobility,
and I'm not at all of such fortune
that you should single me out
to have a love affair with.
If you get what you want from me,   125
I have no doubt about it:
you'll soon get tired of me,
and I'll be far worse off than before.
If I should love you
and satisfy your desire,   130
love wouldn't be shared equally

between the two of us.
Because you're a powerful king
and my husband is your vassal,
I'm sure you believe   135
your rank entitles you to my love.
Love is worthless if it's not mutual.
A poor but loyal man is worth more—
if he also possesses good sense and virtue—
and his love brings greater joy   140
than the love of a prince or a king
who has no loyalty in him.
Anyone who aims higher in love
than his own wealth entitles him to
will be frightened by every little thing that occurs.   145
The rich man, however, is confident
that no one will steal a mistress away
whose favor he obtains by his authority over her."
     Equitan answered her,
"Please, my lady! Don't say such things!   150
No one could consider himself noble
(rather, he'd be haggling like a tradesman)
who, for the sake of wealth or a big fief,
would take pains to win someone of low repute.
There's no woman in the world—if she's smart,   155
refined, and of noble character,
and if she places a high enough value on her love
that she isn't inconstant—
whom a rich prince in his palace
wouldn't yearn for   160
and love well and truly,
even if she'd nothing but the shirt on her back.
Whoever is inconstant in love
and gives himself up to treachery
is mocked and deceived in the end;   165
I've seen it happen many times like that.
It's no surprise when someone loses out
who deserves to because of his behavior.
My dear lady, I'm offering myself to you!
Don't think of me as your king,   170

but as your vassal and your lover.
I tell you, I promise you
I'll do whatever you want.
Don't let me die on your account!
You be the lord and I'll be the servant—   175
you be the proud one and I'll be the beggar!"
        The king pleaded with her,
begged her so often for mercy,
that she promised him her love
and granted him possession of her body.   180
Then they exchanged rings,
and promised themselves to each other.
They kept their promises and loved each other well;
they died for this in the end.
        Their affair lasted a long time,   185
without anyone hearing of it.
At the times set for their meetings,
when they were to speak together at the king's palace,
the king informed his followers
that he wanted to be bled privately.   190
The doors of his chamber were closed,
and no one was so daring,
if the king didn't summon him,
that he would ever enter there.
Meanwhile, the seneschal held court   195
and heard pleas and complaints.
The king loved the seneschal's wife for a long time,
had no desire for any other woman;
he didn't want to marry,
and never allowed the subject to be raised.   200
His people held this against him,
and the seneschal's wife
heard about it often; this worried her,
and she was afraid she would lose him.
So when she next had the chance to speak to him—   205
when she should have been full of joy,
kissing and embracing him
and having a good time with him—
she burst into tears, making a big scene.

The king asked   210
what the matter was,
and the lady answered,
"My lord, I'm crying because of our love,
which has brought me to great sorrow:
you're going to take a wife, some king's daughter,   215
and you will get rid of me;
I've heard all about it, I know it's true.
And—alas!—what will become of me?
On your account I must now face death,
for I have no other comfort than you."   220
The king spoke lovingly to her:
"Dear love, don't be afraid!
I promise I'll never take a wife,
never leave you for another.
Believe me, this is the truth: 225
If your husband were dead,
I'd make you my lady and my queen;
no one could stop me."
The lady thanked him,
said she was very grateful to him;   230
if he would assure her
that he wouldn't leave her for someone else,
she would quickly undertake
to do away with her lord.
It would be easy to arrange   235
if he were willing to help her.
He agreed to do so;
there was nothing she could demand of him
that he wouldn't do, if he possibly could,
whether it turned out well or badly.   240
        "My lord," she says, "please
come hunting in the forest,
out in the country where I live.
Stay awhile at my husband's castle;
you can be bled there,   245
and on the third day after that, take a bath.
My lord will be bled with you
and will bathe with you as well;

make it clear to him—and don't relent—
that he must keep you company!   250
I'll have the baths heated
and the two tubs brought in;
his will be so boiling hot
that no man on earth
could escape being horribly scalded   255
as soon as he sat down in it.
When he's scalded to death,
send for his men and yours;
then you can show them exactly how
he suddenly died in his bath."   260
The king promised her
that he'd do just as she wished.
      Less than three months later,
the king went out into the countryside to hunt.
He had himself bled to ward off illness,   265
and his seneschal bled with him.
On the third day, he said he wanted to bathe;
the seneschal was happy to comply.
"Bathe with me," said the king,
and the seneschal replied, "Willingly."   270
The wife had the baths heated,
the two tubs brought;
next to the bed, according to plan,
she had them both set down.
Then she had boiling water brought   275
for the seneschal's tub.
The good man got up
and went outside to relax for a moment.
His wife came to speak to the king
and he pulled her down beside him;   280
they lay down on her husband's bed
and began to enjoy themselves.
They lay there together.
Because the tub was right before them,
they set a guard at the bedroom door;   285
a maidservant was to keep watch there.
Suddenly the seneschal returned,

and knocked on the door; the girl held it closed.
He struck it so violently
that he forced it open.   290
There he discovered the king and his own wife
lying in each other's arms.
The king looked up and saw him coming;
to hide his villainy
he jumped into the tub feet first,   295
stark naked.
He didn't stop to think what he was doing.
And there he was scalded to death,
caught in his own evil trap,
while the seneschal remained safe and sound.   300
The seneschal could see very well
what had happened to the king.
He grabbed his wife at once
and thrust her head first into the tub.
Thus both died,   305
the king first, the wife after him.
Whoever wants to hear some sound advice
can profit from this example:
he who plans evil for another
may have that evil rebound back on him.   310
       It all happened just as I've told you.
The Bretons made a *lai* about it,
about Equitan, his fate,
and the woman who loved him so much.

Laustic

I shall tell you an adventure
about which the Bretons made a *lai*.
Laüstic was the name, I think,
they gave it in their land.
In French it is *rossignol*,   5
and *nightingale* in proper English.
At Saint-Malo, in that country,
there was a famous city.
Two knights lived there,
they both had strong houses.   10

From the goodness of the two barons
the city acquired a good name.
One had married a woman
wise, courtly, and handsome;
she set a wonderfully high value on herself,   15
within the bounds of custom and usage.
The other was a bachelor,
well known among his peers
for bravery and great valor;
he delighted in living well.   20
He jousted often, spent widely
and gave out what he had.
He also loved his neighbor's wife;
he asked her, begged her so persistently,
and there was such good in him,   25
that she loved him more than anything,
as much for the good that she heard of him
as because he was close by.
They loved each other discreetly and well,
concealed themselves and took care   30
that they weren't seen
or disturbed or suspected.
And they could do this well enough
since their dwellings were close,
their houses were next door,   35
and so were their rooms and their towers;
there was no barrier or boundary
except a high wall of dark stone.
From the rooms where the lady slept,
if she went to the window   40
she could talk to her love
on the other side, and he to her,
and they could exchange their possessions,
by tossing and throwing them.
There was scarcely anything to disturb them,   45
they were both quite at ease;
except that they couldn't come together
completely for their pleasure,
for the lady was closely guarded

when her husband was in the country.   50
Yet they always managed,
whether at night or in the day,
to be able to talk together;
no one could prevent
their coming to the window   55
and seeing each other there.
For a long time they loved each other,
until one summer
when the woods and meadows were green
and the orchards blooming.   60
The little birds, with great sweetness,
were voicing their joy above the flowers.
It is no wonder if he understands them,
he who has love to his desire.
I'll tell you the truth about the knight: 65
he listened to them intently
and to the lady on the other side,
both with words and looks.
At night, when the moon shone
when her lord was in bed,   70
she often rose from his side
and wrapped herself in a cloak.
She went to the window
because of her lover, who, she knew,
was leading the same life,   75
awake most of the night.
Each took pleasure in the other's sight
since they could have nothing more;
but she got up and stood there so often
that her lord grew angry   80
and began to question her, to ask
why she got up and where she went.
"My lord," the lady answered him,
"there is no joy in this world
like hearing the nightingale sing.   85
That's why I stand there.
It sounds so sweet at night
that it gives me great pleasure;

it delights me so and I so desire it
that I cannot close my eyes."   90
When her lord heard what she said
he laughed in anger and ill will.
He set his mind on one thing:
to trap the nightingale.
There was no valet in his house   95
that he didn't set to making traps, nets, or snares,
which he then had placed in the orchard;
there was no hazel tree or chestnut
where they did not place a snare or lime
until they trapped and captured him.   100
When they had caught the nightingale,
they brought it, still alive, to the lord.
He was very happy when he had it;
he came to the lady's chambers.
"Lady," he said, "where are you?   105
Come here! Speak to us!
I have trapped the nightingale
that kept you awake so much.
From now on you can lie in peace:
he will never again awaken you."   110
When the lady heard him,
she was sad and angry.
She asked her lord for the bird
but he killed it out of spite,
he broke its neck in his hands—   115
too vicious an act—
and threw the body on the lady;
her shift was stained with blood,
a little, on her breast.
Then he left the room.   120
The lady took the little body;
she wept hard and cursed
those who betrayed the nightingale,
who made the traps and snares,
for they took great joy from her.   125
"Alas," she said, "now I must suffer.
I won't be able to get up at night

or go and stand in the window
where I used to see my love.
I know one thing for certain: 130
he'd think I was pretending.
I must decide what to do about this.
I shall send him the nightingale
and relate the adventure."
In a piece of samite,   135
embroidered in gold and writing,
she wrapped the little bird.
She called one of her servants,
charged him with her message,
and sent him to her love.   140
He came to the knight,
greeted him in the name of the lady,
related the whole message to him,
and presented the nightingale.

When everything had been told and revealed to the knight,   145
after he had listened well,
he was very sad about the adventure,
but he wasn't mean or hesitant.
He had a small vessel fashioned,
with no iron or steel in it;   150
it was all pure gold and good stones,
very precious and very dear;
the cover was very carefully attached.
He placed the nightingale inside
and then he had the casket sealed—   155
he carried it with him always.

This adventure was told,
it could not be concealed for long.
The Bretons made a *lai* about it
which men call *The Nightingale*.   160

from *Inferno*

Dante Alighieri
Translated by Allen Mandelbaum

INFERNO

CANTO I

Nel mezzo del cammin di nostra vita
mi ritrovai per una selva oscura,
ché la diritta via era smarrita.

Ahi quanto a dir qual era è cosa dura   4
esta selva selvaggia e aspra e forte
che nel pensier rinova la paura!

Tant' è amara che poco è più morte;   7
ma per trattar del ben ch'i' vi trovai,
dirò de l'altre cose ch'i' v'ho scorte.

Io non so ben ridir com' i' v'intrai,   10
tant' era pien di sonno a quel punto
che la verace via abbandonai.

Ma poi ch'i' fui al piè d'un colle giunto,   13
là dove terminava quella valle
che m'avea di paura il cor compunto,

guardai in alto e vidi le sue spalle   16
vestite già de' raggi del pianeta
che mena dritto altrui per ogne calle.

Allor fu la paura un poco queta,   19
che nel lago del cor m'era durata
la notte ch'i' passai con tanta pieta.

E come quei che con lena affannata,   22
uscito fuor del pelago a la riva,
si volge a l'acqua perigliosa e guata,

così l'animo mio, ch'ancor fuggiva,   25
si volse a retro a rimirar lo passo
che non lasciò già mai persona viva.

Poi ch'èi posato un poco il corpo lasso,   28
ripresi via per la piaggia diserta,
sì che 'l piè fermo sempre era 'l più basso.

The voyager-narrator astray by night in a dark forest. Morning and
the sunlit hill. Three beasts that impede his ascent. The encounter
with Virgil, who offers his guidance and an alternative path through
two of the three realms the voyager must visit.

W hen I had journeyed half of our life's way,
    I found myself within a shadowed forest,
for I had lost the path that does not stray.

    Ah, it is hard to speak of what it was,   4
that savage forest, dense and difficult,
which even in recall renews my fear:

    so bitter—death is hardly more severe!   7
But to retell the good discovered there,
I'll also tell the other things I saw.

    I cannot clearly say how I had entered   10
the wood; I was so full of sleep just at
the point where I abandoned the true path.

    But when I'd reached the bottom of a hill—   13
it rose along the boundary of the valley
that had harassed my heart with so much fear—

    I looked on high and saw its shoulders clothed   16
already by the rays of that same planet
which serves to lead men straight along all roads.

    At this my fear was somewhat quieted;   19
for through the night of sorrow I had spent,
the lake within my heart felt terror present.

    And just as he who, with exhausted breath,   22
having escaped from sea to shore, turns back
to watch the dangerous waters he has quit,

    so did my spirit, still a fugitive,   25
turn back to look intently at the pass
that never has let any man survive.

    I let my tired body rest awhile.   28
Moving again, I tried the lonely slope—
my firm foot always was the one below.

Ed ecco, quasi al cominciar de l'erta,   31
una lonza leggiera e presta molto,
che di pel macolato era coverta;
   e non mi si partia dinanzi al volto,   34
anzi 'mpediva tanto il mio cammino,
ch'i' fui per ritornar più volte vòlto.
   Temp' era dal principio del mattino,   37
e 'l sol montava 'n sù con quelle stelle
ch'eran con lui quando l'amor divino
   mosse di prima quelle cose belle;   40
sì ch'a bene sperar m'era cagione
di quella fiera a la gaetta pelle
   l'ora del tempo e la dolce stagione;   43
ma non sì che paura non mi desse
la vista che m'apparve d'un leone.
   Questi parea che contra me venisse   46
con la test' alta e con rabbiosa fame,
sì che parea che l'aere ne tremesse.
   Ed una lupa, che di tutte brame   49
sembiava carca ne la sua magrezza,
e molte genti fé già viver grame,
   questa mi porse tanto di gravezza   52
con la paura ch'uscia di sua vista,
ch'io perdei la speranza de l'altezza.
   E qual è quei che volontieri acquista,   55
e giugne 'l tempo che perder lo face,
che 'n tutti suoi pensier piange e s'attrista;
   tal mi fece la bestia sanza pace,   58
che, venendomi 'ncontro, a poco a poco
mi ripigneva là dove 'l sol tace.
   Mentre ch'i' rovinava in basso loco,   61
dinanzi a li occhi mi si fu offerto
chi per lungo silenzio parea fioco.
   Quando vidi costui nel gran diserto,   64
"*Miserere* di me," gridai a lui,
"qual che tu sii, od ombra od omo certo!"
   Rispuosemi: "Non omo, omo già fui,   67
e li parenti miei furon lombardi,
mantoani per patrïa ambedui.

And almost where the hillside starts to rise—   31
look there!—a leopard, very quick and lithe,
a leopard covered with a spotted hide.
    He did not disappear from sight, but stayed;   34
indeed, he so impeded my ascent
that I had often to turn back again.
    The time was the beginning of the morning;   37
the sun was rising now in fellowship
with the same stars that had escorted it
    when Divine Love first moved those things of beauty;   40
so that the hour and the gentle season
gave me good cause for hopefulness on seeing
    that beast before me with his speckled skin;   43
but hope was hardly able to prevent
the fear I felt when I beheld a lion.
    His head held high and ravenous with hunger—   46
even the air around him seemed to shudder—
this lion seemed to make his way against me.
    And then a she-wolf showed herself; she seemed   49
to carry every craving in her leanness;
she had already brought despair to many.
    The very sight of her so weighted me   52
with fearfulness that I abandoned hope
of ever climbing up that mountain slope.
    Even as he who glories while he gains   55
will, when the time has come to tally loss,
lament with every thought and turn despondent,
    so was I when I faced that restless beast,   58
which, even as she stalked me, step by step
had thrust me back to where the sun is speechless.
    While I retreated down to lower ground,   61
before my eyes there suddenly appeared
one who seemed faint because of the long silence.
    When I saw him in that vast wilderness,   64
"Have pity on me," were the words I cried,
"whatever you may be—a shade, a man."
    He answered me: "Not man; I once was man.   67
Both of my parents came from Lombardy,
and both claimed Mantua as native city.

Nacqui *sub Iulio,* ancor che fosse tardi,   70
e vissi a Roma sotto 'l buono Augusto
nel tempo de li dèi falsi e bugiardi.

Poeta fui, e cantai di quel giusto   73
figliuol d'Anchise che venne di Troia,
poi che 'l superbo Ilïón fu combusto.

Ma tu perché ritorni a tanta noia?   76
perché non sali il dilettoso monte
ch'è principio e cagion di tutta gioia?"

"Or se' tu quel Virgilio e quella fonte   79
che spandi di parlar sì largo fiume?"
rispuos' io lui con vergognosa fronte.

"O de li altri poeti onore e lume,   82
vagliami 'l lungo studio e 'l grande amore
che m'ha fatto cercar lo tuo volume.

Tu se' lo mio maestro e 'l mio autore,   85
tu se' solo colui da cu' io tolsi
lo bello stilo che m'ha fatto onore.

Vedi la bestia per cu' io mi volsi;   88
aiutami da lei, famoso saggio,
ch'ella mi fa tremar le vene e i polsi."

"A te convien tenere altro vïaggio,"   91
rispuose, poi che lagrimar mi vide,
"se vuo' campar d'esto loco selvaggio;

ché questa bestia, per la qual tu gride,   94
non lascia altrui passar per la sua via,
ma tanto lo 'mpedisce che l'uccide;

e ha natura sì malvagia e ria,   97
che mai non empie la bramosa voglia,
e dopo 'l pasto ha più fame che pria.

Molti son li animali a cui s'ammoglia,   100
e più saranno ancora, infin che 'l veltro
verrà, che la farà morir con doglia.

Questi non ciberà terra né peltro,   103
ma sapïenza, amore e virtute,
e sua nazion sarà tra feltro e feltro.

Di quella umile Italia fia salute   106
per cui morì la vergine Cammilla,
Eurialo e Turno e Niso di ferute.

And I was born, though late, *sub Julio,*   70
and lived in Rome under the good Augustus—
the season of the false and lying gods.

    I was a poet, and I sang the righteous   73
son of Anchises who had come from Troy
when flames destroyed the pride of Ilium.

    But why do you return to wretchedness?   76
Why not climb up the mountain of delight,
the origin and cause of every joy?"

    "And are you then that Virgil, you the fountain   79
that freely pours so rich a stream of speech?"
I answered him with shame upon my brow.

    "O light and honor of all other poets,   82
may my long study and the intense love
that made me search your volume serve me now.

    You are my master and my author, you—   85
the only one from whom my writing drew
the noble style for which I have been honored.

    You see the beast that made me turn aside;   88
help me, o famous sage, to stand against her,
for she has made my blood and pulses shudder."

    "It is another path that you must take,"   91
he answered when he saw my tearfulness,
"if you would leave this savage wilderness;

    the beast that is the cause of your outcry   94
allows no man to pass along her track,
but blocks him even to the point of death;

    her nature is so squalid, so malicious   97
that she can never sate her greedy will;
when she has fed, she's hungrier than ever.

    She mates with many living souls and shall   100
yet mate with many more, until the Greyhound
arrives, inflicting painful death on her.

    That Hound will never feed on land or pewter,   103
but find his fare in wisdom, love, and virtue;
his place of birth shall be between two felts.

    He will restore low-lying Italy   106
for which the maid Camilla died of wounds,
and Nisus, Turnus, and Euryalus.

Questi la caccerà per ogne villa,   109
fin che l'avrà rimessa ne lo 'nferno,
là onde 'nvidia prima dipartilla.

 Ond' io per lo tuo me' penso e discerno 112
che tu mi segui, e io sarò tua guida,
e trarrotti di qui per loco etterno,

 ove udirai le disperate strida,   115
vedrai li antichi spiriti dolenti,
ch'a la seconda morte ciascun grida;

 e vederai color che son contenti   118
nel foco, perché speran di venire
quando che sia a le beate genti.

 A le quai poi se tu vorrai salire,   121
anima fia a ciò più di me degna:
con lei ti lascerò nel mio partire;

 ché quello imperador che là sù regna, 124
perch' i' fu' ribellante a la sua legge,
non vuol che 'n sua città per me si vegna.

 In tutte parti impera e quivi regge; 127
quivi è la sua città e l'alto seggio:
oh felice colui cu' ivi elegge!"

 E io a lui: "Poeta, io ti richeggio   130
per quello Dio che tu non conoscesti,
a ciò ch'io fugga questo male e peggio,

 che tu mi meni là dov' or dicesti,   133
sì ch'io veggia la porta di san Pietro
e color cui tu fai cotanto mesti."

 Allor si mosse, e io li tenni dietro. 136

And he will hunt that beast through every city 109
until he thrusts her back again to Hell,
from which she was first sent above by envy.

Therefore, I think and judge it best for you 112
to follow me, and I shall guide you, taking
you from this place through an eternal place,

where you shall hear the howls of desperation 115
and see the ancient spirits in their pain,
as each of them laments his second death;

and you shall see those souls who are content 118
within the fire, for they hope to reach—
whenever that may be—the blessed people.

If you would then ascend as high as these, 121
a soul more worthy than I am will guide you;
I'll leave you in her care when I depart,

because that Emperor who reigns above, 124
since I have been rebellious to His law,
will not allow me entry to His city.

He governs everywhere, but rules from there; 127
there is His city, His high capital:
o happy those He chooses to be there!"

And I replied: "O poet—by that God 130
whom you had never come to know—I beg you,
that I may flee this evil and worse evils,

to lead me to the place of which you spoke, 133
that I may see the gateway of Saint Peter
and those whom you describe as sorrowful."

Then he set out, and I moved on behind him. 136

1·2

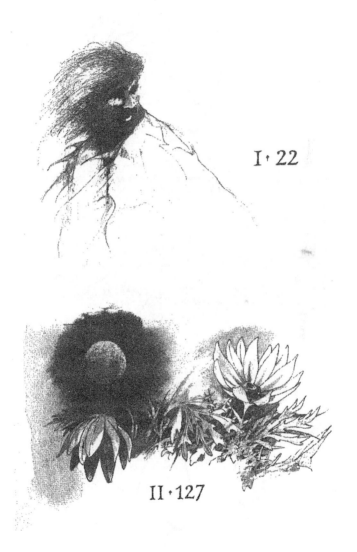

I·22

II·127

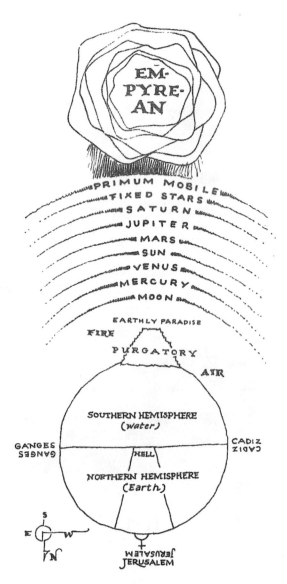

THE UNIVERSE OF DANTE

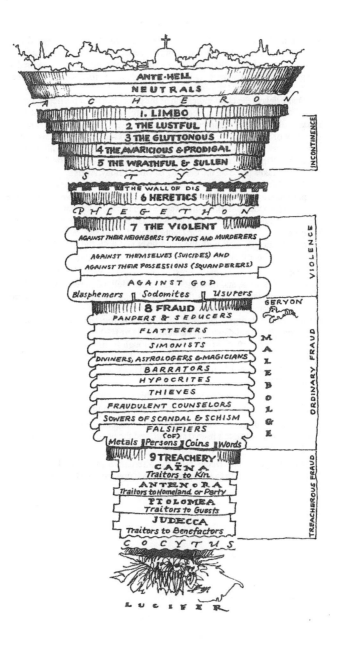

Notes

CANTO I

1–3 It is not known exactly when Dante began to write the *Inferno*. But he was surely writing while in exile from Florence; and he was constructing a fiction dated before both his exile and his act of writing began. This predating gives him some advantage in "foreseeing" events that occurred between the date of the tale and the date of the telling.

Dante delays the chief indication of the possible date of his fictive voyage until Canto XXI, 112–114 (see note there for a fuller account). That latter passage allows most commentators to define the night in the dark wood as the night of Maundy Thursday, the night before Good Friday, the evening of April 7 in the year 1300. The day of Good Friday is then spent with the three beasts and Virgil in Canto I, so that the entry into Ante-Hell at the beginning of Canto II takes place on the evening of Good Friday, April 8.

"*Our* life"—with its "possessive of human solidarity" (Spitzer)—links the particularity of Dante the wayfarer to the universality of everyman. In the *Convivio* (IV, xxiii, 6–10), Dante fixes 35 years as the midpoint of man's life, following Psalm 89:10 (90:10 in the King James), which sets 70 years as the length of man's days. Thus, for Dante himself, who was born in 1265, the year 1300 accords well with the cited texts and with the passage in Isaiah (38:10), "In the middle of my days, I shall go to the gates of Hell."

2 The "shadowed" or dark forest is our way station to many images of darkness, blindness, and obscurity that obsess Hell—that realm in which the sun never appears, as it does throughout Purgatory—though Virgil, somewhat clairvoyantly, will refer to the movement of the unseen skies on the earth above "starless" (III, 23) Hell. (While *Inferno* begins at night, *Purgatorio* begins at dawn and *Paradiso* at noon.)

But the forest precedes the journey through Hell. It is the dark wood of life on earth when lived in sin; it is Dante's interior wood; and it is the wood of political darkness, of Florence, of Italy, of papal corruption, of the absence of imperial authority.

5 In accord with most commentators, this translation sees *forte* as "difficult" (that is, difficult to traverse—or, perhaps better, to escape from).

8 The "good discovered there" has a host of probable meanings, but it certainly anticipates Dante's rescue by Virgil and the beginning of the long journey to salvation.

13–18 At this point Dante sees the alternative to the dark forest: the "hill"—that is, the path to virtue, which leads upward. The hill is illuminated by the sun, which Dante does not see directly but whose rays stand for the light of God's illuminating grace. Dante's access to the hill, however, is blocked by the three beasts he encounters—beasts symbolic of different aspects of human sinfulness (see 31–60).

17 In the Ptolemaic system, the sun is a "planet" revolving around the earth. For the cosmos of Dante see the diagram on p. 343.

21 In terms of the physiology of Dante's time, "the lake of my heart" refers to that inner chamber of the heart thought to be the physical seat of the emotion of fear.

22–25 This first simile of the poem already draws on an important theme of imagery throughout the *Comedy*: the sea. It is not unrelated to the Red Sea of the Exodus (Singleton) and, given Dante's use of *pelago* here for "sea," to the exhausted Trojan survivors of the storm in *Aen.* I, 242; 251–252 (Hollander) or to the landing from the *pelago* that precedes Aeneas's own entry into the underworld *(Aen.* VI, 1–3).

30 The difficulty of interpreting this line has given pause to many commentators. Boccaccio's literal reading was that those who climb always tend to support themselves more on that foot which remains below. This translation is compatible with his reading—and with the view that the firm foot may, alternately, be the left, then the right. Recent allegorists (Freccero, Mazzoni) identify the firm foot as *one* foot, the left—the foot weighed down by appetites, concupiscence, limping will—as against the right—the foot of the intellect. For them, *fermo* means "halting, dragging, inhibiting."

31–60 For most early commentators—and, after many alternate proposals, for many moderns—the leopard represents lust; the lion, pride; the she-wolf, avarice or cupidity. Whatever specific area of sin is assigned to each animal, the Italian certainly links them alliteratively to each other—*lonza—leone— lupa* (Ragonese in the *E.D.)* (which this translation cannot do)—and to Lucifer of Canto XXXIII (Sarolli). The translation's "leopard" keeps the text close, as early commentators do, to Jer. 5:6, which speaks of a lion, a wolf, and a leopard. But *lonza* may be a lynxlike animal (see *Aen.* I, 458) or a strange hybrid.

37–40 The world was believed to have been created in spring, with the sun in the constellation of Aries; and Dante's own voyage takes place in the springtime.

60 Dante's use of synesthesia—the merging of the visual ("the sun") and the auditory ("speechless")—recurs in line 63.

63 This translation's "faint" for *fioco* echoes the auditory and visual connotations of the Italian, though leaning here to the visual: Dante sees Virgil indistinctly—in a shadowed space where the "sun is speechless." This initiates and reinforces Dante's uncertainty, which gives rise to the "whatever you may be" of line 66. But this shadowed space also resonates as time—the long ages in which Virgil did not have the full voice he will now find again through and in Dante.

70–72 Virgil (70–19 B.C.) was born *sub Julio,* in the time of Julius Caesar, though too late to win Caesar's esteem. Though "false and lying gods" is close indeed to Augustine's *"deos falsos fallacesque" (City of God* II, xxix, 2), Dante's own use of pagan gods in the machinery of the *Comedy* would reframe this assertion: the pagan gods were "false and lying" when seen as sufficient ends in themselves, but they carried some truth as prefigurations of the Christian God.

73–75 "The righteous son of Anchises" is Aeneas, hero of the *Aeneid,* to which Dante refers repeatedly in the *Inferno.*

82–87 "The noble style" is the tragic style, the style of epic narrative and of the exalted, spacious, ethically-intellectually committed lyric. Dante can claim to "have been honored" for his achievement in the latter category before 1300, but Virgil was hardly his chief mentor then. This passage seems, rather, to carry wishful meaning, the force and weight of desire, as if Dante were saying, "You, Virgil, using the ancient but ever-living tongue of the Latins, gave full life to the stately tragic style, the noble upper register, in epic; my mixed, comic style, drawing on all three styles—the upper, the middle, the lower—for this my modern, Christian, prophetic epic in the maternal tongue of the Italians, the modern Latins, needs you as exemplary inspiration and would achieve honor comparable to yours."

Boccaccio, glossing "for which I have been honored" with "here he uses the past tense for the future, producing a solecism," senses the same intention.

101 The Greyhound of this prophetic passage, the redeemer who "will restore low-lying Italy" (106), has been identified in very diverse ways: as an ecclesiastic; as a secular political figure; as Christ; as Dante himself; as Cangrande della Scala of Verona, Dante's benefactor and an Imperial viceroy; and as others. Most probably the term connotes a political prophecy; almost as probably it foretells and hopes for a Holy Roman Emperor or his viceroy; and possibly it may refer to Henry VII, who was elected Holy Roman Emperor on November 27, 1308.

103–104 Earthly goods and nourishment are represented by "land or pewter" (which here would stand for "money"); spiritual goods by the attributes of the Trinity—wisdom, the Son; love, the Holy Ghost; virtue, the Father. This is not, however, a necessary argument for reading the Greyhound as a papal or ecclesiastical figure: for Dante elsewhere in his works, temporal authority, too, has its direct source in God.

105 Those who opt for Cangrande della Scala as the Greyhound capitalize the two *Feltros,* referring them to Feltre and Montefeltro, towns that mark the rough limits of Cangrande's domains. But this translation renders a lowercase *feltro* as "felt": the "two felts" would be the two felt-lined urns in which "Yes" and "No" ballots, respectively, were deposited in elections in Dante's time; such urns could call up the image of electing a Holy Roman Emperor. In that case, the "place of birth" would refer, not to the Greyhound's physical birth, but to his birth in and his assumption of office.

106 Virgil's *humilemque videmus Italiam,* "we sight ... the low coastline of Italy" *(Aen.* III, 681–682), is a geographic observation: Dante's *umile Italia,* "low-lying Italy," on the other hand, has moral overtones.

106–107 Those mentioned in these lines are all figures in Virgil's *Aeneid* who died in the war between the Trojans and the Latins. Camilla was a faithful woman warrior who aided Turnus, King of the Rutulians, in the war of the Latins against Aeneas *(Aen.* VII, 1055–1072; XI, 854–1126). Nisus and Euryalus were close friends who died together after a night attack on a Rutulian camp *(Aen.* IX, 232–597). Turnus was killed in the single combat with Aeneas that is placed at the end of the *Aeneid* (XII, 928–1271). This is one point where Dante shares Virgil's overarching compassion, which embraces the victors and the vanquished; Dante alternates Latin, Trojan, Latin, Trojan—and cites two Trojans who were, themselves, sacrificed in the course of the Trojans' victorious campaign.

117 This translation sees "the second death" as the state of damned souls rejoined with their bodies after the Last Judgment, and translates *grida* as "laments"—a use of this word that presents some difficulty. But as F. Mazzoni, who is followed here, notes: this line is "more tormented and disputed than, in itself, it deserves to be."

118–120 The souls in Purgatory.

121 "These" are "the blessed people" in Paradise.

122 "A soul more worthy than I am" is Beatrice, born in 1266, the year after Dante's birth, loved by Dante from his boyhood, and celebrated by him—after her death in 1290—in his *Vita Nuova.* Boccaccio and other 14th-century commentators, including Dante's son Pietro, identify her as one of the daughters of Folco Portinari; Boccaccio also mentions her marriage to a Simone de' Bardi. Folco Portinari's will of 1288 confirms this last detail for Beatrice Portinari. In the *Comedy,* the historical Beatrice is spokeswoman for the divine science of theology.

125–126 Because, as a pagan, Virgil did not worship God, he is not allowed entry to His city. For a fuller explanation of pagans' status in the Christian scheme of the afterlife, see Canto IV, 24; 52–61, and notes.

Virgil's description of Heaven as a city makes explicit the analogy drawn throughout the *Comedy,* and especially in the *Inferno,* between the Roman Empire (see II, 13–24, and note) and the heavenly City of God.

134 Since Virgil is to lead Dante through, but not beyond, Purgatory, it is best to read "the gateway of St. Peter" as the gate of Purgatory, where the vicar of St. Peter is custodian, rather than the entry to Paradise (which, in any case, in Dante's account, has no gate).

The Wife of Bath

Geoffrey Chaucer
translated by A. Kent Hieatt and Constance Hieatt

The Prologue of the Wife of Bath's Tale

Experience, even if there were no other authority
in this world, would be grounds enough for me
to speak of the woe that is in marriage;
for, my lords, since I was twelve years old,
thanks be to eternal God,   5
I have had five husbands at the church door—
if I may have been legally married so often;
and all were worthy men in their different ways.
But I was definitely told, not long ago,
that since Christ went but once   10
to a wedding, in Cana of Galilee,
by that example he taught me
that I should not be married more than once.
Also, consider what sharp words
Jesus, God and man, spoke beside a   15
well in reproof of the Samaritan:
'Thou hast had five husbands,' he said,
'and he whom thou now hast
is not thy husband'; thus he spoke, certainly;
what he meant by it, I cannot say.   20
But I ask this, why was the fifth man
no husband to the Samaritan?
How many was she allowed to have in marriage?
Never yet in my life have I heard
this number defined.   25
People may guess and interpret the text up and down,
but I know well, without a doubt, God bade
us expressly to increase and multiply;

that pleasant text I can well understand.
And also I well know that he said my husband   30
should leave father and mother, and take me;
but he made no mention of number—
of bigamy or of octogamy;
why should men speak evil of it?
    "Look at the wise king, Lord Solomon;   35
I think he had more than one wife; I would to God
I could be refreshed half so often as he!
What a gift from God he had with all his wives!
No man living in this world has such.   40
God knows this noble king to my thinking
had many a merry bout with each of them
the first night; he had a good life.
Blessed be God that I have married five!
Welcome the sixth, whenever he comes along.   45
For indeed, I don't want to keep myself entirely chaste;
when my husband has gone from the world,
some Christian man shall wed me soon.
for the Apostle says that then I am free
to marry in God's name where I please.   50
He says it's no sin to be married;
it is better to marry than to burn.
What do I care if folk speak evil
of cursed Lamech and his bigamy?
I know very well that Abraham was a holy man,   55
and Jacob too, as far as I can see;
and each of them had more than two wives,
and so did many another holy man.
Tell me, where, in any time,
did God on high expressly prohibit marriage?   60
I pray you, tell me;
or where did he command virginity?
I know as well as you do—not a doubt!—
that the Apostle, when he spoke of maidenhood,
said that he had no commandment for it.   65
One may counsel a woman to be a virgin,
but counseling is not commandment;
he left it to our own judgment.

For if God had decreed maidenhood, then
he would have condemned marriage in effect;   70
and certainly if there were no seed sown,
then where should virginity grow from?
Paul did not dare in the least to decree
a thing for which his master gave no order.
The prize is set up for virginity;   75
grab it who may, let's see who wins the race.
   "But this saying does not apply to every man,
but only where it pleases God to give it, of his might.
I very well know that the Apostle was a virgin;
but nevertheless, although he wrote and said   80
that he wished that everyone were such as he,
all this is only advice in favor of virginity;
and he gave me, as an indulgence, leave
to be a wife; so it is no reproach
for me to marry if my mate dies;   85
it is without any taint of bigamy—
although it may be good not to touch a woman
(he meant in a bed or couch;
for it is dangerous to assemble fire and tow—
you know what this example means).   90
This is the sum of the matter, he held virginity to be
more perfect than marrying in the frailty of the flesh.
It is frailty, that is, unless the man and woman
intend to live all their lives in chastity.
   "I grant it freely; I'm not envious,   95
although maidenhood be preferred to bigamy.
It pleases some to be pure, body and soul;
I won't make any boast about my own estate.
As you well know, a lord doesn't have every
vessel in his household made of gold;   100
some are made of wood, and are serviceable to their lord.
God calls people to him in sundry ways,
and each one has an appropriate gift of God,
some this, some that—as it pleases him to provide.
   "Virginity is a great perfection,   105
and also devoted continence,
but Christ, who is the well of perfection,

did not bid every man to go and sell
all that he had and give it to the poor,
and in that way to follow in his footsteps; 110
He spoke to them that wished to live perfectly:
and by your leave, my lords, that isn't me.
I will bestow the flower of my whole life
in the acts and fruits of marriage.
    "Tell me also, to what end 115
were reproductive organs made,
why are people made so perfectly?
Believe me, they were not made for nothing.
whoever wants to, let him enlarge on the matter
    and argue to
and fro that they were made for the purgation 120
of urine, and that both our private parts
were made to distinguish a female from a male,
and for no other cause—do you say no?
Experience knows well it is not so;
So that the clerics won't be angry with me, 125
I'll say this: they were made for both;
that is to say, for necessary business and for pleasure
in engendering, when we do not displease God.
Why else should men set it down in their books
that a man shall yield his wife her debt? 130
Now how shall he make his payment
unless he uses his simple instrument?
Then, they were given to creatures
for purging urine and also for propagation.
    "But I don't say that everyone who has 135
such equipment as I mentioned is bound
to go and use it in engendering;
then we wouldn't care about chastity.
Christ, who was formed as a man, was a virgin,
and many a saint since the world began 140
lived always in perfect chastity.
I won't envy them virginity:
let them be white bread of finest wheat,
and let us wives be called barley bread;
and yet, with barley bread, as Mark tells us, 145

Our Lord Jesus refreshed many a man.
In such estate as God has called us to
I'll persevere; I'm not particular.
In marriage I'll use my equipment
as freely as my maker sent it;   150
If I should be grudging, God give me sorrow!
My husband shall have it both evening and
    morning,
whenever he wants to come forth and pay his debt.
I'll have a husband—I won't make it difficult—
who shall be both my debtor and my slave,   155
and have his trouble
in the flesh while I'm his wife.
All through my life I have the power
over his own body, and not he.
Just so the Apostle explained it to me,   160
and he bade our husbands to love us well.
Every bit of this lesson pleases me—"
    Just then the Pardoner started up;
"Now, dame," he said, "by God and by Saint John,
you are a noble preacher in this matter!   165
I was about to wed a wife; alas,
why should I purchase it so dearly with my flesh?
I'd rather not wed a wife this year!"
    "Wait," said she, "my tale is not begun;
no, you'll drink from another barrel   170
before I am through—one that shall taste worse
    than ale.
And when I have told you my tale
of the tribulation of marriage,
in which I have been an expert all my life—
that is to say, I myself have been the whip—   175
then you may choose whether you wish to sip
of the tun that I shall broach.
Be wary of it, before you approach too near;
for I shall tell more than ten examples.
By him who won't be warned by other men   180
shall other men be warned.
These same words were written by Ptolemy;
read in his *Almagest*, and find it there."

"Dame, I pray you, if it be your will,"
said this Pardoner, "tell your tale   185
as you began; leave off for no man,
and teach us young men some of your practice."
    "Gladly" said she, "since it may please you.
But yet I pray all this company
that if I speak according to my fancy,   190
you do not take what I say amiss;
for I only intend to amuse you.
    "Now, sirs, I'll go on with my tale.—
As ever I hope to drink wine or ale,
I'll tell the truth; of those husbands that I had,   195
three of them were good and two were bad.
The first three men were good, and rich, and old;
they were scarcely able to keep the statute
by which they were bound to me—
you know quite well what I mean by this, by heaven!   200
So help me God, I laugh when I think
how pitifully I made them work at night;
and by my faith I set no store by it.
They had given me their land and their treasure;
I no longer needed to be diligent   205
to win their love, or show them reverence.
They loved me so well, by God above,
that I didn't prize their love!
A wise woman will concentrate on getting
that love which she doesn't possess;   210
but since I had them wholly in my hand,
and since they had given me all their land,
why should I take pains to please them,
unless it should be for my own profit and
    pleasure?
I so set them to work, by my faith,   215
that many a night they sang 'alas!'
The prize of bacon some people have in
Essex at Dunmow was never brought to them, I know.
I governed them so well in my way
that each of them was most happy and eager   220
to bring me gay things from the fair.

They were glad indeed when I spoke pleasantly
    to them;
for God knows I chided them cruelly.
    "'Now hear how suitably I behaved myself,
you wise wives who can understand.   225
You should speak thus and put them in the wrong;
for no man can perjure himself and lie
half so boldly as a woman can.
I don't say this for wives that are wise,
except when they have made a mistake.   230
A wise wife, if she knows what is good for her,
will convince her husband that the chough is mad,
and call as a witness her own maid,
who conspires with her; but listen to how I spoke:
    "'Old sluggard, is this the way you dress me?   235
Why is my neighbor's wife so smart?
She is honored everywhere she goes;
I sit at home, I have no decent clothes.
What do you do at my neighbor's house?
Is she so fair? Are you so amorous?   240
What are you whispering to our maid, for
    heaven's sake?
Old sir, lecher, stop your tricks!
Why, if I have a friend or acquaintance
in all innocence, you chide like a fiend
if I walk to his house and visit!   245
You come home as drunk as a mouse
and preach from your bench, bad luck to you!
You tell me it is a great misfortune
to marry a poor woman, as far as cost is concerned;
and if she is rich and of high lineage,   250
then you say that it is a torment
to suffer her pride and her melancholy.
And if she is fair, you knave,
you say that every lecher wants to have her;
she who is assaulted on every side   255
can't remain chaste very long.
    "'You say some men desire us for wealth,
some for our shapeliness, and some for our beauty;

some want a woman because she can sing or dance,
some because she is well-bred and flirtatious;   260
some like her hands and her graceful arms;
thus we all go to the devil by your account.
You say no one can keep a castle wall
when it is assailed all around for so long a time.
  "'And if she is ugly, you say that she   265
covets every man she sees;
for she will leap on him like a spaniel
until she finds some man who will buy her wares;
there is no goose swimming in the lake, you say,
that is so gray it cannot find a mate.   270
And you say it is very hard to manage
a thing that no man will willingly keep.
You say this, you wretch, as you go to bed,
and that no wise man needs to marry,
nor any man who aspires to heaven.   275
May wild thunderbolts and fiery lightning
break your withered neck!
  "'You say that leaking houses and smoke
and nagging wives make men flee
out of their own houses; bless us,   280
what ails such an old man to scold so?
You say we wives will hide our vices
until we are safely married, and then we will show them;
that's certainly a fit proverb for a scolding curmudgeon!
You say that oxen, asses, horses, and hounds   285
are tested at various times;
and so are basins and washbowls, before people
    buy them—
spoons and stools and all such household goods,
and so are pots, clothes and adornments;
but men don't try out wives   290
until they are married; scolding old dotard!
And then, you say, we'll show our vices.
  "'You also say that I am displeased
unless you praise my beauty,
and pore constantly on my face,   295
and call me "fair dame" everywhere;

and unless you hold a feast on my
birthday, and give me gay new clothing,
and unless you honor my nurse
and my chambermaid,   300
and my father's relatives and connections;—
you say all this, old barrel full of lies!
   "'Moreover, you have caught a false
suspicion of our apprentice Jankin,
because he has curly hair, shining like purest gold,   305
and squires me everywhere;
I wouldn't want him even if you died tomorrow.
   "'But tell me this, why do you hide—sorrow to you!—
the keys of your chest away from me?
It is my property as well as yours, by heaven.   310
Do you think you can make an idiot of the mistress
     of the
house? Now by the lord who is called Saint James,
you shall not be master of both my body and my goods,
even if you rage with anger;
you'll go without one of them, like it or not.   315
What use is it to snoop and spy on me?
I think you'd like to lock me in your chest!
You should say, "Wife, go where you like;
amuse yourself, I won't believe any gossip.
I know you for a true wife, Dame Alice."   320
We don't love a man who carefully watches
where we go; we want to be at large.
   "'Beyond all other men, may the wise
astrologer Lord Ptolemy be blessed,
for in his *Almagest* he speaks this proverb: 325
"The wisest of all men is he
that never cares who has the world in his hand."
You should understand by this proverb
that if you have enough, why should you care
how merrily other folks fare?   330
For certainly, old dotard, by your leave,
you'll have quite sex enough at night.
He who forbids another man to light a candle
at his lantern is too great a niggard;

he'll have none the less light, by heaven;   335
if you have enough, you needn't complain.
  "'You also say that if we make ourselves attractive
with fine clothing and adornments
it imperils our chastity;
and further—sorrow take you—you must back
    yourself up   340
by saying these words in the Apostle's name:
"You women shall adorn yourselves
in shamefastness and sobriety," said he,
"and not in braided hair and gay jewels,
as pearls or gold, or rich array"";   345
I won't conform to this text and
rubric one gnat's worth!
You said this: that I was like a cat;
for if someone singes a cat's fur,
then the cat will stay in its dwelling;   350
and if the cat's fur is sleek and attractive,
she won't stay in the house half a day,
but out she'll go, before the break of day,
to show her fur and go a-caterwauling;
this is to say, sir grouch, that if I'm gaily dressed,   355
I'll run out to show off my clothes.
"'You old fool, what use is it for you to spy?
Even if you ask Argus, with his hundred eyes,
to be my bodyguard (as he can do it best),
in faith, he can't guard me unless I please;   360
I still could deceive him, as I hope to thrive.
  "'You also said that there are three things
which trouble all this earth,
and that no man can endure a fourth;
O dear sir tartar, Jesus shorten your life!   365
Still you preach and say that a hateful wife
is reckoned as one of these misfortunes.
Are there no other kind of comparisons
you can apply your parables to—
must a poor wife be one of them?   370
  "'You compare a woman's love to hell,
to barren land where water can't remain.

You compare it also to wild fire:
the more it burns, the more it wants
to consume everything that will burn.   375
You say that just as worms destroy a tree,
just so a wife destroys her husband; and
that all who are bound to wives know this.'
      "My lords, just so, as you have learned,
I boldly accused my old husbands   380
of speaking in their drunkenness;
and all was false, but I called on
Jankin and my niece as witnesses.
Oh Lord, the pain and woe I gave them,
though they were guiltless, by God's sweet suffering!   385
For I could bite and whinny like a horse;
I could complain, though I was the guilty one;
else many time I would have been ruined.
Whoever comes first to the mill, grinds first;
I complained first, and so our fight was ended.   390
They were quite glad to excuse themselves quickly
for things they had never been guilty of in their lives.
      "I would accuse them about wenches
when they were so sick they could hardly stand.
Yet it tickled a husband's heart, since he   395
thought I showed such great fondness for him.
I swore that all my walking out by night
was to spy out the wenches he lay with;
under this pretense I had many a merry time,
for all such wit is given us at our birth;   400
God has given women by nature deceit, weeping,
and spinning, as long as they live.
And thus I can boast of one thing:
in the end I got the better of them in every case,
by trick, or force, or by some kind of method,   405
such as continual complaining or whining;
in particular, they had misfortune in bed,
where I would chide and give them no pleasure;
I would no longer stay in the bed
if I felt my husband's arm over my side   410
until he had paid his ransom to me;

then I'd allow him to do his bit of business.
Therefore I tell this moral to everyone—
profit whoever may, for all is for sale:
you cannot lure a hawk with an empty hand;   415
for profit I would endure all his lust,
and pretend an appetite myself;
and yet I never had a taste for aged meat—
that's what made me scold them all the time.
For even if the pope had sat beside them,   420
I wouldn't spare them at their own board;
I swear I requited them word for word.
So help me almighty God,
even if I were to make my testament right now,
I don't owe them a word which has not been repaid.   425
I brought it about by my wit
that they had to give up, as the best thing to do,
or else we would never have been at rest.
For though he might look like a raging lion,
yet he would fail to gain his point.   430
    "Then I would say, 'Dear friend, notice
the meek look on Wilkin, our sheep;
come near, my spouse, let me kiss your cheek!
You should be quite patient and meek,
and have a scrupulous conscience,   435
since you preach so of the patience of Job.
Always be patient, since you preach so well;
for unless you do, we shall certainly teach you
that it is a fine thing to have a wife in peace.
One of us two must bend, without a doubt;   440
and since a man is more reasonable
than a woman is, you must be patient.
What ails you to grumble and groan so?
Is it because you want to have my thing to yourself?
Why take it all, then, have every bit of it!   445
Peter! I swear you love it well!
Now if I would sell my *belle chose*,
I could walk as fresh as a rose;
but I will keep it for your own taste.
You're to blame, by God, I tell you the truth.'   450

"We would have words like this.
Now I will speak of my fourth husband.
"My fourth husband was a reveller—
that is to say, he had a paramour;
and I was young and full of wantonness,   455
stubborn and strong and merry as a magpie.
How gracefully I could dance to a harp,
and sing just like a nightingale,
when I bad drunk a draught of sweet wine!
Metellius, the foul churl, the swine,   460
who took his wife's life with a staff
because she drank wine—if I had been his wife
he wouldn't have daunted me from drink;
and after wine I must needs think of Venus:
for just as surely as cold brings hail,   465
a lickerish mouth must have a lecherous tail.
A drunken woman has no defense;
this, lechers know by experience.
"But Lord Christ! When I remember
my youth and my gaeity,   470
it tickles me to the bottom of my heart;
to this day it does my heart good
that I have had my world in my time.
But age, alas, that poisons everything,
has robbed me of my beauty and my pith;   475
let it go, farewell, the devil with it!
The flour is gone, there is no more to say:
now I must sell the bran, as best I can;
but still I will contrive to be right merry.
Now I'll tell about my fourth husband.   480
"I tell you I was angry in my heart
that he had delight in any other.
But he was repaid, by God and by Saint Joce!
I made him a staff of the same wood—
not with my body in a filthy way,   485
but indeed my manner with other men was such
that I made him fry in his own grease
for anger and pure jealousy.
By God, I was his purgatory on earth,

by which help I hope his soul is in glory. 490
For God knows he often sat and sang out
when his shoe pinched him bitterly.
No one but God and he knew
how sorely I wrung him in many ways.
He died when I came back from Jerusalem, 495
and lies buried under the rood-beam,
although his tomb is not so elaborate
as the sepulchre of that Darius was
which Appelles wrought so skillfully;
it would have been just a waste to bury him expensively. 500
Farewell to him, may God rest his soul;
he is now in his grave and in his coffin.
 "Now I will tell of my fifth husband:
God never let his soul go down to hell!
And yet he was the most brutal to me; 505
that I can feel on my ribs, all down the row,
and always shall, to my dying day.
But in our bed he was so tireless and wanton,
and moreover he could cajole me so well
when he wanted to have my *belle chose*, 510
that even if he had beaten me on every bone,
he could soon win my love again.
I think I loved him best because
he was so cool in his love to me.
We women have, to tell the truth, 515
an odd fancy in this matter;
whatever we cannot easily get
we will cry after and crave all day.
Forbid us a thing, and we desire it;
press it upon us, and then we will flee. 520
Faced with coyness we bring out all our wares;
a great crowd at the market makes wares expensive,
and what is too cheap is held to be worth little;
every wise woman knows this.
 "My fifth husband, God bless his soul, 525
whom I took for love and not money,
was at one time a scholar at Oxford,
and had left school, and went home to board

with my close friend, who dwelt in our town:
God bless her soul! Her name was Alison.   530
She knew my heart and private affairs
better than our parish priest, as I may thrive!
To her I revealed all my secrets.
For whether my husband had pissed on a wall
or done something which should have cost him his life,   535
to her, and to another worthy wife,
and to my niece, whom I loved well,
I would have betrayed every one of his secrets.
And so I did often enough, God knows,
and that often made his face red and hot   540
for very shame, so that he blamed himself
for having told me so great a confidence.
   "And so it happened that once, in Lent
(thus many times I went to my friend's house,
for I always loved to be merry,   545
and to walk, in March, April, and May,
from house to house, to hear various tidings),
that Jankin the clerk and my dear friend Dame Alice
and I myself went into the fields.
My husband was at London all that Lent;   550
I had the better leisure to enjoy myself
and to see, and be seen by,
lusty people; how could I know how my favor
was destined to be bestowed, or where?
Therefore I made my visits   555
to feast-eves and processions,
to sermons and these pilgrimages,
to miracle plays and to marriages,
and wore my gay scarlet clothes:
on my life, worms or moths or mites   560
never ate a bit of them;
and do you know why? Because they were
      used constantly.
   "Now I'll tell what happened to me.
As I was saying, we walked in the fields,   565
until truly this clerk and I enjoyed
such dalliance that in my foresight

I spoke to him and told him that
if I were a widow he should marry me.
For certainly (I don't say it as a boast)
I was never yet unprovided for   570
in marriage, and other matters too;
I hold that a mouse that has but one hole
to run to has a heart not worth a leek;
for if that should fail, then all is finished.
    "I made him believe he had enchanted me;   575
my mother taught me that trick.
And also I said I had dreamed of him all night:
he wanted to slay me as I lay on my back,
and all my bed was full of blood;
but yet I expected that he would bring me luck;   580
for blood signifies gold, as I was taught.
And all this was false, I had dreamed none of it;
I was just following my mother's lore, as I
always did, in this as well as in other matters.
    "But now sir, let me see, what am I talking about?   585
Aha! By God, I have my tale back again.
    "When my fourth husband was on his bier,
I wept, all the same, and acted sorrowful,
as wives must, for it is customary,
and covered my face with my handkerchief;   590
but since I was provided with a mate,
I wept but little, that I guarantee.
    "My husband was brought to church in the morning,
with neighbors who mourned for him;
and Jankin our clerk was one of them.   595
So help me God, when I saw him walk
behind the bier, it seemed to me he had a pair
of legs and feet so neat and handsome
that I gave all my heart into his keeping.
He was, I think, twenty years old,   600
and I was forty, if the truth be told;
but yet I always had a colt's tooth.
I was gap-toothed, and that became me well;
I had the print of St. Venus's seal.
So help me God, I was a lusty one,   605

and fair and rich and young and well off;
and truly, as my husbands told me,
I had the best *quoniam* that might be.
For certainly, my feelings all come
from Venus, and my heart from Mars: 610
Venus gave me my lust, my lecherousness,
and Mars gave me my sturdy hardiness,
because Taurus was in the ascendant when I was
        born, and
Mars was in that sign. Alas, alas, that ever love was sin!
I always followed my inclination 615
according to the stellar influences at my birth;
I was so made that I could not withhold
my chamber of Venus from a good fellow.
I still have the mark of Mars on my face,
and also in another private place. 620
For, as surely as God is my salvation,
I never had any discrimination in love,
but always followed my appetite,
be he short or tall, dark or fair;
I didn't care, so long as he pleased me, 625
how poor he was, nor of what rank.
    "What should I say, except that at the end of the
        month
this gay clerk Jankin, that was so pleasant,
wedded me with great ceremony,
and to him I gave all the lands and property 630
that had ever been given to me before;
but afterward I repented this sorely:
he would not allow anything I wanted.
By God, he hit me once on the ear
because I had torn a leaf out of his book; 635
as a result of that stroke, my ear became totally deaf.
I was stubborn as a lioness,
and as for my tongue, an absolute ranter;
and I'd walk, as I'd done before,
from house to house, although he'd sworn I wouldn't; 640
because of this he would often preach
and teach me of the deeds of ancient Romans:

how Simplicius Gallus left his wife
and forsook her for the rest of his life
just because he saw her looking out 645
of his door bareheaded one day.
   "He told me by name of another Roman
who also, because his wife was at a summer
game without his knowledge, forsook her.
And then he would seek in his Bible 650
for that proverb of Ecclesiasticus
where he makes a command strictly forbidding
a man to allow his wife to go roaming about;
then you could be sure he would say this:
   'Whoever builds his house of willows, 655
   and rides his blind horse over plowed land,
   and allows his wife to visit shrines,
   is worthy to be hanged on the gallows.'
But all for nought; I didn't care a berry
for his proverbs and old saw, 660
nor would I be corrected by him.
I hate that man who tells me my vices,
and so, God knows, do more of us than I.
This made him utterly furious with me;
I wouldn't give in to him in any case. 665
   "Now I'll tell you truly, by Saint Thomas,
why I tore a leaf out of his book,
for which he hit me so that I became deaf.
He had a book that he always loved to read
night and day to amuse himself. 670
He called it Valerius and Theophrastus;
at which book he was always laughing heartily;
and also there was at some time a clerk at Rome,
a cardinal, that was called St. Jerome,
who wrote a book against Jovinian; 675
in this book there was also Tertulian,
Chrysippus, Trotula, and Heloise,
who was an abbess not far from Paris;
and also the Parables of Solomon,
Ovid's *Art of Love*, and many other books, 680
and all these were bound in one volume.

And every day and night it was his custom,
when he had leisure and could rest
from other worldly occupation,
to read in this book of wicked wives. 685
He knew more legends and lives of them
than there are of good wives in the Bible.
For believe me, it is an impossibility
for any clerk to speak good of wives—
unless it be of the lives of holy saints, 690
but never of any other woman.
Who painted the lion, tell me who?
By God, if women had written stories,
as clerks have in their oratories,
they would have written more of men's wickedness 695
than all of the sex of Adam can redress.
The children of Mercury and of Venus
are quite contrary in their ways;
Mercury loves wisdom and learning,
and Venus loves revelry and expenditure. 700
And, because of their diverse dispositions,
each loses power when the other is dominant;
and thus, God knows, Mercury is powerless
in the Sign of the Fish, where Venus is dominant;
and Venus falls when Mercury ascends; 705
therefore no woman is praised by any clerk.
The clerk, when he is old, and unable to do
any of Venus's work worth his old shoe,
then sits down and writes in his dotage
that women cannot keep their marriage vows! 710
    "But now to the purpose, as to why I was beaten,
as I told you, because of a book, for heaven's sake.
One night Jankin, who was the head of the household,
read in his book as he sat by the fire,
first, concerning Eve, that all mankind was brought 715
to wretchedness by her wickedness,
for which Jesus Christ himself was slain,
who redeemed us with his heart's blood.
Here you can expressly find this of woman:
that woman caused the fall of all mankind. 720

"Then he read to me how Samson lost his hair:
while he was sleeping, his mistress cut it with her shears;
through this treason he lost both his eyes.
"Then he read to me, and this is no lie,
about Hercules and his Dejanira,   725
who caused him to set himself on fire.
"He forgot none of the sorrow and woe
    that Socrates had with his two wives;
how Xantippe cast piss upon his head;
this poor man sat as still as if he were dead;   730
he wiped his head; he dared to say no more
than, 'Before the thunder stops, comes the rain.'
    "The tale of Pasiphaë, who was the queen of Crete,
he maliciously thought sweet;
fie, speak no more—it is a grisly thing—   735
about her horrible lust and her preference.
"Of Clytemnestra, who because of her lechery
with falseness caused her husband's death,
he read with great devotion.
    "He told me also why   740
Amphiaraus lost his life at Thebes;
my husband had a story about his wife,
Eriphyle, who for a trinket of gold
secretly told the Greeks
where her husband had hidden himself,   745
which is why he had sad luck at Thebes.
    "He told me of Livia and of Lucilla;
they both caused their husbands to die,
one for love and the other for hate;
Livia, late one night, poisoned   750
her husband, because she was his foe.
Lustful Lucilla loved her husband so
that in order to make him think of her always
she gave him a love potion of such a kind
that he was dead before morning;   755
and thus husbands always suffer.
    "'Then he told me how one Latumius
complained to his friend Arrius
that in his garden there grew a tree

on which, he said, his three wives   760
had spitefully hanged themselves.
  "'O dear brother,' said this Arrius,
'give me a cutting of that blessed tree,
and it shall be planted in my garden.'
  "He read of wives of a later date   765
some of whom had slain their husbands in their beds,
and let their lechers make love to them all the night
while the corpse lay flat on the floor.
And some have driven nails into their husband's brain
while they slept, and thus slain them.   770
Some have given them poison in their drink.
He told of more evil than the heart can imagine;
and along with that, he knew more proverbs
than there are blades of grass or herbs in the world.
  "'It is better,' said he, 'to dwell   775
with a lion or a foul dragon
than with a woman accustomed to scold.
It is better,' said he, 'to stay high on the roof
than with an angry wife down in the house;
they are so wicked and contrary   780
they always hate what their husbands love.'
He said, 'A woman casts her shame away
when she casts off her smock,' and furthermore,
'A fair woman, unless she is also chaste,
is like a gold ring in a sow's nose.'   785
Who would suppose or imagine
the woe and pain that was in my heart?
  "And when I saw he would never stop
reading in this cursed book all night,
suddenly I plucked three leaves   790
out of his book, right as he was reading, and also
I hit him on the cheek with my fist, so
that he fell down into our fire backward.
He started up like a raging lion
and hit me on the head with his fist   795
so that I lay on the floor as if I were dead.
And when he saw how still I lay,
he was aghast, and would have fled away,

until at last I awoke from my swoon:
'Oh! Have you slain me, false thief?' I said,   800
'And have you murdered me thus for my land?
Before I die, I yet want to kiss you.'
    "He came near, and kneeled down gently,
and said, 'Dear sister Alisoun,
so help me God, I shall never hit you again;   805
what I have done, you are to blame for yourself.
Forgive me for it, I beseech you.'
But yet again I hit him on the cheek,
and said, 'Thief, this much I am avenged;
now I shall die, I can speak no longer.'   810
But at last, after much care and woe,
we fell into accord between ourselves.
He gave the bridle completely into my hand
to have control of house and land,
and also of his tongue and hand;   815
and I made him burn his book right then.
And when I had got for myself,
through superiority, all the sovereignty,
and he had said, 'My own true wife,
do as you wish the rest of your life,   820
preserve your honor, and my public position, too,'
after that day we never argued.
So God help me, I was as kind to him
as any wife from Denmark to India,
and as true, and so was he to me.   825
I pray to God who sits in majesty
to bless his soul, for his dear mercy's sake!
Now I'll tell my tale; if you will listen."

Behold the words between the Summoner and the Friar

The Friar laughed when he had heard all this:
"Now, dame," said he, "as I may have joy or bliss,   830
this is a long preamble to a tale!"
And when the Summoner heard the Friar exclaim,
"Lo!" said the Summoner, "By God's two arms!
A friar will always be butting in.
See, good people, a fly and a friar   835

will fall into every dish and also every matter.
What do you mean, talking about perambulation?
Oh, amble or trot or pace, or go sit down;
you're spoiling our fun by behaving in this manner."
    "Oh, is that so, sir Summoner?" said the Friar,   840
"Now by my faith, before I go, I'll
tell such a tale or two about a summoner
that everyone here shall laugh."
    "Now, Friar, damn your eyes,"
said this Summoner, "and damn me   845
if I don't tell two or three tales
about friars before I get to Sittingbourne,
so that I shall make your heart mourn;
I can easily see that your patience is gone."
    Our Host cried "Peace! And that at once!"   850
And said, "Let the woman tell her tale.
You behave like people who have got drunk on ale.
Tell your tale, dame; that is best."
    "All ready, sir," said she, 'just as you wish,
if I have the permission of this worthy Friar."   855
    "Yes, dame," said he, "tell on and I will listen."

Here begins the Wife of Bath's Tale

In the old days of King Arthur,
of whom Britons speak great honor,
this land was all filled with fairies.
The elf queen with her jolly company
danced often in many a green meadow—   5
this was the old belief, as I have read;
I speak of many hundred years ago.
But now no one can see elves anymore,
for now the great charity and prayers
of limiters and other holy friars,   10
who search every field and stream,
as thick as specks of dust in a sunbeam,
blessing halls, chambers, kitchens, bedrooms,
cities, towns, castles, high towers,
villages, barns, stables, dairies: 15
this is the reason that there are no fairies.

For where an elf was wont to walk,
there now walks the limiter himself,
in afternoons and in mornings,
and says his Matins and his holy things,   20
as he goes about within his limits.
Women may go up and down safely;
in every bush or under every tree
there is no other incubus but he—
and he won't do anything but dishonor to them.   25
    It so happened that this King Arthur
had in his house a lusty bachelor,
who one day came riding from the river;
and it happened that he saw a maiden
walking before him, alone as she was born.   30
And from this maiden then, against her will,
and by pure force, he took her maidenhood.
Because of this violation, there was such a clamor
and such petitioning to King Arthur
that this knight was condemned to die   35
according to law, and should have lost his head—
it happened that such was the statute then—
except that the queen and various other ladies
prayed to the king for grace so long
that he granted him his life on the spot,   40
and gave him to the queen, completely at her will,
to choose whether she would save or destroy him.
    The queen thanked the king heartily,
and then spoke thus to the knight,
one day, when she saw a fitting time: 45
"You are still in such a position," said she,
"that you have no guarantee of your life as yet.
I will grant you life if you can tell me
what thing it is that women most desire.
Be wary, and keep your neck from the ax.   50
And if you cannot tell it to me now,
I will still give you leave to go
a year and a day to seek and learn
a sufficient answer in this matter.
And I want a guarantee, before you go,   55

that you will yield up your person in this place."
    The knight was woeful, and he sighed sorrowfully;
but then, he could not do as he pleased.
And in the end he decided to go off,
and to come back again just at the end of the year,   60
with such an answer as God would provide for him;
he took his leave and went forth on his way.
    He sought in every house and every place
where he hoped to find favor,
in order to learn what thing women most love;   65
but he reached no land where he could find
two people who were in agreement
with each other on this matter.
    Some said women love riches best;
some said honor; some said amusement;   70
some, rich apparel; some said pleasure in bed,
and often to be widowed and remarried.
Some said that our hearts are most soothed
when we are flattered and pampered:
he came near the truth, I will not lie;   75
a man can win us best with flattery,
and with constant attendance and assiduity
we are ensnared, both high and low.
    And some said that we love best
to be free, and do just as we please,   80
and to have no man reprove us for our vice,
but say that we are wise and not at all foolish.
For truly, if anyone will scratch us
on a sore spot, there is not one of us
who will not kick for being told the truth;   85
try it, and he who does shall find this out.
No matter how full of vice we are within,
we wish to be thought wise and clean from sin.
    And some said that we take delight
in being thought reliable and able to keep a secret   90
and hold steadfast to a purpose
and not betray anything that people tell us.
But that idea isn't worth a rake handle;
by heaven, we women can't conceal a thing;

witness Midas; would you hear the tale? 95
   Ovid, among other brief matters,
said Midas had two ass's ears growing
on his head under his long hair;
which evil he hid from everyone's sight
as artfully as he could, 100
so that no one knew of it except his wife.
He loved her most, and also trusted her;
he prayed her not to tell anyone
of his disfigurement.
   She swore to him that not for all the world 105
would she do such villainy and sin
as to give her husband so bad a name;
out of her own shame she wouldn't tell it.
But nonetheless she thought that she would die
for having to keep a secret so long; 110
it seemed to her that her heart swelled so painfully
some word must needs burst from her;
and since she dared not tell it to anybody,
she ran down to a marsh close by—
her heart was on fire until she got there— 115
and, as a bittern booms in the mire,
she laid her mouth down to the water:
   "Betray me not, you water, with your sound,"
said she. "To you I tell it, and to no one else:
my husband has two long ass's ears! 120
Now my heart is all cured, for the secret is out!
I simply couldn't keep it any longer."
In this you can see that though we wait a time,
yet out it must come: we cannot hide a secret.
If you wish to hear the rest of the tale, 125
read Ovid, and there you can learn of it.
   When this knight whom my tale specially concerns
saw that he couldn't come by it—
that is to say, what women love most—
his spirit was very sorrowful within his breast; 130
but home he went, he might not linger:
the day was come when he must turn homeward.
And on his way, burdened with care, he happened

to ride by the edge of a forest,
where he saw more than twenty-four   135
ladies moving in a dance;
he drew eagerly toward that dance
in the hope that he might learn something.
But indeed, before he quite got there,
the dancers vanished, he knew not where.   140
He saw no living creature,
except a woman sitting on the green:
no one could imagine an uglier creature.
This old woman rose before the knight
and said, "Sir knight, no road lies this way.   145
Tell me, by your faith, what you seek for.
Perhaps it may be the better;
these old folks know many things," said she.
    "Dear mother," said this knight, "certainly
I am as good as dead unless I can say   150
what thing it is that women most desire;
if you could tell me, I would repay your trouble well."
    "Give me your promise, here upon my hand," said she,
"that you will do the next thing I require
of you, if it lies in your power,   155
and I will tell it to you before nightfall."
"Here is my promise," said the knight, "I grant it."
    "Then," said she, "I dare to boast
that your life is safe, for I'll swear
upon my life that the queen will say as I do.   160
Let's see whether the proudest of all those
that wear a coverchief or headdress
dares deny what I shall teach you;
let's go on without any more talk."
Then she whispered a message in his ear,   165
and told him to be glad and not afraid.
    When they had come to the court, this knight
said he had kept his day as he had promised,
and his answer, he said, was ready.
Many a noble wife and many a maiden,   170
and many a widow (since widows are so wise),
were assembled to bear his answer

with the queen herself sitting as judge;
and then the knight was ordered to appear.
  Everyone was commanded to keep silence,   175
and the knight was commanded to tell in open assembly
what thing it is that secular women love best.
This knight did not stand in beastlike silence,
but answered to his question at once
with manly voice, so that all the court heard it: 180
  "My liege lady," he said, "generally
women desire to have dominion
over their husbands as well as their lovers,
and to be above them in mastery;
this is your greatest desire, though you may kill me;   185
do as you please, I am at your will here."
  In all the court there was neither wife nor maiden
nor widow who contradicted what he said,
but all said he deserved to have his life.
  And at that word up jumped the old woman   190
whom the knight had seen sitting on the green:
"Mercy," said she, "my sovereign lady queen!
Before your court depart, do right by me,
I taught this answer to the knight;
for this he gave me his promise there   195
that he would do the first thing
I required of him, if it lay in his power.
Before the court, then, I pray you, sir knight,"
said she, "to take me as your wife;
for well you know that I have saved your life.   200
If I say false, deny me, on your faith!"
  The knight answered, "Alas and woe is me!
I know quite well that such was my promise.
For the love of God ask for something else;
take all my property and let my body go."   205
  "No then," said she. "Curse the two of us!
For though I am ugly and old and poor,
I wouldn't want all the metal or ore
that is buried under the earth or lies above
unless I were your wife and your love as well."   210
  "My love?" said he; "No, my damnation!

Alas, that any of my birth
should ever be so foully disgraced!"
But it was all for nothing; the end was this, that he
was forced to accept the fact that he must needs wed her;   215
and he took his old wife and went to bed.

    Now some people might say, perhaps,
that out of negligence I am not bothering
to tell you about the joy and the pomp
at the feast that day,   220
to which objection I shall answer briefly:
I am telling you that there was no joy or feast at all,
there was nothing but gloom and much sorrow;
for he married her privately in the morning
and afterward hid himself like an owl all day—   225
he was so dejected because his wife looked so ugly.

    Great was the woe in the knight's mind
when he was brought with his wife to bed;
he tossed and he turned to and fro.
His old wife lay smiling all the time,   230
and said, "O dear husband, bless my soul!
Does every knight behave with his wife as you do?
Is this the law of King Arthur's house?
Is every one of his knights so cold?
I am your own love and your wife;   235
I am she who saved your life;
and certainly I never yet did wrong to you.
Why do you act thus with me the first night?
You act like a man who has lost his mind.
What am I guilty of? For God's sake, tell me,   240
and it shall be corrected, if I can manage it."

    "Corrected?" said this knight, "Alas, no, no!
It will never be corrected!
You are so loathsome and so old,
and what is more, of such low birth,   245
that it is little wonder if I toss and turn.
I wish to God my heart would break!"

    "Is this," said she, "the cause of your unrest?"

    "Yes, certainly," said he, "it's no wonder."

    "Now, sir," said she, "I could rectify all this,   250

if I wanted to, before three days were up,
if you behaved yourself to me well.
    "But in the matter of your speaking of such nobility
as descends from ancient wealth,
claiming that because of it you are supposed to be   255
noblemen—such arrogance is not worth a hen.
Find the man who is always the most virtuous,
privately and publicly, and who always tries hardest
to do what noble deeds he can,
and consider him the greatest nobleman.   260
Christ wants us to claim our nobility from him,
not from our ancestors because of their ancient wealth:
for though they give us all their heritage,
on the strength of which we claim to be of noble descent,
yet they cannot bequeath by any means   265
or to any of us their virtuous manner of life
which made them be called noblemen;
and which summoned us to follow them at the
      same level.
    "Well can the wise poet of Florence
who is called Dante speak on this subject;   270
in this sort of rhyme is Dante's tale:
'Not oft by branches of a family tree
Does human prowess rise; for gracious God
Wants us to claim from him nobility.'
For from our elders we may claim nothing   275
but perishable matter, to which man may do hurt
and injury. And everyone knows as well as I that
if nobility were implanted by nature
in a certain lineage, down the line of descent,
they would never cease, in private or public,   280
to do the fair offices of nobility;
they could do nothing shameful or evil.
    "Take fire, and bear it into the darkest house
from here to the Mount of Caucasus,
and let men shut the doors and go away;   285
yet the fire will blaze and burn as well
as if twenty thousand men were looking at it;
it will maintain its natural function always

until it dies, I'll stake my life.
    "By this you can easily see that nobility 290
is not tied to possessions,
since people do not perform their function
without variation as does the fire, according to
      its nature.
For, God knows, men may very often find
a lord's son committing shameful and vile deeds; 295
and he who wishes to have credit for his nobility
because he was born of a noble house,
and because his elders were noble and virtuous,
but will not himself do any noble deeds
or follow the example of his late noble ancestor, 300
he is not noble, be he duke or earl;
for villainous, sinful deeds make him a churl.
This kind of nobility is only the renown
of your ancestors, earned by their great goodness,
which is a thing apart from yourself. 305
Your nobility comes from God alone;
then our true nobility comes of grace,
it was in no way bequeathed to us with our station
      in life.
    "Think how noble, as Valerius says,
was that Tullius Hostilius 310
who rose out of poverty to high nobility.
Read Seneca, and read Boethius, too;
there you shall see expressly that there is no doubt
that he is noble who does noble deeds.
And therefore, dear husband, I thus conclude 315
even if my ancestors were low,
yet God on high may—and so I hope—
grant me grace to live virtuously;
then I am noble, from the time when I begin
to live virtuously and avoid sin. 320
    "And as for the poverty you reprove me for,
high God in whom we believe
chose to live his life in willing poverty;
and certainly every man, maiden, or wife
can understand that Jesus, heaven's king, 325

would not choose a vicious way of life.
Contented poverty is an honorable thing, indeed;
this is said by Seneca and other learned men.
Whoever is content with his poverty
I hold to be rich, even if he hasn't a shirt.   330
He who covets anything is a poor man,
for he wants to have something which is not in
    his power.
But he who has nothing and desires nothing is rich,
although you may consider him nothing but a
    lowly man.
   "True poverty sings of its own accord;   335
Juvenal says of poverty, 'Merrily can
the poor man sing and joke before the
thieves when he goes by the road.'
Poverty is a good that is hated, and, I guess,
a great expeller of cares;   340
a great amender of knowledge, too,
to him that takes it in patience.
Poverty is this, although it seem unhealthy:
possession of that which no man will challenge.
Poverty will often, when a man is low,   345
make him know his God and himself as well.
Poverty is a glass, it seems to me,
through which he can see his true friends.
And therefore, sir, since I do not harm you by it,
do not reprove me for my poverty anymore.   350
   "Now, sir, you reprove me for age;
but certainly, sir, aside from bookish
authority, you nobles who are honorable
say that one should honor an old person,
and call him father, for the sake of your nobility;   355
and I can find authors to that effect, I imagine.
   "Now as to the point that I am ugly and old—
then you need not dread being a cuckold;
for ugliness and age, as I may thrive,
are great wardens of chastity.   360
But nevertheless, since I know what pleases you,
I shall fulfill your fleshly appetite.

"Choose now," said she, "one of these two things:
to have me ugly and old until I die,
and be a faithful, humble wife to you,   365
and never displease you in all my life;
or else to have me young and fair,
and take your chances on the flocking
of people to your house because of me—
or to some other place, it may well be.   370
Now choose yourself, whichever you like."
    The knight considered and sighed sorely,
but at last he spoke in this manner,
"My lady and my love, and wife so dear,
I put myself under your wise control;   375
you yourself choose which may be most pleasurable
and most honorable to you and to me also.
I don't care which of the two I get;
for whatever pleases you suffices for me."
    "Then have I got mastery over you," said she,   380
"since I may choose and rule as I please?"
    "Yes, certainly, wife," said he, "I consider that best."
    "Kiss me," said she, "we won't be angry anymore;
for I swear I will be both these things to you;
that is to say, both fair indeed and good.   385
I pray to God that I may die mad
if I am not just as good and true to you
as ever was wife since the world began.
And, if I am not tomorrow as fair to see
as any lady, empress, or queen   390
between the east and the west,
do with the question of my life and death just as
        you wish.
Raise the curtain, and see how it is."
    And when the knight actually saw all this—
that she was so fair and so young, too,   395
he seized her in his two arms for joy,
his heart was bathed in bliss;
he kissed her a thousand times in a row.
And she obeyed him in everything
that might give him pleasure or joy.   400

   And thus they lived to the end of their lives
in perfect joy; and Jesus Christ sends us
husbands who are meek, young, and lively in bed,
and grace to outlive those that we marry.
And also I pray Jesus to shorten the lives   405
of those that won't be governed by their wives;
and as for old and angry niggards with their money,
God send them soon a true pestilence.